Smollett: Author of the First Distinction

SMOLLETT: AUTHOR OF THE FIRST DISTINCTION

edited by
Alan Bold

VISION
and
BARNES & NOBLE

Vision Press Limited
11–14 Stanhope Mews West
London SW7 5RD

and

Barnes & Noble Books
81 Adams Drive
Totowa, NJ 07512

ISBN (UK) 0 85478 434 9
ISBN (US) 0 389 20240 1

Printed and bound by
Mansell (Bookbinders) Ltd.,
Witham, Essex.
Phototypeset by Galleon Photosetting,
Ipswich, Suffolk.
MCMLXXXII

Contents

Introduction

by ALAN BOLD

A primary reason for this symposium is a desire to help restore Smollett to the company classified by Matthew Bramble as 'authors of the first distinction'. Smollett has, through a long process of academic neglect and consequent public indifference, become a classic in name rather than in fact; available but not, apparently, irresistible. Readers may be prepared to bow in the direction of his great name but are hardly encouraged to come to terms with his great work. In this book the contributors have combined in a collective exploration of the vitality and importance of Smollett's writing and have generally come to the conclusion that, in view of his immense talent and range, he is ripe for reassessment and ready for a revival.

As the symposium is about declaring interests I should acknowledge that my own interest in Smollett is as a Scot, and a quintessential one at that. That fact is what first drew me to his fiction. Smollett's first novel, *The Adventures of Roderick Random*, aggressively demonstrates the author's national genius and its remarkable emotional repertoire is derived from Smollett's own diverse and adventurous background (as well as the general 'disposition of the Scots, addicted to travelling'). The novel was first published in 1748, in the traumatic period following the cultural catastrophe of Culloden (which, as Damian Grant reminds us, provoked 'The Tears of Scotland' in Smollett). Smollett certainly wanted to show the Scot as a combative character—in his own image, in other words, for Sir Walter Scott rightly drew attention (in *The Lives of the Novelists*) to Smollett's propensity for 'wrangles and brawls' intellectual and otherwise. Random may not be the Compleat Smollett (any more than Matthew Bramble is) but persuasively comes over as a portrait of the artist as a young Scot. That Random is larger than life is due to Smollett's ability to shape his common source material into an extraordinary human drama.

Roderick Random has all the contradictions we associate with

Scotland and Scottish fiction. It is full of conflict, tense as a Scottish night out. It combines squalor and sentimentality, self-doubt and self-aggrandisement, feminine fragility and masculine violence. The Scottish tendency to dwell on misfortune is summed up in the synopsis of the second chapter:

> *I grow up—am hated by my relations—sent to school—neglected by my grandfather—maltreated by my master—seasoned to adversity—form cabals against the pedant—debarred access to my grandfather—hunted by his heir—demolish the teeth of his tutor.*

Give or take a few details and you have a tale of woe that could be endorsed by many who have endured a Scottish childhood. On a literary level here is a theme (an assault on life as revenge for the brutal betrayal of childhood's dreamy promise) that will, with variations, sustain Scottish novelists as they constantly renew the tradition initiated by Smollett. Francis Russell Hart opened his account of *The Scottish Novel* (1978) with a discussion of Smollett and found our author 'seeking new ways and matters for the expression of a vision he has had all along . . . that vision of a monstrously perverse, fallen, but animated world; that powerful conflation of the terrible, the horrible, and the ludicrous which we call the grotesque. In Scottish Gothic, the grotesque plays an essential role.'

Smollett's own life unfolded as a particularly Scottish melodrama and had its grotesque moments. He selfconsciously carried the cross of early failure (in the name of his tragedy *The Regicide*); he valued quantity as much as quality or, to put it another way, industry as much as inspiration. Though Tom Scott claims convincingly that Smollett could have been a great verse satirist he was not a sensuous writer as his celebrated, and static, lines on Leven Water confirm:

> The springing trout in speckled pride,
> The salmon, monarch of the tide,
> The ruthless pike intent on war,
> The silver eel, and mottled par.

Smollett is merely going through the motions there and his muse is never really alive unless motivated by malice or moral indignation or mockery.

8

By acquiring his art in action (rather than theoretical reflection) Smollett set an impressive precedent for the pugnacious writer. He truly mastered his medium so that by the time of *Humphry Clinker* he could luxuriate a bit, enjoy the spectacle of his skill to the extent of exhibiting it. Here, as a good example of Smollett's virtuosity, is Jery Melford's description of his aunt:

> Mrs Tabitha Bramble is a maiden of forty-five. In person, she is tall, raw-boned, aukward, flat-chested, and stooping; her complexion is sallow and freckled; her eyes are not grey, but greenish, like those of a cat, and generally inflamed; her hair is of a sandy, or rather dusty hue; her forehead low; her nose long, sharp, and, towards the extremity, always red in cool weather; her lips skinny, her mouth extensive, her teeth straggling and loose, of various colours and conformation; and her long neck shrivelled into a thousand wrinkles—

The prose is both vivid and vivacious and the incidental density of the narrative traps the reader, forces him (or her) to go further.

Smollett was a voluminous writer who tried his hand at most aspects of literature; here we concentrate on his creative achievement and see him principally as a novelist whose imagination was more than equal to his astounding powers of observation. All that is required for Smollett to reclaim his position as a genuinely popular novelist is for the public to be made aware of the authentic character of his work. First, though, Smollett must be made a topic of discussion and once his words circulate his contemporary relevance (to pick up a point from the end of David Daiches's essay) will be evident.

I would like to thank all the contributors for their cooperation in this project and Alan Moore of Vision Press for his enthusiastic interest. Two of the essays have appeared elsewhere: David Daiches's 'Smollett Reconsidered' featured in a German *Festschrift* and a collection in honour of Edgar Johnson; Paul-Gabriel Boucé's analysis of the thematic structure of *Ferdinand Count Fathom* originally formed part of his *The Novels of Tobias Smollett* published in 1976 by Longman to whom we are extremely grateful for permission to reproduce it. I hope what follows conforms to the intentions outlined in the Preface to

Roderick Random: 'The attention is not tired with a bare Catalogue of characters, but agreeably diverted with all the variety of invention; and the vicissitudes of life appear in their peculiar circumstances, opening an ample field for wit and humour.'

Part One

SMOLLETT IN GENERAL

1

Smollett Reconsidered

by DAVID DAICHES

Smollett is something of an odd man out in the history of our literature. He has not come in for modern revaluation as one of the pioneers of the English novel, as have Defoe, Richardson and Fielding. He is not discussed, except for an occasional casual aside, in Ian Watt's influential study *The Rise of the Novel*: indeed, Watt specifically excludes Smollett, observing that he 'has many merits as a social reporter and as a humorist, but the manifest flaws in the central situations and the general structure of all his novels except *Humphry Clinker* . . . prevent him from playing a very important role in the main tradition of the novel.' He is of course wholly excluded from F. R. Leavis's 'great tradition' of English fiction, and he is not given separate mention in the index to the twenty volumes of *Scrutiny* though he is briefly alluded to in a review of a book on Dickens as being one of the sources of Dickens's brand of humour, with the additional comment: 'Smollett had no subtlety; he is coarse and crude in a way that Fielding never is, and this element, toned down to Victorian requirements, is very obvious in Dickens.' The Americans have concentrated either on his biography and personal relationships, as in the work of Lewis Knapp, or on constructing hypotheses concerning the influence on his handling of character and action of eighteenth century Scottish philosophers, as in Morris Golden's interesting but doctrinaire *Smollett and the Scottish School*. Few seem concerned with a critical reappraisal of Smollett's work.

Students of English literature read *Humphry Clinker*, his last and undoubtedly his best novel, but as a rule know of *Roderick*

13

Random and *Peregrine Pickle* only by repute as robust picaresque novels of adventure which hold no special attractions for the modern reader. His third novel, *Ferdinand Count Fathom*, is unknown to most modern university students of English even by name, and in any case the history of an out-and-out rogue who undergoes a sudden and puzzling conversion to virtue at the end of the book can hardly be expected to compete for students' attention either with the genuine rogue literature of the Elizabethans or with Fielding's gravely ironical *Jonathan Wilde the Great* or Thackeray's *Barry Lyndon*. Smollett's fourth and penultimate novel, *Sir Launcelot Greaves*, is pretty well universally dismissed by critics, when they concern themselves with it at all, as a feeble attempt to produce an eighteenth century *Don Quixote*.

Yet I think that it is with *Sir Launcelot Greaves* that a reappraisal of Smollett might well begin. For preposterous though the idea of an eighteenth-century knight in armour riding round the English countryside to redress wrongs, and absurd, melodramatic, contrived and coincidental as the course of action in the novel is, *Sir Launcelot Greaves* is the novel in which Smollett exposes most directly the moral centre which lies at the heart of all his fiction and gives it proportion and meaning. Smollett is not generally presented as a moralist. His own deep sense of personal grievance, his crotchetiness, his masochistic descriptions of motiveless violence and cruelty, his belligerent coarseness in writing of smells and excretions—all this, combined with the apparently episodic nature of his plots which seem to have no other function than to entertain the reader until the author is too fatigued to carry on, suggests the amoral if not immoral writer whose only object is to amuse and shock simultaneously. Nevertheless, Smollett was essentially a moralist and a man of feeling, deeply moved by human suffering especially if it was caused by deliberate injustice or wanton cruelty. All his novels contain scenes in which a good man is brought into personal contact with some terrible example of injustice and suffering and is enabled to undo the injustice and punish the perpetrator of it. Sometimes these scenes take on the dimensions almost of a harrowing of Hell and a deliverance of the innocents who are held captive there. A notable example of this, and a virtually archetypal scene in Smollett, is provided in

Chapters 11 and 12 of *Sir Launcelot Greaves*. Sir Launcelot, in the course of his questing around the country in search of occasions to perform good deeds, finds himself in the jail of an unnamed market town as a result of the ignorance and malice of a certain Justice Gobble. In the jail he meets various other victims of Justice Gobble's cruelty and malevolence:

> . . . a crew of naked wretches crowded around him, and, like a congregation of rooks, opened their throats all at once, in accusation of Justice Gobble. The knight was moved at this scene, which he could not help comparing, in his own mind, to what would appear upon a much more awful occasion, when the cries of the widow and the orphan, the injured and oppressed, would be uttered at the tribunal of an unerring Judge, against the villainous and insolent authors of their calamity.

He learns that Justice Gobble was the son of a tailor who, by cunning and marrying his master's widow, had worked his way up from a journeyman hosier to a position of wealth and power in this country neighbourhood. Once settled in the country and having acquired a commission as justice of the peace through the influence of a peer who owed him money, Gobble proceeded to ruin certain shopkeepers in the country town who had voted contrary to his interests. By various devices he drove these individuals to financial ruin and a debtor's prison. Among his victims in the jail was a woman who had been driven half mad by her terrible misfortunes, deliberately inflicted on her by Gobble: a gentlewoman born, she had married a wealthy farmer, and on his death determined to manage the farm herself with the help of her hopeful son, who was engaged to a daughter of a prosperous farmer in the neighbourhood. But because Mrs. Gobble once fancied herself insulted by the young man's fiancée, she and the justice together conspired to take revenge: the young man was pressed for a soldier, to be killed in action soon afterwards, and his forlorn fiancée 'wept and pined until she fell into a consumption'. The widow, consumed by grief and without the help of her son, was unable to manage the farm and lost both her goods and her reason. 'Then' (in Smollett's words) 'the landlord seized for his rent, and she was arrested at the suit of Justice Gobble, who had bought up one of her debts in order to distress her, and now pretended that her madness was

15

feigned.' When he learns the details of the unhappy woman's story (from one of her fellow prisoners) Sir Launcelot discovers that she is his own former nurse, 'the very woman who watched over my infancy, and even nourished me with her milk!' On his realizing this, 'a tear stole softly down each cheek'. Eventually, because of his rank and wealth, Sir Launcelot is able to intimidate Justice Gobble and to find means of proving his total corruption. He forces Gobble to make amends to those whom he had persecuted. Everyone is discharged from prison, their debts cancelled or paid. The widow, Mrs. Oakley, recovers her reason—and her son, for it turns out that the report of his death had been false and he returns home just after Sir Launcelot has completed his mission of restoring justice all round. Mother and son meet again in a 'tender scene' which Smollett refuses to elaborate on: 'let it suffice to say, their mutual happiness was unspeakable.' Suky, the young man's fiancée, 'though very weak, and greatly emaciated', is found still alive, and of course recovers quickly on the return of her sweetheart. And the chapter ends thus:

> This adventure of our knight was crowned with every happy circumstance that could give pleasure to a generous mind. The prisoners were released, and reinstated in their former occupations. The justice performed his articles from fear, and afterwards turned over a new leaf from remorse. Young Oakley was married to Suky, with whom he received a considerable portion. The new-married couple found a farm ready stocked for them on the knight's estate; and the mother enjoyed a happy retreat in the character of housekeeper at Greavesbury-hall [Sir Launcelot's country house].

It is interesting that here, as in similar scenes throughout Smollett, we find retributive justice, the redressing of wrongs, sensibility, and the restoration of order. Smollett believed in order; he believed in people acting decently and humanely in the particular rank of life to which they were called. He also had an ideal of rustic felicity and accepted that modified Horatian ideal of contented country living which so many eighteenth-century writers found attractive. 'The new-married couple found a farm ready stocked for them on the knight's estate': it is a characteristic Smollett happy ending. Towards the end of *Humphry Clinker*—a novel which is organized so as to point steadily to the superiority of a peaceful, ordered country life over anything the bustling and wicked city can provide—Mr. Dennison describes to Matthew Bramble (who is in many respects Smollett himself) how he 'became enamoured of a country life' and how in consequence he established himself in the country: this description provides one of the moral centres of the novel. 'I drained bogs,' Dennison tells Bramble, 'burned heath, grubbed up furze and fern; I planted copse and willows where nothing else would grow; I gradually inclosed all my farms, and made such improvements that my estate now yields me clear twelve hundred pounds a year—All this time my wife and I have enjoyed uninterrupted health, and a regular flow of spirits, except on a very few occasions, when our cheerfulness was invaded by such accidents as are inseparable from the condition of life.' The combination of healthy rural activity, financial prosperity, and personal content marred only by the inevitable misfortunes to which human life is subject, sums up Smollett's ideal of the good life—an ideal he conspicuously failed to realize in his own chequered career.

Again and again we find in Smollett that the ultimate in human felicity is to land up with a country estate, loved and esteemed by one's tenants and the surrounding rustics. *Sir Launcelot Greaves*, which is the morally simplest of his novels and sets out his principles in almost allegorical terms, has a conclusion in which the knight and his newly married wife (who is of course the beautiful and sensitive girl from whom he had long been parted by the unscrupulous machinations of a wicked relative) return to Greavesbury-hall in a scene of ritual celebration. Sir Launcelot

> was met by about five thousand persons of both sexes and every age, dressed out in their gayest apparel, . . . and the rector from the knight's own parish. They were preceded by music of different kinds, ranged under a great variety of flags and ensigns; and the women, as well as the men, bedizened with fancy-knots and marriage favours. At the end of the avenue, a select bevy of comely virgins arrayed in white, and a separate band of choice youths, distinguished by garlands of laurel and holly interweaved, fell into the procession, and sung in chorus a rustic epithalamium composed by the curate.

The solemn ritual note here is almost reminiscent of Milton's

17

account of Lycidas' reception into heaven, where he

> hears the unexpressive nuptial song,
> In the blest kingdoms meek of joy and love.
> There entertain him all the saints above,
> In solemn troops and sweet societies . . .

It is indeed a symbolic and exemplary conclusion, as the next paragraph makes clear:

> The perfect and uninterrupted felicity of the knight and his endearing consort diffused itself through the whole adjacent country as far as their example and influence could extend. They were admired, esteemed, and applauded, by every person of taste, sentiment, and benevolence; at the same time beloved, revered, and almost adored, by the common people, among whom they suffered not the merciless hand of indigence or misery to seize one single sacrifice.

The relation between Smollett's realism and his moral sensibility—his sentimentality if you like—is a central question in all his work. All his novels are punctuated by scenes of moral edification in which virtue triumphs to the accompaniment of tears of sensibility on the part of the virtuous; these scenes provide, at a deliberately different level of realism from the bulk of the narrative, directions to the reader on how to interpret the author's intentions and moral standards. Professor A. A. Parker, in his illuminating study of the picaresque novel entitled *Literature and the Delinquent*, emphasizes that the picaresque novel in Spain arose 'out of [a] climate of a social satire born of the urge to religious reform'. If we change the phrase 'religious reform' to 'moral reform', this applies exactly to Smollett's novels. The incidents of high moral sensibility which Smollett interpolates amid his scenes of violence, comic coarseness and brutal realism, and which operate at a different level of probability from these scenes, are analogous to the moralizing digressions in Mateo Alemán's *Guzmán de Alfarache*, the novel which Parker calls 'the first fully-developed picaresque novel and the first full-length realistic novel in European literature'. Guzmán, as Parker reminds us, 'has been persistently criticized for attempting to cover up in hypocritical moralizing a relish for unsavoury delinquency.' A similar charge has been made against Daniel Defoe's *Moll Flanders* and other of his novels, and it could be made too against Smollett, though in Smollett's case it is not so much hypocrisy as a radical difference in style and feeling between the vividly realistic passages and the highly stylized scenes of moral edification that may disturb the reader. But these stylized scenes are crucial: they provide the moral justification for the vivid exhibition of the wickedness of the world. The motiveless malignity of individuals—and it is worth noting how many of Smollett's villains, from Captain Oakum and Doctor Mackshane in *Roderick Random* to Justice Gobble in *Sir Launcelot Greaves*, seem to act out of impersonal malice—can drive morally neutral people to crime in order to make a living, and in both Roderick Random and Peregrine Pickle projects the hero into a life of adventuring and fortune-hunting which often strains the reader's belief in him as an acceptable hero. But so long as he remains open to the assault of sensibility he is redeemable, and Smollett sees to it that all his heroes— even, at the end, the atrocious villain Ferdinand Count Fathom—do remain open to such an assault. As a result, the hero is *educable* by experience. Roderick Random, having been united with his long-lost father by one of those positively stunning coincidences in which Smollett's novels abound, and which always serve a moral purpose, tells his father about the life he has led:

> I recounted the most material circumstances of my fortune, to which he listened with wonder and attention, manifesting from time to time those different emotions which my different situations may have raised in a parent's breast, and, when my detail was ended, blessed God for the adversity I had undergone, which, he said, enlarged the understanding, improved the heart, steeled the constitution, and qualified a young man for all the duties and enjoyments of life, much better than any education which affluence could bestow.

Roderick Random is thus a *Bildungsroman*, as in some degree are all Smollett's novels. The significant phrase in the passage I have just quoted is 'improved the heart'. The culture of the heart was of course a theme that much exercised eighteenth-century philosophers, especially those in Scotland. Ten years after Smollett's death Henry Home, Lord Kames, published a book with this very title, *The Culture of the Heart*, in which he argued that 'the culture of the heart during childhood, is the chief branch of education.' And it was in the year of Smollett's death that Henry Mackenzie published *The Man of Feeling*, generally regarded as the prime document in the history of the cult of sensibility in Britain. But Smollett had been there before him. Matthew Bramble, in *Humphry Clinker*, is as much a Man of Feeling as Mackenzie's Harley. Both are given to weeping tears of sensibility. Bramble, however, usually covers his sensibility in public with an appearance of gruff irascibility. The reason is given quite explicitly by his nephew, Jeremy Melford. 'He is as tender as a man without a skin,' Melford writes to his friend Sir Watkin Phillips, 'who cannot bear the slightest touch without flinching. What tickles another would give him torment; . . .' Bramble's bad-temperedly vivid descriptions of everything that offends the senses when people are gathered together in public places in Bath or London are done with a kind of masochistic relish which represents the other side of his sensibility. When he is faced with one of those ritually presented symbolic situations which occur in all Smollett's novels, his reaction is one of pure sensibility:

As we stood at the window of an inn that fronted the public prison, a person arrived on horseback, genteelly, tho' plainly, dressed in a blue frock, with his own hair cut short, and a gold-laced hat upon his head.—Alighting, and giving his horse to the landlord, he advanced to an old man who was at work in paving the street, and accosted him in these words: 'This is hard work for such an old man as you.'—So saying, he took the instrument out of his hand, and began to thump the pavement.—After a few strokes, 'Have you never a son (said he) to ease you of this labour?' 'Yes, an please your honour (replied the senior), I have three hopeful lads, but, at present, they are out of the way.' 'Honour not me (cried the stranger); but more becomes me to honour your grey hairs.—Where are these sons you talk of?' The ancient paviour said, his eldest son was a captain in the East Indies; and the youngest had lately inlisted as a soldier, in hopes of prospering like his brother. The gentleman desiring to know what was become of the second, he wiped his eyes, and owned, he had taken upon him his old father's debts, for which he was now in the prison hard by.

The traveller made three quick steps towards the jail, then turning short, 'Tell me (said he), has that unnatural captain sent you nothing to relieve your distress?' 'Call him not unnatural (replied the other); God's blessing be upon him! he sent me a great deal of money; but I made a bad use of it; I lost it by being security for a gentleman that was my landlord, and was stript of all I had in the world besides.' At that instant a young man, thrusting out his head and neck between two iron bars in the prison-window, exclaimed, 'Father! father! if my brother William is in life, that's he!' 'I am!—I am!—(cried the stranger, clasping the old man in his arms, and shedding a flood of tears)—I am your son Willy, sure enough!' Before the father, who was quite confounded, could make any return to this tenderness, a decent old woman bolting out from the door of a poor habitation, cried, 'Where is my bairn? where is my dear Willy?'—The captain no sooner beheld her, than he quitted his father, and ran into her embrace.

I can assure you, my uncle [i.e. Matthew Bramble: the story is being told by Melford in a letter to a friend], who saw and heard every thing that passed, was as much moved as any one of the parties concerned in this pathetic recognition—He sobbed, and wept, and clapped his hands, and hollowed, and finally ran down into the street. By this time, the captain had retired with his parents, and all the inhabitants of the place were assembled at the door.—Mr. Bramble, nevertheless, pressed thro' the crowd, and entering the house, 'Captain (said he), I beg the favour of your acquaintance—I would have travelled a hundred miles to see this affecting scene; and I shall think myself happy if you and your parents will dine with me at the public house.'

In the end 'the whole family retired to the inn with my uncle, attended by the crowd, the individuals of which shook their townsman by the hand, while he returned their caresses without the least sign of pride or affectation'.

Now this is not one of the scenes in *Humphry Clinker* that admirers of the novel are likely to quote. They, understandably and up to a point justly, prefer the racy humour in the self-characterization of Bramble and of his sister Tabitha in their letters, the unconsciously suggestive malapropisms of Win Jenkins, the absurd yet convincing and in its way moving character of Lieutenant Lismahago, and the progressive mellowing of Bramble's character as he moves northwards to Smollett's native Scotland. They enjoy picking out the didactic threads, identifying the moral satire, showing how Smollett mediates between the extremes of primitive barbarity and corrupting luxury in developing his ideal of the good country life, and pointing to the vitality and humour of the novel. They pass over the preposterous coincidences such as Humphry Clinker, a casually discovered young pauper, turning out to be Bramble's illegitimate son and the actor Wilson, with whom Bramble's niece has been having a clandestine love affair, turning out to be the son of Bramble's worthy friend Dennison and the very person Bramble wants his niece to marry. Up to a point they are right to do so, for the life of the novel resides elsewhere. Yet what we might call the scenes of stylized sentiment provide a sort of emblematic acting out of the moral pattern on which the whole novel is based. One cannot help being struck, in the scene from which I have quoted, by its almost primitive allegorical quality—an old man mending a road, a stranger on horseback accosting him, the brother putting his head out of the prison window to recognize the stranger. It is like a primitive book illustration, a sixteenth-century woodcut illustrating a moral tale. Everybody in the story is simultaneously visible. The prison happens to be right beside the place where the old man is working; the mother emerges from a house equally near; and the whole scene is looked down on by Bramble from the window of his inn which is, as it were, another panel of the same woodcut. This is typical of Smollett's moral vignettes. They operate on a different level of probability from the main narrative of his novels, just as the preposterous coincidences—long-lost friends meeting in the most improbable places, people believed dead on the strongest evidence turning out to be alive, transformations of identity which turn A into the much lamented or long sought B, and so on—are contrivances to force moral crises. For Smollett's actual narrative art is episodic—at its best, vividly and brilliantly episodic. It cannot by itself shape the episodes into a moral or indeed into any sort of pattern. To achieve the moral pattern, he needs the coincidence and the stylized moral vignette.

I began by taking *Sir Launcelot Greaves* as not the best but the most central of Smollett's novels. It is the novel in which his seething indignation in the face of injustice found its 'objective correlative' in an actual knight errant who went about the country redressing wrongs. But of course that is a very unsophisticated technique for an eighteenth-century novelist who wanted to attack the vices of contemporary society. And in endeavouring to give it some plausibility he had to invent melodramatically sentimental reasons for his knight's becoming sufficiently touched in the head so as to embark on his venture. He is not really crazy of course, and it is interesting to see how cagily Smollett keeps bringing in touches of essential sanity after Sir Launcelot's initial introduction as a latter-day Don Quixote. The discovery that his lady love had never really betrayed him, as he had been led to believe, restores him to sanity completely. The fact is that Smollett shows considerable uneasiness about the whole business, and it is this uneasiness that hastens the book (the shortest of his novels) to its rapid conclusion. The reader today will turn to it for help in understanding Smollett, but having got that help it is not likely that he will return.

Sir Launcelot is a wholly good man from the beginning; but what about Roderick Random and Peregrine Pickle, who after a long period of pretty dubious adventuring are rewarded with wealth, social position, and the hand of the beautiful girl they have long loved? The *Bildungsroman* is not necessarily a success story; to be educated by life is not necessarily to get everything you want in the end (and while you are still young enough to enjoy it); but this is how Smollett evidently sees it. The happy endings here can hardly be regarded as stylized moral vignettes, like the ending of *Sir Launcelot Greaves*, for they concentrate quite specifically on matters of finance and personal vindication. 'Fortune seems determined to make ample amends for her former cruelty,' writes Roderick Random at the end of the novel he tells in the first person; 'for my proctor writes, that notwithstanding the clause in my father-in-law's will, on which the squire founds his claim, I shall certainly recover my wife's fortune, in consequence of a codicil annexed, which explains that clause, and limits her restriction to the age of nineteen, after which she was at her own disposal.' As for Peregrine Pickle (whose story is told in the third person):

Many persons of consequence, who had dropped the acquaintance of Peregrine in the beginning of his decline, now made open efforts to cultivate his friendship anew; but he discouraged all these advances with the most mortifying disdain; and one day, when the nobelman whom he had formerly obliged [and who had behaved ungratefully] came up to him in the drawing-room, with the salutation of—'your servant, Mr. Pickle,' he eyed him with a look of inaffable contempt, saying,—'I suppose your lordship is mistaken in your man,' and turned his head another way, in presence of the whole court.

Of course part of the reason for the happy endings here is that they had become—as they were long to remain—a convention of the novel. Readers expected and wanted them. Another reason, at least as far as *Roderick Random* is concerned, for, in its early part at least, this novel has considerable autobiographical elements, is that the happy ending represents a degree of wish fulfilment. Further, a happy ending provides a way in which the author can thumb his nose at the spite and malice of those who hinder a young man's getting on in the world. In this connection, it is worth looking at what Smollett says in his Preface to *Roderick Random*:

> I have attempted to represent modest merit struggling with every difficulty to which a friendless orphan is exposed from his own want of experience, as well as from the selfishness, envy, malice, and base indifference of mankind. To secure a favourable prepossession, I have allowed him the advantage of birth and education, which, in the series of his misfortunes, will, I hope, engage the ingenuous more warmly in his behalf; . . .

Roderick is a young man of 'modest merit'—reasonably moral, but with plenty of weaknesses. His sufferings are wholly the result of 'the selfishness, envy, malice, and base indifference' of others. It is therefore particularly satisfying to see the forces of selfishness, envy and malice deliberately affronted by the hero's final success. It is true that there are parts of the novel in which Roderick acts as a shameless fortune hunter, trying to maintain himself in wealth and reputation by sheer imposture, but even this is shown as the product of desperate necessity, not of malice. His behaviour to the faithful and humble Strap is far from admirable. Yet weakness, vanity, inexperience, credulity, rather than any cruelty of disposition (which he conspicuously lacks) account for his bad behaviour. And if he is forced into trickery to maintain himself, the fault is clearly shown to be in society, which does not reward honesty, industry, openness or kindness, but estimates people entirely by the degree of persuasiveness with which they can act the part of the wealthy and well-connected person of influence. We see this even more clearly in *Peregrine Pickle*. Peregrine is far more the shameless adventurer than Roderick, and is a far from attractive character. But from the beginning he is persecuted by the motiveless malice of his mother (a character treated by Smollett with an obsessive savagery); vanity and unbridled passion are his chief vices, and these are no more the gravest vices for Smollett than they were for Fielding. It is society that forces him to be a fortune-hunter, not, as with Ferdinand Count Fathom, an evil disposition.

So the happy ending in *Roderick Random* and *Peregrine Pickle* can be explained partly as a convention of the novel, partly as wish-fulfilment, partly as nose-thumbing at the spiteful and the malicious people whom Smollett believed to have been responsible for his own lack of success in a variety of fields. But there is something more than this. The happy ending is an expression of what in the last analysis was a moral optimism on Smollett's part. This may sound an outrageous observation to anyone who knows Smollett's life and character. Was he not peevish, irascible, proud, thin-skinned, with a constant chip on his shoulder? Yes he was; yet he was optimistic in the sense that he believed that moral problems could be solved by the good heart, by moral sensibility, and that the combination of a basically good heart and abundant fortune could in the end anchor a young man in a life of exemplary virtue. If in his assumption that people not innately vicious can be forced into a life of tricky fortune-hunting by the way society judges its members and the way it treats them Smollett reminds us of the Thackeray of *Vanity Fair* (and Becky Sharp is more of a Smollett heroine than has been generally recognized), then in his bringing of his heroes to a haven of wealth and regenerated moral feeling he reminds us of Defoe. Of the final prosperity and religious conversion of Defoe's Moll Flanders and Colonel Jack, Professor Parker has this to say:

> Conversion, which had been so real and important an element in the picaresque tradition, is now merely a literary and social convention—the adjunct to a respectable life, which has come to

mean a prosperous one. Respectability had been attained by Guzmán on the torture-rack, by Simplicissimus [the hero of Jacob Christoffel von Grimmelshausen's picaresque novel set during the Thirty Years War] in the cavern on the unhabited island.

It is not fair to apply this to Smollett, for neither Roderick nor Peregrine are 'converted' to virtue as a result of acquiring prosperity, while Ferdinand Count Fathom, the villain who really *is* converted at the end, is converted by his misery, by seeing that vice doesn't pay. But it is true to say that for Smollett vice, though ubiquitous, is unnatural, and virtue results from the natural and easy promptings of the good heart. The good heart manifests itself in acts of benevolence and acts of benevolence can best be performed by men of wealth. Virtue is not the forgiving of your torturers while you are suffering on the rack. True, in Smollett a poor man can give his last penny to a friend or to someone worse off than himself (consider how Strap helps Roderick Random) and in a debtor's prison, a place we see so often in Smollett, the less desperately off can help the desperate. But for Smollett the *model* act of virtue is exercised by benevolent wealth through good feeling. If you are to harrow Hell and redeem the innocent that lie there you must have the physical means to enable you to do it as well as the good heart to prompt the action. Ideal virtue is effortless, and with a rich estate, a good and beautiful wife, loyal and affectionate retainers, and a good heart, a man is in a position to yield to the moral promptings of his heart and be effortlessly virtuous. This is the position in which we see Roderick Random, Peregrine Pickle and Sir Launcelot Greaves at the end of the novels of which they are respectively the heroes. Dickens, who learned so much from Smollett, had a more complex moral vision. Even in the early *Pickwick Papers* the benevolent and prosperous Mr. Pickwick's period in prison is less a harrowing of Hell (though there is an element of this about it, derived from Smollett) than a part of his own education. And in *Great Expectations*, that mature *Bildungs-roman*, gentlemanliness, wealth and virtue are seen to be, if not inevitably incompatible, at least in a very disturbing and problematical relationship.

All this is very abstract, it might well be objected. We don't read Smollett (when we do read him) for the moral ideas underlying the novels, but for the texture of the narrative, the violence, colour, vitality, physical reality, of the sights, sounds, smells, actions he so vividly presents. There can be no doubt that we do find these qualities in Smollett. *Roderick Random* provides an amazing list of strong adventures.

'Blood and wounds!' cried Weazel, 'd'ye question the honour of my wife, Madam? Hell and damnation! no man in England durst say so much. I would flea him—carbonado him! Fury and destruction! I would have his liver for my supper.' So saying, he drew his sword, and flourished with it, to the great terror of Strap; while Miss Jenny, snapping her fingers, told him she did not value his resentment a louse. In the midst of this quarrel, the master of the waggon alighted, who, understanding the cause of the disturbance, and fearing the captain and his lady would take umbrage, and leave his carriage, was at great pains to have everything made up, which he at last accomplished, and we sat down to supper altogether. At bed-time we were shown to our apartments: the old usurer, Strap, and I, to one room; the captain, his wife, and Miss Jenny, to another. About midnight, my companion's bowels being disordered, he got up, in order to go backward; but, in his return, mistaking one door for another, entered Weazel's chamber, and without any hesitation, went to bed to his wife, who was fast asleep; the captain being at the other end of the room, groping for some empty vessel, in lieu of his own chamber pot, which was leaky. As he did not perceive Strap coming in, he went towards his own bed, after having found a convenience; but no sooner did he feel a rough head, covered with a cotton night-cap, than it came into his mind, that he had mistaken Miss Jenny's bed instead of his own, and that the head he felt was that of some gallant, with whom she had made an assignation. Full of this conjecture, and scandalized at the prostitution of his apartment, he snatched up the vessel he had just before filled, and emptied it at once on the astonished barber and his own wife, who, waking on that instant, broke forth into lamentable cries, which not only alarmed the husband beyond measure, but frightened poor Strap almost out of his senses; for he verily believed himself bewitched; especially when the incensed captain seized him by the throat, with a volley of oaths, asking him how he durst have the presumption to attempt the chastity of his wife. Poor Strap was so amazed and confounded, that he could say nothing but—'I take God to witness, she's a virgin for

27

me.' Mrs. Weazel, enraged to find herself in such a pickle, through the precipitation of her husband, arose in her shift, and, with the heel of her shoe, which she found by the bed-side, belaboured the captain's bald pate, till he roared—'Murder.' 'I'll teach you to empty your stink-pots on me,' cried she, 'you pitiful hop-o'-my-thumb coxcomb. What! I warrant you're jealous, you man of lath. Was it for this I condescended to take you to my bed, you poor withered sapless twig?' The noise occasioned by this adventure had brought the master of the waggon and me to the door, where we overheard all that passed with great satisfaction. In the mean time, we were alarmed with the cry of—'Rape! murder! rape!' which Miss Jenny pronounced with great vociferation. 'O! you vile abominable old villain!' said she, 'would you rob me of my virtue? but I'll be revenged of you, you old goat! I will. Help! for heaven's sake! help! I shall be ravished, ruined! help!' Some servants of the inn, hearing this cry, came running up stairs with lights, and such weapons as chance afforded, when we beheld a very diverting scene. In one corner stood the poor captain shivering in his shirt, which was all torn to rags, with a woful visage scratched all over by his wife, who had by this time wrapped the counterpane about her, and sat sobbing on the side of her bed. In the other end lay the old usurer, sprawling on Miss Jenny's bed, with his flannel jacket over his shirt, and his tawny meagre limbs exposed to the air; while she held him fast by the two ears, and loaded him with execrations. . . .

We can leave this 'very diverting scene' while it is still going full blast, observing only that there are literally hundreds more of the same kind in this novel. It is like an expansion of a quintessential mediaeval *fabliau*. It is all there—entering the wrong room or bed in the dark, the emptying of the chamber pot, the screams and accusations and counter-accusations, the grotesque figures, scantily clad, sprawling with their limbs in the air, the misunderstandings, the insults. This is presented as comedy, and there can be no doubt at all that a relish for this kind of simple-minded comedy co-existed in Smollett with the over-riding moral sensibility I have already discussed. It would be a very naïve view of human nature indeed that would dismiss them as incompatible. (Incidentally, it is interesting that this kind of night-time misadventure recurs several times, derived from Smollett, in Dickens' *Pickwick Papers*, but suitably purged of frank sex talk and chamber-pots.) Altogether darker in tone are the scenes set on board the *Thunder*. Here Smollett drew on his own experiences on board the *Cumberland* where he served as surgeon's mate during the ill-fated Carthagena expedition of 1740–41. The appalling brutality of life on board an eighteenth-century man-of-war, where most of the crew were found by the press-gang, is presented with a vividness that makes one positively wince. Yet, though much in these chapters is documentary, the scenes as a whole are far from simple documentaries. The brutal actions are described as acts of calculated malice on the part of individuals of evil character. In some characters Smollett puts all the evil characteristics he can think of; Mackshane, for example, the new ship's surgeon, 'was grossly ignorant, and intolerably assuming, false, vindictive, and unforgiving; a merciless tyrant to his inferiors, an abject sycophant to those above him.' And this description is borne out by numbers of particular incidents. The Captain, too, is a monster and acts accordingly. Life is made possible for Roderick by the kindness of other individuals, particularly by the friendship of the first mate, the proud and eccentric Mr. Morgan, a stage Welshman whose speech contains distinct echoes of Shakespeare's Fluellen and Sir Hugh Evans yet who remains a vivid and persuasive character (though scarcely three-dimensional) who brings much needed comic relief into these grim scenes.

Chapter 33 gives an account of the actual attack on Carthagena, which Smollett later developed in a separate pamphlet. He almost steps out of Roderick's character in giving his ironical explanation of the stupid behaviour of the admiral: this is clearly Smollett speaking. First he tells the reader that there were those who 'taxed this commander with want of honesty, as well as sense; and alleged that he ought to have sacrificed private pique to the interest of his country; that where the lives of so many brave fellow-citizens were concerned, he ought to have concurred with the general, without being solicited, or even desired, towards their preservation and advantage; . . .' He then lists other accusation made by some against the admiral, before concluding: 'But all these suggestions surely proceeded from ignorance and malevolence or else the admiral would not have found it such an easy matter, at his return to England, to justify his conduct to a ministry at once so upright and so discerning.' This, of course, is political satire, and the discursive episodic form of the novel enables Smollett to inject political and social satire at many points, often paying back personal scores, as in his account in Chapter 62 of the poet Melopoyn and his scurvy treatment by theatrical managers and other influential people when he tried vainly over a long period to have his tragedy put on the stage. Smollett himself had left Scotland for London in 1739, at the age of nineteen, with a tragedy *The Regicide, or, James the First of Scotland*, which he could persuade no one to put on, much to his indignation. The account of his vain struggle to have it accepted which he gives in the preface to the published edition of the play shows how autobiographical the Melopoyn episode is: in this episode he tried to *pay back* those who, out of deliberate malice as he believed, kept his play off the stage. (It never occurred to him that it was a bad play: it is in fact a highly rhetorical performance in imitation-Shakespearean blank verse, and though of very little merit it is no worse than many plays that were successful on the eighteenth-century stage.) Though Smollett believed in the good heart he was always a great one for paying back: as I have suggested, his happy endings are a way of paying back his heroes' and so his own enemies.

The account of Roderick's adventures loses something of its brutal vividness after he leaves the ship. His encounter with Narcissa, whom at the end of the book he marries, is described, as are all Smollett's accounts of the heroes' meetings with their future wives, with a studied elegance of romantic feeling that is in sharp contrast with other parts of the narrative: the object is to show the hero possessed of genuine sensibility, which is brought out by the ideal woman. Indeed, the tough adventurism which Roderick has hitherto displayed and which has enabled him to survive great physical hardships now gives way to the soft languishing of a lover which he expresses in an ode:

> Thy fatal shafts unerring move,
> I bow before thine altar, Love.
> I feel thy soft resistless flame
> Glide swift through all my vital frame!
>
> For while I gaze, my bosom glows,
> My blood in tides impetuous flows;
> Hope, Fear, and Joy, alternate roll,
> And floods of transports 'whelm my soul!

This is a far cry from the world of broken heads and emptied chamber-pots of which we have hitherto seen so much. But again it must be emphasized that for Smollett the world of sensibility co-existed with the world of violence and provided the moral standard on which we recognized the world of violence as undesirable, even though it might be interesting and entertaining. In *Humphry Clinker* a similar modulation into the verse of sensibility occurs when Matthew Bramble reaches Smollett's own native part of Scotland. In a letter to his friend Dr. Lewis, Bramble waxes enthusiastic over Loch Lomond and the Water of Leven, an area which he calls 'the Arcadia of Scotland'. To express his enthusiasm, he encloses in his letter a 'copy of a little ode to this river, by Dr. Smollett, who was born on the banks of it'—by this device disclaiming responsibility for Bramble's authorship of the poem, though, as we know that Bramble is in many respects Smollett, the device is pretty transparent. But what a remarkable poem it is for the outwardly satirical and misanthropic Bramble to admire!

> Pure stream! in whose transparent wave
> My youthful limbs I wont to lave;
> No torrents stain thy limpid source;
> No rocks impede thy dimpling course,
> That sweetly warbles o'er its bed,
> With white, round polish'd pebbles spread; . . .

Is this really Smollett? we cannot help asking. Isn't it Henry Vaughan, who wrote similar lines in his poem 'The Water-fall' a hundred years earlier?

> Dear Stream! dear bank, where often I
> Have sate, and pleas'd my pensive eye, . . .

The resemblance must be a coincidence, but it is significant nonetheless. Though Vaughan uses the beauty and clarity of the stream to symbolize the fountain of life and the mystical truths of religion and Smollett is led on to describe an ideal community of happy pastoral workers, both attitudes stem from a sensibility that represents a variety of the Renaissance development of the *beatus ille* tradition. That tradition, of seeking happiness in a garden, in rural retirement, in meditation in the midst of nature, in country content, has been studied in all its varieties by Maren-Sofie Røstvig in her two-volume work entitled *The Happy Man: Studies in the Metamorphoses of a Classical Ideal*. It would take me too far afield to examine the ways in which this tradition reached Smollett, but the fact that it is possible to refer to this tradition at all in discussing Smollett is itself significant.

But to return to Roderick. Having lost all his money at the gaming table he is imprisoned for debt in the Marshalsea. This is the first of the many prison scenes in Smollett; in this underworld microcosm he is able to make points about the nature of society both through direct satire and through the presentation of symbolic situations. Both Scott and Dickens learned from Smollett here. When, in *The Fortunes of Nigel*, the desperate hero takes refuge in Whitefriars, 'then well-known by the cant name of Alsatia', Scott gives us a picture of an underworld society in which 'bankrupt citizens, ruined gamesters, irreclaimable prodigals, desperate duellists, bravoes, homicides, and debauched profligates of every description, all leagued together to maintain the immunities of their asylum'. Dickens knew and admired Scott's picture of life in Alsatia, although of course he had direct access to Smollett as well. The underground world, at the same time realistically and symbolically treated, is an important tradition in the nineteenth-century novel, and it owes much more to Smollett than to earlier picaresque and rogue literature.

Roderick is rescued from prison by his benevolent uncle, Lieutenant Bowling, the first of the series of naval characters in Smollett's novels, and after that the novel proceeds fairly rapidly to its happy ending. Before leaving *Roderick Random*, I must mention another of its features—the inset 'history of Miss Williams'. Such inset histories were of course common in eighteenth-century fiction—one thinks at once of the history of the Man of the Hill in Fielding's *Tom Jones*—and Smollett introduces them in most of his novels. But the point I want to make about Miss Williams' story is that it is the story of a good woman of respectable birth who is driven by betrayal and misfortune to prostitution. She tells the story of her life in a style of conscious elegance, as does, to an even greater extent, the 'Lady of Quality' who tells the extremely long story of *her* life in *Peregrine Pickle*. The good prostitute, the prostitute of sensibility, who in the end is redeemed (and in this novel marries Roderick's faithful retainer Strap), has traditionally been an interest of the Man of Feeling. This is another tradition that stems from Smollett.

Lieutenant Bowling is a very subdued seaman compared to Commodore Hawser Trunnion in Smollett's second novel *Peregrine Pickle*. Trunnion is a stage sailor, with his violently nautical language and kind heart underneath, an eccentric, a 'humour' in the Jonsonian sense; he and his companions, Hatchway and Pipes, living together in a fortified house which Dickens remembered when he described Wemmick's 'fortress' in *Great Expectations*, lie behind a host of later military and naval fictional characters from Uncle Toby in *Tristram Shandy* to Captain Cuttle in *Dombey and Son*, and beyond. Such characters are the products of a flamboyant imagination, which Smollett certainly possessed, and in spite of being two-dimensional can operate with great moral force in the novel in which they play their part. I say *moral* force, because Trunnion, with his combination of good heart and picturesque violence of nautical language, can speak out on the side of the good in critical situations in a way that clears the moral atmosphere and lays bare the moral pattern which sustains the work as a whole. And in *Peregrine Pickle* we need every possible device to suggest a pattern, for the shape of the novel continually gets lost in its doggedly episodic progression. The novel lacks the brutal vigour and the sense of earthy reality we find in so much of *Roderick Random*, and its succession of practical jokes, tricks, acts of vengeance, beatings up, absurd physical accidents and farcical situations sometimes seem to be the products of a desperately searching inventiveness. Smollett took a peculiar pleasure in accidents involving gross physical discomfort. A good example of this is in Chapter XLII, where Peregrine is in Paris. He has fallen in with a couple of eccentric Englishmen, a stupid and ignorant painter named Pallett and a self-important young doctor who always swears that the ancients did everything better than the moderns. To demonstrate this, the doctor arranges a dinner in the manner of the ancient Romans, to which are invited not only Peregrine and Pallett but also (at Peregrine's malicious suggestion) 'a French marquis, an Italian count, and a German baron, whom [Peregrine] knew to be egregious coxcombs, and therefore most likely to enhance the joy of the entertainment'. Here is part of Smollett's account of the dinner:

> The Frenchman, having swallowed the first spoonful, made a full pause, his throat swelled as if an egg had stuck in his gullet, his eyes rolled, and his mouth underwent a series of involuntary contractions and dilations. Pallet, who looked steadfastly at this connoisseur, with a view of consulting his taste, before he would himself venture on the soup, began to be' disturbed at these emotions, and observed, with some concern, that the poor gentleman seemed to be going into a fit; when Peregrine assured him, that these were symptoms of ecstacy, and, for further confirmation, asked the marquis how he found the soup. It was with infinite difficulty that his complaisance could so far master his disgust, as to enable him to answer, 'Altogether excellent, upon my honour!' and the painter, being certified of his approbation, lifted the spoon to his mouth without scruple; but far from justifying the elogium of his taster, when this precious composition diffused itself upon his palate, he seemed to be deprived of all sense and motion, and sat like the leaden statue of some river god, with the liquor flowing out at both sides of his mouth.
>
> The doctor, alarmed at this indecent phenomenon, earnestly inquired into the cause of it; and when Pallet recovered his recollection, and swore that he would rather swallow porridge made of burning brimstone than such an infernal mess as that which he had tasted, the physician, in his own vindication, assured the company, that, except the usual ingredients, he had mixed nothing in the soup but some sal ammoniac, instead of the ancient nitrum, which could not now be procured; and appealed to the marquis, whether such a succedaneum was not an improvement on the whole. The unfortunate petit maitre, driven to the extremity of his condescension, acknowledged it to be a masterly refinement; and feeling himself obliged, in point of honour, to evince his sentiments by his practice, forced a few more mouthfuls of this disagreeable potion down his throat, till his stomach was so much offended, that he was compelled to start up of a sudden; and, in the hurry of his elevation, over-turned his plate into the bosom of the baron. The emergency of his occasions would not permit him to stay and make apologies for his abrupt behaviour; so that he flew into another apartment, where Pickle found him puking, and crossing himself with great devotion; . . . when our hero returned to the dining-room, the German got up, and was under the hands of his own lacquey,

34

who wiped the grease from a rich embroidered waistcoat, while he, almost frantic with his misfortune, stamped upon the ground, and in High Dutch cursed the unlucky banquet, and the impertinent entertainer, who all this time, with great deliberation, consoled him for the disaster, by assuring him, that the damage might be repaired with some oil of turpentine and a hot iron. Peregrine, who could scarce refrain from laughing in his face, appeased his indignation, by telling him how much the whole company, and especially the marquis, was mortified at the accident; and the unhappy salacabia being removed, the places were filled with two pyes, one of dormice, liquored with syrup of white poppies, which the doctor had substituted in the room of roasted poppy-seed, formerly eaten with honey, as a dessert; and the other composed of an hock of pork baked in honey.

And so the party proceeds, until the final course is brought in. The doctor describes it to his guests:

'That which smokes in the middle,' said he, 'is a sow's stomach, filled with a composition of minced pork, hog's brains, eggs, pepper, cloves, garlic, aniseed, rue, ginger, oil, wine, and pickle. On the right-hand side are the teats and belly of a sow, just farrowed, fried with sweet wine, oil, flour, lovage, and pepper. On the left is a fricassee of snails, fed, or rather purged, with milk. At that end next Mr. Pallet are fritters of pompions, lovage, origanum, and oil; and here are a couple of pullets, roasted and stuffed in the manner of Appicius.'

The painter, who by wry faces testified his abhorrence of the sow's stomach, which he compared to a bagpipe, and the snails which had undergone purgation, no sooner heard him mention the roasted pullets, than he eagerly solicited the wing of the fowl; upon which the doctor desired he would take the trouble of cutting them up, and accordingly sent them round, while Mr. Pallet tucked the table-cloth under his chin, and brandished his knife and fork with singular address; but scarce were they set down before him, when the tears ran down his cheeks, and he called aloud, in a manifest disorder,—'Zounds! this is the essence of a whole bed of garlic!' That he might not, however, disappoint or disgrace the entertainer, he opened his instruments to one of the birds; and, when he opened up the cavity, was assaulted by such an irruption of intolerable smells, that, without staying to disengage himself from the cloth, he sprung away, with an exclamation of 'Lord Jesus!' and involved the whole table in havoc, ruin, and confusion.

Before Pickle could accomplish his escape, he was sauced with a syrup of the dormice pye, which went to pieces in the general wreck: and as for the Italian count, he was overwhelmed by the sow's stomach, which, bursting in the fall, discharged its contents upon his leg and thigh, and scalded him so miserably, that he shrieked with anguish, and grinned with a most ghastly and horrible aspect.

There are no moral implications in an incident of this kind. It is knock-about farce, presented as pure entertainment. There is more of it in *Peregrine Pickle* than in any other of Smollett's novels, and the reader has to have a very strong appetite for this sort of thing not to get occasionally wearied. Some accidents and misadventures, on the other hand, do have moral implications, such as the farcical coincidences which prevent Peregrine from carrying out his seduction of the lady he met in the diligence on the way to Ghent or some of the troubles he met with in Paris as a result of his quarrelsomeness, arrogance and lust. For Peregrine is a much more dubious character than Roderick Random, and for large parts of the novel carries with him much less of the reader's sympathy. He even attempts to drug and so seduce the beautiful and virtuous Emilia, who of course in the end forgives him and whom he marries in the happy ending. True, he is persecuted (for reasons never convincingly explained) by his mother, and by his weak-minded father who is subservient to his mother, but on the other hand he is loved and protected by Trunnion, and he goes abroad not as a desperate fortune-hunter but well provided with money and servants, in order to learn more of the world. For all his faults, he has at bottom a generous heart, and a capacity for shedding tears of sensibility. His relations with his sister, the only member of his immediate family who will have anything to do with him, are tender and loving; when they met after a long absence she 'shed a flood of tears in his bosom' and he reciprocated: 'he embraced her with all the piety of fraternal tenderness, wept over her in his turn, assured her that this was one of the happiest moments of his life, and kindly thanked her for having resisted the example and disobeyed the injunctions of his mother's unnatural aversion.' Then there is his tender reconciliation with Mr. Gauntlet, Emilia's brother, after learning his history:

36

Peregrine's generous heart was wrung with anguish, when he understood that this young gentleman, who was the only son of a distinguished officer, had carried arms for the space of five years, without being able to obtain a subaltern's commission, though he had always behaved with remarkable regularity of spirit, and acquired the friendship and esteem of all the officers under whom he had served.

He would at that time, with the utmost pleasure, have shared his finances with him; . . .

—but he wants to find indirect ways of doing this since he doesn't want to wound Gauntlet's sensitivities. All in all, Smollett allows Peregrine's 'pride and vanity' (which he describes as 'the ruling foibles of our adventurer') to take him as far as possible on the road to unscrupulous behaviour without allowing him to lose his potential capacity for sensibility. Such a capacity does not, of course, in any way inhibit his relish for mischief. Time and again we are told how Peregrine promises himself 'store of entertainment' by stage-managing embarrassments or fights or ludicrous situations for other people, such as the occasions when he contrives to get the doctor and the painter to fight a duel (in a scene reminiscent of the way Sir Toby provokes Sir Andrew Aguecheek into challenging the disguised Viola in *Twelfth Night*), or his device for making Pallet believe that the rabbit he was eating was really a cat. This last, incidentally, is an incident deriving from *Gil Blas*, which Smollett had translated (or the translation of which he had supervised) and which clearly had a strong influence on all his work, to an even greater degree than Cervantes, Defoe and Swift, from whom he also learned.

As always in Smollett there are autobiographical elements, and private grudges are ventilated in the presentation of some of the characters. There are also interesting traces of humane political sympathies in his account of the Jacobite exiles of Boulogne making their daily pilgrimage to the shore to look across the Channel towards their native land to which they could not return. We are reminded that, though, in the words of an early biographer, Smollett 'had been bred a Whig', the Battle of Culloden and its aftermath had provoked him to write 'The Tears of Scotland', a poem of patriotic indignation:

Mourn, hapless Caledonia, mourn
Thy banish'd peace, thy laurels torn!
Thy sons, for valour long renown'd,
Lie slaughter'd on their native ground!
Thy hospitable roofs no more
Invite the stranger to the door;
In smoky ruins sunk they lie,
The monuments of cruelty. . . .

After the death of his protector Commodore Trunnion, Peregrine is his own master, and he embarks on a series of misadventures, humiliations and disgraces during which he seems to be more the object of the author's satire than a hero. But these do not last long. After his encounter with the 'Lady of Quality', whose excessively long reminiscences divide the novel roughly into two and whose style of sentimental elegance in narrating her misfortunes reminds us of the very similar style in which John Cleland clothed his bawdy *Memoirs of a Woman of Pleasure* (otherwise known as *Fanny Hill*), he sets up with his misanthropic friend Cadwallader Crabtree as a fake fortune-teller, before proceeding to a variety of other adventures which eventually land him in the Fleet. Once again the prison gives Smollett an opportunity to present not only inset moral stories told by some of the inhabitants (again, stylized to a degree, as all such inset moral stories are in Smollett) but also morally significant situations and incidents, such as the determination of the faithful Hatchway and Pipes to share his fate—something that Dickens remembered when he made Sam Weller insist on sharing prison life with Mr. Pickwick. The death of his unkind father, intestate, restores him to fortune and happiness. Peregrine 'found himself delivered from confinement and disgrace, without being obliged to any person upon earth for his deliverance; he had it now in his power to retort the contempt of the world in a manner suited to his most sanguine wish; he was reconciled to his friend, and enabled to gratify his love, even upon his own terms; and saw himself in possession of a fortune more ample than his first inheritance, with a stock of experience that would steer him clear of all those quicksands among which he had been formerly wrecked'. A *Bildungsroman* indeed!

Peregrine's fortune is now £80,000, £10,000 more than the £70,000 left to Ernest Pontifex by his Aunt Alethea in Samuel

Butler's *The Way of all Flesh*, which enables Ernest to revenge himself upon his parents. Ernest's laughing reply to his detested father when his father asks him why the money was not handed over to himself or to his brother John savours of the same kind of vengeful use of final prosperity of which I earlier noted a trace in Peregrine Pickle. Only Butler's revenge is more savage:

> Theobald flushed scarlet. 'But why,' he said, and these were the first words that actually crossed his lips—'if the money was not his to keep, did [Mr. Overton, Alethea's trustee] not hand it over to my brother John and me?' . . .
>
> 'Because, my dear father,' said Ernest still laughing, 'my aunt left it to him in trust for me, not in trust either for you or for my Uncle John—and it has accumulated till it is now over £70,000. . . .'

It may seem a long way from Smollett to Butler, but we can go even further, to Butler's great admirer Bernard Shaw. For Chapter LXXXVII of *Peregrine Pickle* contains a story which was almost certainly the inspiration of Shaw's *Pygmalion*. Peregrine finds on the road an attractive, but ragged, filthy and ill-spoken beggar girl, and he is seized with the whim to turn her into a presentable lady by improving her speech, manners and clothes. He has her sent to his home, where the first thing that she has to undergo is an unaccustomed bath and a thorough scrubbing. Peregrine had 'observed, that the conversation of those who are dignified with the appellation of polite company, is neither more edifying nor entertaining than that which is met among the lower classes of mankind; and that the only essential difference, in point of demeanour, is the form of an education, which the meanest capacity can acquire without much study or application. Possessed of this notion, he determined to take the young mendicant under his own tutorage and instruction. In consequence of which, he hoped he should, in a few weeks, be able to produce her in company, as an accomplished young lady of uncommon wit and an excellent understanding.' He succeeded brilliantly, though he had difficulty in overcoming the lady's 'inveterate habit of swearing'. The time came when she could be safely presented to the *beau monde*, and this was duly done. All seemed to be going well until

> one evening, being at cards with a certain lady whom she detected in the very act of unfair conveyance, she taxed her

roundly with the fraud, and brought upon herself such a torrent of sarcastic reproof as overbore all her maxims of caution, and burst open the floodgates of her own natural repartee, twanged off with the appellation of b—— and w——, which she repeated with great vehemence, in an attitude of manual defiance, to the terror of her antagonist and the astonishment of all present: nay, to such an unguarded pitch was she provoked that, starting up, she snapped her fingers in testimony of disdain, and, as she quitted the room, applied her hand to that part which was the last of her that disappeared, inviting the company to kiss it by one of its coarsest denominations.

For a novelist as little read as Smollett, his influence has proved surprisingly pervasive.

The Adventures of Ferdinand Count Fathom, Smollett's third novel, is the only one of his novels which can be classed as picaresque in the sense in which Professor Parker has defined that *genre*, for it has a true delinquent as hero. Indeed, Parker calls it 'the last European novel of any consequence that is directly within the tradition started by *Guzmán de Alfarache*'. Smollett was a little nervous of working within the rogue tradition, as his preface indicates:

> Let me not, therefore, be condemned for having chosen my principal character from the purlieus of treachery and fraud, when I declare my purpose is to set him up as a beacon for the benefit of the inexperienced and unwary, who, from the perusal of these memoirs, may learn to avoid the manifold snares with which they are continually surrounded in the paths of life; while those who hesitate on the brink of iniquity may be terrified from plunging into that irredemiable gulf, by surveying the deplorable fate of *Ferdinand Count Fathom*.

Smollett is not being hypocritical here, and we do not have here the problem we have in, say, Defoe's *Moll Flanders*, where obvious enjoyment in the presentation of a criminal life co-exists with the professed aim of edification. Though *Ferdinand Count Fathom* sustains the reader's interest with the provocative liveliness of its main narrative, the instances of treachery, betrayal, double-crossing and perfidy on the part of his hero really do arouse the reader's moral indignation, as they are intended to. We do not need the interpolation of moral vignettes, in the standard Smollett manner, to establish the moral pattern, for nowhere are we tempted to admire Ferdinand or to have any feeling towards him other than one of moral detestation, even though his adventures are continually *interesting*. To sustain interest without sympathy is difficult in any kind of narrative, and Smollett's technical feat is considerable.

But Smollett did not trust his account of his villain's villainy to make its own moral point. 'That the mind might not be fatigued, nor the imagination disgusted, by a succession of vicious objects,' his preface continues, 'I have endeavoured to refresh the attention with occasional incidents of a different nature; and raised up a virtuous character, in opposition to the adventurer, with a view to amuse the fancy, engage the affection, and form a striking contrast which might heighten the expression, and give a *relief* to the moral of the whole.'

At one point, when Ferdinand has apparently driven to her death the beautiful and innocent fiancée of his friend and benefactor, after having maliciously estranged them from each other in the hope of seducing the girl himself, Smollett breaks out: 'Perfidious wretch! thy crimes turn out so atrocious, that I half repent me of having undertaken to record thy memoirs.' But he goes on to point out that

> such monsters ought to be exhibited to public view, that mankind may be upon their guard against imposture; that the world may see how fraud is apt to overshoot itself; and that as virtue, though it may suffer for a while, will triumph in the end, so iniquity, though it may prosper for a season, will at last be overtaken by that punishment and disgrace which are its due.

Smollett's answer to the old question, 'Why do the wicked prosper?', is that in the long run they don't; sooner or later, and quite often sooner, they over-reach themselves and are destroyed or forced to repentance. You will see why earlier I called Smollett an optimist.

Ferdinand, like all Smollett's villains, is villainous by nature; we are not given any psychological explanation of his evil disposition, unless his mother's having been a *femme de guerre* with various European armies and having had the habit after a battle of murdering wounded soldiers for their possessions can be considered as providing a hereditary reason for his delinquency. But he early acquires a generous patron, and is given an excellent start in life. He is a brilliant actor and consummate

41

hypocrite, dissimulation and deceit being at the centre of his villainy. He even lacks physical courage, but what Smollett calls his 'sagacity and presence of mind' manage to supply the place of it. Throughout the whole of his life as a villain he is playing a part, in order to obtain money or position or to seduce a girl or sometimes simply to amuse himself. If in Dickens hypocrisy is so central a clue to moral evil, here again we can see the influence of Smollett.

In displaying the virtuosity of Ferdinand's hypocritical role-taking, Smollett is able to attack a host of contemporary social follies and villainies, for generally it is the folly or villainy (or both) of society that makes it possible for the hypocrite to prosper. Ferdinand's career as a medical practitioner enabled his creator, who had studied medicine at Glasgow and had himself practised as a doctor, to give his views of the abuses of medical practice. Anyone interested in the social role of the doctor in the eighteenth century, and in the difference in function and social prestige between the apothecary, the surgeon and the physician, will find much illumination in this novel. I have myself found the novel richer in social details than any other of Smollett's. For instance, I had occasion not long ago to inquire into the degree to which the habit of whisky-drinking (as distinct from gin-drinking) had come into London from Scotland and Ireland by the third quarter of the eighteenth century, and sure enough we find that Ferdinand, in order to make people think that he was busy with his medical practice, would keep his carriage conspicuously waiting while he, supposedly attending patients, would in fact 'glide into some obscure coffeehouse, and treat himself with a dram of usquebaugh'.

Ferdinand's double-crossing of his friend and benefactor Renaldo, a type of the virtuous man of feeling, and his driving of Renaldo's fiancée Monimia to apparent death, precipitates the climax of the plot. For, in a characteristic Smollett *anagnorisis*, Monimia turns out in the end not only to be alive, but to be identical with Serafina, the daughter of the Spanish Don Diego whom Roderick had swindled out of all his money in Paris. Don Diego had fled from Spain in the belief that he had been responsible for the deaths of his wife and daughter (a belief now revealed to have been totally unfounded). His discovery that he was innocent of the deaths of these two women together with the revelation that Monimia-Serafina was not dead after all, is what makes the happy ending possible. For Don Diego was not the virtual murderer he thought he was, and Ferdinand, evil though his behaviour had been, was not after all responsible for the ruin and death of Monimia. Ferdinand's most ambitious and complicated plot not only failed, but hadn't really taken place: he *thought* he had committed this evil, but in fact he hadn't. This reminds us of Shakespeare's *Measure for Measure*, where forgiveness all round is possible because in the end it is revealed that nobody (except Lucio) was actually guilty of what they believed themselves to be guilty of: Angelo had not viciously trapped Isabella into yielding her body to him, for the girl he had spent the night with, unknown to him, was his own former fiancée and virtual wife. This device is taken to extraordinary lengths in Ferdinand Count Fathom, where in the end the past is, one might say, *undone*; it is revealed *not to have occurred*—and this in spite of the vivid detail in which it was earlier described.

But, after all, this is only a device to enable Smollett to wind up the novel in the true spirit of moral edification and to provide a context in which Ferdinand's penitence, which comes about as a result of the final failure of all his schemes and his subsequent imprisonment and degradation, can be accepted. It also enables Smollett to shift the emphasis in the end to Renaldo and Serafina and to their triumphant union as an ideal and an ideally happy couple. The last section of the book is mostly taken up with the restored fortunes of this couple and of Don Diego. That their fortunes are restored is largely due to the good offices of a benevolent and sentimental Jewish money-lender (once again, Dickens remembered this, in the character of Riah in *Our Mutual Friend*). This Jewish man of feeling, who provides interest-free loans to enable gentlemen in distress to recover their fortunes and gives plain gifts on other occasions, is a new phenomenon in English fiction. At the various revelations of the identity of lost characters there is of course weeping all round, and when Don Diego discovers his supposedly dead daughter Serafina even Joshua, the Jew, bursts into tears of sensibility, Smollett's final seal of approval.

> . . . as for Joshua, the drops of true benevolence flowed from his eyes, like the oil on Aaron's beard, while he skipped about the

room in an awkward ecstacy, and in a voice resembling the
hoarse notes of the long-eared tribe, cried,—'O father Abraham!
such a moving scene hath not been acted since Joseph disclosed
himself unto his brethren in Egypt!'

In the end Ferdinand Count Fathom weeps too. Renaldo, to
whom he has behaved with such baseness, forgives and helps
him. The penitent Ferdinand seeks an interview with his
benefactor, who has now married his Serafina and entered into
his inheritance to become Count Melvil:

> Overwhelmed as I am with Count Melvil's generosity, together
> with a consciousness of my own unworthiness, it ill becomes a
> wretch like me to importune him for further favour; yet I could
> not bear the thought of withdrawing (perhaps for ever) from the
> presence of my benefactor, without soliciting his permission to
> see his face in mercy, to acknowledge my atrocious crimes, to
> hear my pardon confirmed by his voice, and that of his accom-
> plished countess, whom I dare not even at a distance behold; and
> to express my fervent wish for their prosperity.

Renaldo replies in words of encouragement and forgiveness,
and extends his hand, which Ferdinand bathes in tears.
Ferdinand, now married to a girl he had seduced quite early in
his career of vice, retires with his wife to his retreat somewhere
in the north of England, 'which he found extremely well
adapted to the circumstances of his mind and fortune', to lead 'a
sober and penitent life'. Our last view of him, however, is not in
this novel at all but in Smollett's last novel, *Humphry Clinker*.
Matthew Bramble runs into Renaldo and Serafina in York-
shire, when all three are on their way to Scotland, and by
another of Smollett's characteristically manipulated coincidences, they find at the same time that a country apothecary
named Grieve is really the reformed Ferdinand. Bramble is
present at the recognition scene, which is precipitated by the
discovery that Grieve's daughter is called Seraphina Melvilia
after 'the two noble persons abroad to whom he had been
obliged for more than life'. Bramble sums up the position in a
letter to his friend Dr. Lewis:

> Being a sincere convert to virtue, he [Ferdinand] had changed
> his name, that he might elude the enquiries of the count, whose
> generous allowance he determined to forego, that he might have
> no dependence but upon his own industry and moderation. He

had accordingly settled in this village as a practitioner in surgery and physic, and for some years wrestled with all the miseries of indigence, which, however, he and his wife bore with exemplary resignation. At length, by dint of unwearied attention to the duties of his profession, which he exercised with equal humanity and success, he had acquired a tolerable share of business among farmers and common people, which enabled him to live in a decent manner. . . . In short, the adventurer Fathom was, under the name of Grieve, universally respected among the commonalty of this district, as a prodigy of learning and virtue. . . . I make no doubt that Grieve will be pressed to leave off business, and re-unite himself to the count's family; and as the countess seemed extremely fond of his daughter, she will, in all probability, insist upon Seraphina's accompanying her to Scotland.

So the wicked Ferdinand Count Fathom is finally absorbed into the moral pattern of Smollett's last novel, a novel where in the end everything—irascibility, petulance, eccentricity, pride, silliness and even evil—softens into a moral landscape in which sensibility and rural content are the principal features. The Man of Feeling has triumphed over the satirist.

The irascibility and the satire remain, however, as an important part of Smollett's literary character. His *Travels in France and Italy* show him nosing his way through those countries with an extraordinary mixture of censoriousness and sheer curiosity. Sterne, whose *Sentimental Journey* appeared two years later in 1768, contrasted his own ability to take pleasure in everything with the querulous attitude of Smollett:

> The learned SMELFUNGUS travelled from Boulogne to Paris— from Paris to Rome—and so on—but he set out with the spleen and jaundice, and every object he pass'd by was discoloured or distorted—He wrote an account of them, but 'twas nothing but the account of his miserable feelings.

But an account of his feelings, whether miserable or not, was precisely what the Man of Feeling was expected to give, and, for all Sterne's antipathy, he and Smollett shared a belief in the primacy of feeling. Of course, feeling could be peevish and splenetic. Smollett's most sustained work of deliberate and even nasty offensiveness is his *Adventures of an Atom*, a hard-hitting (and wide-hitting) political satire attacking pretty well everything that had happened in English politics for several generations, in the thinly disguised form of an account of an early period of Japanese history; it is very much a work of personal feeling. Satire and sensibility, censoriousness and a capacity for deep yet easily released emotion, the man of wrath and the Man of Feeling, are closely allied. Smollett's literary career shows this clearly. His work provides an important clue to the development of taste, ethical attitudes and patterns of moral emotion in eighteenth-century England—and Scotland. It provided all kinds of suggestions and situations for later novelists, including Scott, Dickens and Thackeray. And if his novels are not among the very greatest in our literature, they are, at their best, vivid, entertaining, provocative and disturbing. A generation which is interested in the nature of violence and in the relation of violence to moral feeling might well find Smollett's novels, in one of their favourite words, extremely 'relevant'.

2

Matthew Bramble's Bath: Smollett and the West Indian Connection

by ROBERT GIDDINGS

'By a kind of magnetic force England draws to it all that is good in the plantations. It is the centre to which all things tend. Nothing but England can we relish or fancy; our hearts are here, wherever our bodies be. If we get a little money, we remit it to England. They that are able, breed up their children in England. All that we can rap and rend is brought to England . . .'—Edward Littleton (Agent for the Island of Barbados) in 1689.

'The sickness still continued to increase among the troops, and even infect the sailors to such a degree that they died in great numbers . . . In order therefore to prevent the total ruin of the army and fleet, preparations were made to quit this inhospitable climate . . . the whole fleet being wooded and watered for the voyage . . . they set sail for Jamaica. Thus ended, in damage and disgrace, the ever memorable expedition to Carthagena, undertaken with an armament, which if properly conducted, might have not only ruined the Spanish settlements in America, but even reduced the whole West Indies under the domination of Great Britain . . .'—Tobias Smollett, *A Compendium of Authentic and Interesting Voyages* (1756).

47

1

Writing on 5 May 1770 Matthew Bramble describes how Bath has declined in gentility and good taste as the result of the contemporary passion for luxury: 'About a dozen years ago,' he writes to Dr Lewis,

> many decent families, restricted to small fortunes, besides those that came hither on the score of health, were tempted to settle in Bath, where they could then live comfortably, and even make a genteel appearance, at a small expense: but the madness of the times has made the place too hot for them . . . Some have already fled to the mountains of Wales, and others have retired to Exeter. Thither, no doubt, they will be followed by the flood of luxury and extravagance, which will drive them from place to place to the very Land's End. . . .

He is touching, of course, upon a theme which was becoming a topic of quite general comment by the close of the eighteenth century. On 14 April 1778 James Boswell and Samuel Johnson dined with General James Edward Oglethorpe, the colonist of Georgia. In the course of the conversation, Oglethorpe began to declaim against luxury. Dr. Johnson argued that luxury produced much good, that no nation was ever hurt by luxury, and asserted that 'every state of society is as luxurious as it can be. Men always take the best they can get.' Oglethorpe countered by claiming that '. . . the best depends much upon ourselves; and if we can be as well satisfied with plain things, we are in the wrong to accustom our palates to what is high-seasoned and expensive.' Typically, Johnson refused to yield the point.

> But hold, Sir; to be merely satisfied is not enough. It is in refinement and elegance that the civilized man differs from the savage. A great part of our industry, and all our ingenuity is exercised in procuring pleasure. . . .

In May 1770, the same month and the same year in which Matthew Bramble wrote about the damaging effects of luxury upon the city of Bath, Oliver Goldsmith published *The Deserted Village*, one of the central statements in our literature on the theme of the social decay effected by the trade in luxury and opulence. In the dedicatory letter to Sir Joshua Reynolds the poet wrote that in regretting the depopulation of the country he was inveighing 'against the increase of our luxuries' and went on to say that he expected therefore to have the 'shout of modern politicians' against him. 'For twenty or thirty years past,' he suggested, 'it has been the fashion to consider luxury as one of the greatest national advantages. . . .' Goldsmith told Sir Joshua Reynolds that he thought 'those luxuries prejudicial to states by which so many vices are introduced, and so many kingdoms . . . undone'.

The disintegration of the old social order in the wake of the rising tide of luxury, mammonism and the mechanization of life develops into one of the dominating themes of western literature (cf. Wordsworth: *The Excursion*, Book VIII, lines 39 and following) but what Smollett puts before us in the sections on the city of Bath in *Humphry Clinker* is not only sharply and accurately observed social comment, but a portrait of society at a particular stage of development, as the nation slowly changed from supporting itself from its own indigenous resources into a country which fed its population and provided for its luxuries by overseas trade. We are looking at the metamorphosis of an agriculturally based economy into a capitalist imperialist nation.

2

Britain was never really an important province of the Roman empire, valuable mainly for its grain, tin and lead. There were a few small country towns and large estates but most settled life was in the South East and South West. Bath (*Aquae Sulis*) belonged to the settled part of southern England. It was easy to get to and to get from, the Fosseway ran from north-east to south-west, joining the four towns of Lincoln, Leicester, Bath and Exeter. In Roman times Bath drew visitors for its Temple of Sul. People also came for the sake of the hot springs. The area was conquered by Saxon invaders in 577. The baths were silted up, buildings fell in and birds nested in the ruins.

Bath developed in the early middle ages within the economic context of feudalism, it became an episcopal and monastic city with a local and in part national reputation for its healing springs. By the tenth century it was presided over by a Reeve— an official of some importance in the Saxon period. It had been Christianized some time in the seventh century and was the site of a monastery of Black Benedictine monks, whose abbey was built here. Refugee monks from Ghent came here in the tenth century and the Flemish influence remained strong for over a century. The *Domesday Boke* contains this reference to the city:

> The king holds Bath. In the time of king Edward it was taxed at the rate of twenty hides, when the county of Somerset was assessed. Here the king has twenty four burgesses, paying him four pounds by the year, and there are ninety burgesses under the protection of other men, paying their sixty shillings per annum. . . .

The city grew into a prosperous medieval town, its importance the result of its becoming a monastic centre and See—Bath and Wells—ordained by Pope Innocent IV in 1245. Bishop John of Tours had a large abbey built here, bigger than that of Winchester or Ely or Norwich. (The present abbey is sixteenth century and in fact covers only the nave of the original church.) Richard I granted Bath its charter in 1189. The wealth of medieval Bath came from its being the centre of the West Country's woollen trade—as Chaucer says:

> Of cloth-making she had such an haunt
> She passed them of Ypres and of Gaunt.

The Monks Mills survived until the eighteenth century. Our best source of knowledge about Bath in the middle ages is John Leyland (1506–52), who noted much evidence of Bath's prosperity, a great gate with a stone arch, sundry churches, and the conveying of the hot spring water by 'pipes of lead' to many houses in the city. The baths were frequented by 'people diseased with Leprosy, Pox, Scabs and Great Aches'. There were several baths, the King's Bath being 'very fine and fair and large . . .'.

The rebuilding of the abbey during the fifteenth century is evidence of Bath's continuing prosperity. Oliver King, who became Bishop of Bath and Wells in 1495, put the ecclesiastical accounts in order and saved money towards the rebuilding of what is, in fact, the priory church at Bath.

The Reformation had a catastrophic effect on Bath Abbey. The Priory was dissolved in 1540. Thomas Cromwell's commissioners presented their evidence about the wealth of the religious establishments in such a way as to discredit them as a preliminary to taking them over. The details were always presented in such a way as to suggest bankruptcy and moral degeneracy. On the Priory at Bath they had this to say:

> It may please your goodness to understand that we have visited Bath . . . we found the Prior a right virtuous man . . . a man simple and not of the greatest wit . . . his monks worse that I have found yet both in buggery and adultery, some of them having ten women, some eight and the rest so fewer. The House well repaired but four hundred pounds in debt. . . .

Reading between the lines we may conclude the establishment was a wealthy one.

The well-to-do citizens of Bath tried to buy King Henry's good favours with presents—including Irish hawks and by granting Cromwell an annuity of £5 a year (approximately £3,000 in today's money, this was before Henry VIII debased the coinage and before the great inflations brought about by the influx of gold from South America). It was to no avail. Immediately before the dissolution the monks sold or granted leases on their lands, revenues and benefices. This was an attempt to capitalize their holdings and to create legal ties in the area. When King Henry's commissioners, John Tregonwell and William Petre, came to Bath to claim the monastic wealth and property, they found the bulk of it disposed of and also that they had to honour the contracts the monks had given the local gentry. This is the basis of several of the local fortunes which descended through various families in the city and were to fund the great rebuilding of Bath in the eighteenth century. The commissioners offered the abbey to the citizens of Bath for 500 marks (a mark = 13s. 4d., two thirds of a pound). The cautious Bathonians refused, for fear of cozening the king, but they took things into their own hands. The beautiful and magnificent priory church was stripped of all its valuables—glass, lead, gold—the lot was sold off to merchants. Only the shell of bishop Oliver King's massive church remained, the walls and certain sections of the roof. King Henry had it sold off to one Humphrey Colles, who in turn sold off the precinct and the church as it stood to Matthew Colthurst. Edmond Colthurst, his son, gave what remained standing of the church to the citizens of Bath for their parish church, and the remainder of the premises he sold to Fulk Morley, from whom it descended to the Duke of

Kingston (family name, Pierrepoint) and Earl Manvers. North Parade and South Parade (1735–40) were built on land owned by the Duke of Kingston, hence Duke Street and Pierrepoint Street: Manvers Street, which runs from Pierrepoint Street to the site now occupied by the Spa Station, commemorates the other titled beneficiary of Bath's priory lands, and Dorchester Street, which joins Manvers Street, was named for Evelyn Pierrepoint, first Marquis of Dorchester.

During most of Queen Elizabeth I's reign the abbey lay in ruins, although the city was prosperous enough. Gradually local charity and individual benevolence provided for the repair of the east end of the north aisle. During the years 1573–80 the Queen authorized collections to be made nationwide for the restoration of the church. By the time of the Armada services could be held in parts of the abbey, which was finally reconstructed and dedicated to saints Peter and Paul while James Montagu was bishop of Bath and Wells 1608–16. Evidence of the wealth of the city is to be found in the fact that Elizabeth granted Bath a charter in 1590, by which Bath was declared to be a sole city on its own, and the citizens to be a body corporate and politic, by the name of 'Mayor, Aldermen and Citizens' with full powers of government.

Bath was still not a fashionable medicinable place, and it was some years before Bath was to receive the royal touch which made her fashionable. Anne of Denmark, wife of James I, visited the city in 1616. A new bath had been constructed but it was still the done thing to bathe in the Cross Bath. She was about to enter when she had a vision of a great flame shooting out from the cistern of the Cross Bath and was so frightened that she refused to get in. Instead she bathed in the new baths, still called the Queen's Bath today. The well-to-do now began to come to Bath and neglected the continent, with them came the hangers-on, card-sharpers, hucksters, tarts and their pimps, social climbers, although bathing was a still pretty rough affair: 'The baths were like so many Bear Gardens', a contemporary wrote,

> and modesty was entirely shut out of them: people of both sexes bathing by Day and Night naked; and Dogs and Cats and even Human Creatures were hurled over the rails into the Water while People were bathing in it. . . .

The visit of Charles II and his court in 1663 put the royal seal of approval on the spa city (one of the best accounts of Bath at this time is to be found in Pepys' diary for June 1668: he noted among other things, 'a pretty good market place, and many good streets, and very fair stone houses . . .').

The creation of Bath as the centre of fashion, for which the Georgian city was built, was the result of a combination of factors: Charles II and his circle created the style of court and society life much as we would recognize it today and places of resort for the well-born and well-to-do had to meet the requirements of those used to metropolitan social life; Bath became a fashionable spa; Richard (Beau) Nash arrived on the scene to organize the city and its entertainments; a combination of war and of trade was beginning to create a massive injection of wealth into British social life; and the landowners (Gay, Pierrepoint, Manvers, Pulteney) got together with the builders and architects (Wood, father and son) to create suitable accommodation to house and to entertain the wealthy in the season (Bath had eight thousand visitors in 1715, the first Pump Room was finished in 1706). The essential links in the story of the creation of Georgian Bath are to be found in the association between Ralph Allen and John Wood. Allen was Bath's wealthy postmaster. He married the illegitimate daughter of General Wade, M.P. for Bath, who left him his fortune and got him a place on the city Council. Allen bought the quarries at Combe Down. John Wood was a surveyor and architect who was inspired by Palladianism. Wealth, ambition, influence, opportunity, ideas—the equation was complete. Nash recognized the potential of Bath and saw that it needed accommodation for the visitors who would flock to spend their wealth during the season at a fashionable resort which combined medical treatment and entertainment. Royal recognition offered the opportunity to men of vision to put Bath on the map. Allen controlled the raw materials. Wood had the imagination to see in Bath the possibility of creating an elegant and imposing city. The landowners and leaseholders were agreeable. Allen was the vital connection with the city Council. Bath became the first city in Britain to make the holiday and tourist industry its main source of income. 'The eighteenth century in time saw in Bath a swift, sharp break with the town's old traditions', writes Bryan Little in *The Building of Bath* (1947), 'a jump forward from the early slow evolution from clothing town to Spa. It was a conscious, highly artificial transformation, as much of a change as Swindon or Dagenham underwent in their respective phases of our modern industrial age. . . .' Bramble had a less favourable view. He writes to tell Dr. Lewis that he finds

> nothing but disappointment at Bath; which is so altered, that I can scarce believe it is the same place that I frequented about thirty years ago . . . this place, which Nature and Providence seem to have intended as a resource from distemper and disquiet, is become the very centre of racket and dissipation. . . .

The cause of the trouble, Bramble diagnosed, was 'the general tide of luxury, which hath overspread the nation . . .'. And where did this wealth come from?

3

On 26 October 1740 Smollett sailed as a surgeon's mate on board the *Chichester*, with eighty guns, one of the largest vessels to leave St. Helens, under the command of Sir Chaloner Ogle, to reinforce the fleet of Admiral Edward Vernon at the West Indies. Britain was at war with Spain. (The terrible conditions of service in the navy during this expedition Smollett described in *Roderick Random* and *A Compendium of Authentic and Interesting Voyages*.) Colonial expansion by means of war, and the wealth from the West Indian slave trade—these are the major sources of the wealth and luxury so frequently noted by commentators of the time. Smollett's associations with both are clear—he served in the West Indian campaign and it was at Jamaica that he met and fell in love with the handsome Creole Anne Lascelles, who became his wife in 1747. She was heiress of an estate and slaves valued then at £3,000. He was to experience great difficulties in laying hands on this wealth. While some of the nation wallowed in luxury at the expense of the West Indies, he was writing, 'I have been hedging and lurching these six weeks in expectation of that cursed ship from Jamaica, which is at last arrived without Letter of Remittance . . .' (a letter to William Hunter, 1751). Three years later he writes: 'Never was I so harrassed . . . as now; a persecution which I owe to the detention of that remittance from Jamaica which I have every day expected since last Christmas . . .' (a letter to George Macaulay, November 1754). To his printer he wrote in October 1757: 'It is a very hard case that I should be troubled . . . when there are actually fifteen hundred pounds . . . due to us at Jamaica . . .' (letter to William Strahan). While the nation thrived, he fretted and went short. *'Magnas inter opes inops'*—he might well recall his Horace. Commerce grew faster than agriculture in the period 1690–1760. Imports of merchandise rose from 16*s*. a head of the population in 1690, to £1 12*s*. a head in 1760, and exports from 18*s*. to £2 2*s*. in the same period, growing at the rate of 1½% per annum throughout this period. Trade with Europe almost stagnated, imports falling 53% at the beginning of the century to 44% by 1750 and to 31% by the end of the century. By contrast trade with the North American Colonies and the West Indies, Africa, India and the Far East increased by leaps and bounds. Independent planters and traders could get wealthier than the directors of overseas trading companies.

This is how the system worked. The American colonies supplied Britain with some necessities, such as naval stores, iron, in the normal way of trade. Much of it was carried in American shipping, the rest of the trade was lucrative (developed under the Navigation Acts) and the gain went to the British mercantile interests. A large part of the colonial imports were re-exported to Europe, and in the process giving a profit of some fifteen per cent of the trade to British shippers and merchants, as well as encouraging new industries such as tobacco-curing and sugar-refining. In addition, British manufacturers were engaged in making goods to exchange for slaves, as well as engaging in the trade itself. Defoe, writing in 1728, said: 'As slaves are the produce of the British Commerce in their *African* Factories . . . they are so far a branch of the *British* Exportation, just as if they were first brought to *England*, landed there, and sent Abroad . . .' (*A Plan of the English Commerce*, 1728). The plantation economy of the West Indies and parts of the American colonies was ultimately financed from England and gave its profits to England. This was also the case with other triangular trade patterns. The wealth created in trade with the West Indies reappeared in Britain in the pockets of returned nabobs, negro-drivers, planters, clerks, factors and hucksters—the wealth they brought back with them was invested in England in titles, in land, or further commercial ventures. This trade in turn created banks, other financial institutions, such as insurance companies, which brought further invisible earnings from abroad. The wealth of the Lascelles family in London, of the Beckford family (William Beckford squandered the family fortune on Fonthill Abbey and Beckford's Tower, in Bath), of the Pinney family in Bristol, of the Pulteney family of Bath, of the Gladstone family in Liverpool—all was based in slave plantations in the West Indies.

Slaving produced wealth not so much because slaves were cheap (they were not) but because there was such a demand for sugar. By the mid-eighteenth century there were two giants among sugar exporting islands, British Jamaica and French Saint-Dominique. A feature of the sugar trade was the habit of the plantocracy to live as absentee landlords in England, leaving estates in the hands of overseers and attorneys, spending income from slaves and sugar at home in England. The essential part of the trick was that slaves made it possible to replace former crops such as coffee, tobacco, indigo, fruit, etc.— all of which could be grown on small acreages for modest or uncertain profits—with a vast monoculture, sugar. It was a rich man's crop, needing huge estates and a massive labour force, based on large investment sunk in the purchase of estate and of slaves.

The tonnage figures of British shipping is striking evidence of the growth of Britain as a trading and commercial nation in this period. In 1702 total British tonnage was 323,000, but by 1763, the year in which the Peace of Paris brought to an end the Seven Years' War and gave Britain the best bits of North America and India, total tonnage was 496,000. The tonnage engaged in foreign trade rose from 123,000 in 1702 to 304,000 in 1773. The figures on entries and clearances at British ports show the same staggering increase: from 827,000 tons in 1686 to 1,450,000 in 1765. The new wealth brought expansion in housing in Britain and more city life. For ordinary people wages were higher than before and opportunities for social betterment were increasing. It was this that attracted migration from country areas to the cities, falling food prices and rising wages. Standards were most evidently rising among the merchant and trading classes. There were more goods to be sold and improved transport led to an increase of trade internally. Shopkeeping thrived: 'A pastrycook's shop, which twenty pounds would have furnished at (one) time,' wrote Defoe, 'could now cost upwards of three hundred pounds' (*Complete English Tradesman* 1725). War itself was another seemingly inexhaustible source of profit. Trade increased at the end of each war in the century (War of the Spanish Succession 1701–14, War of Jenkins' Ear 1739–41, War of the Austrian Succession 1740–48, the Seven Years' War 1756–63 and the struggle in the American colonies lasted from 1775 to 1783). Some industries thrived in war, such as iron and non-ferrous metal smelting, coal, animal breeding, the leather trades (James Brydges, first Duke of Chandos, 1673–1744, M.P. for Hereford, paymaster of the forces abroad 1707–12, made a fortune from supplying the footwear for Marlborough's armies and became Handel's patron), canvas, woollens, shipbuilding, chemicals—war created demand and eliminated the need for 'wastage'.

As merchants made it, they moved out to the plusher suburbs. That the period was one in which suburbia extended outwards from the central city may be evidenced from the growth of London at this stage which by 1760 had a population of over 1,000,000. The pattern in Bath was unusual, as the housing need here was not only residential-suburban, but urban-seasonal. Consumption was the obvious sign of the new affluence—coffee- and tea-drinking (hence the need for all that sugar!), chocolate-drinking, the use of china, lacquer, wallpaper (from China), furniture-making as a delicate art, which relied so heavily on the import of mahogany from the West Indies (Chippendale's *Gentleman and Cabinet Maker's Director*, the first comprehensive trade catalogue of its kind, was published in 1754). 'An ordinary tradesman now . . . shall spend more money by the year than a gentleman . . . and shall increase and lay up every year too . . . a shoemaker in London shall keep a better house, spend more money, clothe his family better, yet grow rich too', commented Defoe, 'It is evident where the difference lies: an estate's a pond, but trade's a spring.' The estimated growth in per capita income between 1688 and 1770 is from £8 a year to £18 a year.

In Charles II's time the well-to-do sipped coffee in the coffee houses of London, but by quite early in the reign of George III the British were swilling tea in the comfort and privacy of their own homes. Arthur Young wrote in *Farmer's Letters* (1767) 'as much superfluous money is expended on tea and sugar as would maintain four million more subjects on bread.' Sir Frederick Eden (*The State of the Poor or An History of the Labouring Classes in England*, 1797) records that, 'even in poor families tea is not only the usual beverage in the morning and evening, but is generally drunk in large quantities at dinner . . .'. Tea was drunk without milk (which was considered unhealthy) and therefore needed to be sweetened. West Indian sugar was on every table. In 1700 the British consumed 10,000 tons of sugar a year, but by 1800 we managed about 150,000 tons—if the population had doubled during the century, it means that the consumption by each Englishman had risen seven-and-a-half times. 'Your very chambermaids have lost their bloom . . . I suppose by sipping tea!' lamented Jonas Hanway (1712–86).

It is tea, with its inescapable need for sugar, which created the West Indian connection and the inevitable economic and social consequences so carefully noted by Smollett. So many had made money by the 1760s that they now wanted to push their way in to the centre of the social scene. People of all classes flocked to Bath. The old cast system seemed to be breaking up. As an anonymous poet commented:

> No seats for peeresses are now appointed
> But rank and title are all disjointed,
> And every great upstart whom great Nash had humbled,
> With Dukes and Princes, counts and Lords is jumbled.

4

Smollett knew Bath well. He visited the city several times in the season and at one time he had entertained the idea of practising here as a physician. He lived variously at South Parade, at the Bear Inn and in Gay Street. In his letters, novels and medical works Bath features quite frequently, and his observations are invariably shrewd and perceptive. By the time he first came to Bath he was a fully qualified physician and had served in the Spanish War of 1739–41 (which provided him with material for some of the most striking scenes in *Roderick*

Random, 2 vols., 1748). In 1752 he published a very detailed account of the use of the waters at Bath, *An Essay on the External Use of Water . . . with Remarks upon the Present Method of Using the Mineral Waters at Bath in Somersetshire, and a Plan for Rendering them more Safe, Agreeable and Efficacious*. The work is valuable still, not so much on medical grounds, as for its accurate contemporary portrait of how the waters were used. This alone would demonstrate how well Smollett knew the city:

> Diseased persons of all ages, sexes and conditions, are promiscuously admitted into an open bath, which affords little or no shelter from the inclemencies of the weather. . . .

He apportions much of the blame for the lack of full and sensible use of the baths to the medical profession (satiric portraits of medical men and comic accounts of the practices are a feature of all his novels); and also blames the mayor and corporation for not fully exploiting the city's most famous natural resource. 'Narrow minds will ever have narrow views', he wrote,

> the Corporation of Bath seems to have forgot that the ease and plenty they now enjoy, and to which their fathers were strangers, are owing to their *Waters*; and that an improvement upon their Baths, would, by bringing a great concourse of company to their town, perpetuate these blessings to them and their posterity. How little is to be expected from them . . . might have been guessed by their conduct to *Mr. Wood* . . . to whose extraordinary genius they are indebted for a great part of the trade and beauty of the place; yet they have industriously opposed his best designs, which . . . would have rendered *Bath*, in point of elegant architecture, the admiration of the whole world. . . .

He is clearly well acquainted, from this evidence alone, with Bath in its hey-day, when its social life was so strictly organized by Nash. (This was Nash's great achievement, his regimen made Bath an entertaining and a safe place for people to come and bring their families: he aimed to free Bath from 'rustic' associations, to replace its primitive amenities and to draw up a code of conduct—he stamped out duelling, laid down rules for dress, created orchestras, waits, card salons, dances, assemblies.) This was Bath before the invasion of the *nouveau riche*, which could boast the architectural glories of the Chandos Building, Ralph Allen's town house, North and South Parades, the

Grammar School, houses in the Vineyards, Trim Street, Queen Square, Kingsmead Square, Gay Street, Widcombe House and Prior Park. It is Bath at this period which he describes in several scenes in *Peregrine Pickle* (4 vols., 1751). The satire here is mild, he mocks the idle and empty world of fashion in the spa, the quacks, the gamblers, the social climbers and rogues of all degree. Many passages in the first edition were cut out from the second and all subsequent editions, among them are passages concerned with Bath doctors who, Smollet says, were scandal-mongers:

> . . . among the secret agents of scandal, none were so busy as the physicians, a class of animals who live in this place like so many ravens hovering about a carcase, and even ply for hire, like scullers at Hungerford-stairs. . . .

Another section describes how Bathonians rely on stray dogs to act as turnspits to roast their Sunday dinners and Peregrine and his mates nab all the dogs one day and the citizens have recourse to various shifts both comic and dramatic to get their dinners cooked:

> One master of a family . . . was obliged to undertake the office of turnspit . . . to the destruction of his appetite and the danger of his health: another being driven to the necessity of cutting the roast into steaks, fell sick of mortification and well nigh lost his wits: and a third, having contrived to suspend the sirloin above the fire . . . the pack thread gave way towards the end of the operation, and the meat falling down, discharged the contents of the dripping pan upon his leg, which was scalded in a miserable manner. . . .

What comes through here is the unspoiled and suburban nature of Bath at the time. There is none of that sense of the hectic and the dislocated which is so characteristic of the Bath scenes in *Humphry Clinker* (3 vols., 1771).

An often (and justly) praised quality in *Humphry Clinker* is Smollett's brilliant exploitation of the multidimensionality offered in the very structure of an epistolary novel. It is worth pondering the effects achieved from seeing reality through the various eyes of Matthew, Jerry, Lydia, Tabitha and Win. The result is not simply that we gradually build up an objective construct of reality from this variety of sources, but that through this necessarily and essentially fragmented texture of perceptions a subjective view almost imperceptively dominates. This is especially (and strikingly) true of the sections on Bath, although I would also urge that a similar case could just as well be based on the sections on London or on Scotland—other areas which we know Smollett felt deeply about.

What comes through in the Bath scenes in *Humphry Clinker* is the sense of collapse, confusion and social disintegration which the rising tide of luxury and its effects on social harmony have clearly started. Consumption and display have become the only human goals; tolerance, compassion and ordinary humanity (such as Matthew himself shows when he rescues young Clinker) have sunk without trace. The dominating view is that of Bramble and it is his insight into what is happening at Bath which is the enduring impression we take from those pages of *Humphry Clinker*. The mature view is dominant, Jerry and Lydia marvel at the wonders and opulence they see around them, but their view is immature and unsound.

> Bath to me is a new world. All is gaiety, good humour and diversion. The eye is continually entertained with the splendour of dress and equipage, and the ear with the sound of coaches. . . . The Squares, the Circus, and the Parades put you in mind of the sumptuous palaces, represented in prints and pictures, and the new buildings . . . look like so many enchanted castles. . . .

But Lydia's gushing commendations stand little chance against Bramble's collective impression of a city brought by folly, luxury, greed and shallowness to the brink of disintegration:

> Every upstart of fortune, harnessed in the trappings of the mode, presents himself at Bath, as in the very focus of observation. Clerks and factors from the East Indies, loaded with the spoil of plundered provinces; planters, negro-drivers and hucksters from our American plantations, enriched they know not how; agents, commissaries and contractors, who have fattened in two successive wars . . . usurers, brokers and jobbers of every kind. . . . Knowing no other criterion of greatness, but the ostentation of wealth . . . all of them hurry to Bath. . . .

It is no accident that he associates the social decay with the stink of physical rottenness. At the Assembly Bramble faints at the smell:

> It was indeed a compound of villainous smells. . . . Imagine to yourself a high exalted essence of mingled odours arising from

61

putrid gums, imposthumated lungs, sour flatulencies, rank arm-
pits, sweating feet, running sores . . . plaster, ointments and
embrocations. . . .

The architecture is given in terms of meretricious flamboyance,
high consumerism: 'The Circus is a pretty bauble, contrived for
shew' and he comments on 'the affected ornaments of the
architrave, which are both childish and misplaced' and talks of
the 'want of beauty and proportion' in the new architecture.
The city has become 'the very centre of racket and dissipation'
inhabited by 'lunatics'. Two impressions are particularly
strong here, the emphasis on dirt and disease, and the sense of
chaos. No reader may easily forget Bramble's words about
'scrophulous ulcers' and 'sweat and dirt, and dandriff, and the
abominable discharges of various kinds, from twenty different
diseased bodies' and the awful suggestion of the source of the
taste and smell of the waters:

> I find that the Roman baths . . . were found covered by an old
> burying ground, belonging to the Abbey; through which, in all
> probability, the water drains in its passage; so that as we drink
> the decoction of living bodies at the Pump Room, we swallow the
> strainings of rotten bones and carcases at the private bath. . . .

The pathological element is indelibly strong: '. . . we know not
what sores may be running into the water while we are bathing,
and what sort of matter we may thus inbibe; the king's evil, the
scurvy, the cancer, and the pox. . . .' The sense of physical
decay is carried over onto the very structure and anatomy of
Bath, which he says are liable to blow down in the wind as they
are built of soft crumbling stone, while their appearance is
suggestive of deformity—'the wreck of streets and squares
disjointed by an earthquake'.

West Indian associations run throughout. Bramble is distressed in the morning to hear 'two negroes, belonging to a
Creole gentleman, who lodged in the same house' practising the
French-horn, and there are the inevitable West Indian heiresses:
'The ball was opened by a Scotch Lord, with a mulatto heiress
from St. Christophers. . . .' Bath was in the process of being
taken over by the West Indian traders, who formed their own
social circle with all the other West Indian families to whom
they were linked by marriage, by business association or neighbourhood. The same names crop up in island social circles and

at Bath—Akerse, Bannister, Douglas, Ottley, Skerrett, Tuite, Kirwan, Phipps, Oliver, Manning. Bath Abbey contains the memorials of numerous members of the West Indian community who found Bath to their liking, and possibly stayed longer than they had at first intended. The family and friends, their children and black servants, together might form a seasonal booking of some hundred and fifty people. It was to accommodate such parties as this from Barbados, Antigua, Jamaica that Sir William Pulteney, himself a wealthy plantation owner in the West Indies, bought and developed the Bathwick Estate. The city of Bath which Smollett captures in *Humphry Clinker* is clearly responding to that significant West Indian connection. It is a paradigm of western European economic development, a city which in microcosm embodies that series of changes from the primitive and the savage, through feudalism, mercantilism and colonial capitalism.

> Thus the number of people, and the number of houses continue to increase; and this will ever be the case, till the streams that swell this irresistible torrent of folly and extravagance, shall either be exhausted, or turned into other channels, by incidents and events which I do not pretend to forsee. . . .

We know now that what Smollett saw was only the beginning; imperialism then had hardly flexed its muscles.

In fact an examination of Smollett's treatment of Bath and the West Indian connection reveals the complex materiality of *Humphry Clinker* as a literary text. Working within an accepted literary convention of the day—the epistolary novel perfected by Richardson, with the denouement of recognition and marriage forming the 'happy ending'—Smollett has symptomatically demonstrated the essential contradiction in the novel as a *genre*—that it was essentially the product of bourgeois capitalism, and yet is quintessentially antagonistic to its very means of production. How extraordinarily apt is that accidental image of the corrupting bodies from the ancient burial ground whose very dissolution created the capital investment in real estate which made the industrial revolution of Bath possible, and whose very corruption seeps through to infect the contemporary world, literally bodying forth Marx's concept of the system's carrying within itself the seeds of its own destruction.

3

Tobias Smollett: The Scot as English Novelist

by K. G. SIMPSON

> You ask me what degrees there are between Scotts Novels and those of Smollet. They appear to me to be quite distinct in every particular—more especially in their aim—Scott endeavours to throw so interesting and romantic a colouring into common and low Characters as to give them a touch of the Sublime—Smollet on the contrary pulls down and levels what other Men would continue Romance.[1]

This is the judgement of Keats, and it is acutely accurate. It can be substantiated by contrasting the battle scenes in *Roderick Random* with Scott's habitual romanticizing of warfare. Keats's comment may be employed to illuminate the marked change in Scottish literary values in the half century or so which separated Scott from Smollett.[2] It is salutary, therefore, to remember that Smollett was a Scot, and that if he wrote in standard English he did so very much as a Scot. The purpose of this essay is to suggest that Smollett brought to the novel in English certain distinctive features of the Scots literary tradition, and that he is a key figure in the particular Scottish experience of the Europe-wide movement of ideas and taste in the eighteenth century from rationalism by way of sensibility and the Gothic to high Romanticism.

Smollett's fictional technique is characterized by range and pace, and by a concomitant lack of depth. The effect is that of watching a succession of crowded slides—some very vivid—with a few ubiquitous characters, but so depicted that there is little to convey individuality of response or development of values. The point of view remains firmly external: the reader is shown people in situations but sees little of their responses beyond the most obviously physical. Energy and inventiveness, rather than any interest in the mind and its workings, inform Smollett's novels. Scott, comparing Smollett's genius with that of Rubens, observed:

> His pictures are often deficient in grace; sometimes coarse, and even vulgar in conception; deficient in keeping, and in the due subordination of parts to each other; and intimating too much carelessness on the part of the artist. But these faults are redeemed by such richness and brilliancy of colours; such a profusion of imagination—now bodying forth the grand and terrible—now the natural, the easy, and the ludicrous; there is so much of life, action, and bustle, in every group he has painted; so much force and individuality of character—that we readily grant to Smollett an equal rank with his great rival Fielding, while we place both far above any of their successors in the same line of fictitious composition.[3]

That Scott, with his consuming interest in Scottish culture, should have failed to relate such qualities in Smollett to a distinctly Scottish tradition, preferring instead to get involved in comparisons with Fielding, is indicative of the extent to which the competitive cultural impulse induced by the Union of 1707 had, by the end of the eighteenth century, turned the Scots (or some of them) into self-conscious and self-distorting North Britons.

The analogy with Rubens, however, is a valid one. Smollett excels, like earlier Scottish writers, in the vivid depiction of bustling communal life. Roderick and Strap descend into an ordinary, and with stylistic gusto Smollett draws a picture of London lower life centred around the farcical misadventure of Strap's fall. But after the inspired invention of this scene it is dropped with considerable haste and some contrivance. The imaginative energy subsides as readily as it has arisen. The scene remains a vivid scene, but it has led to nothing. Such episodes endorse Coleridge's evaluation of Smollett's method:

'we find that a number of things are put together to counterfeit humour, but there is no growth from within.'[4] In the main when Smollett has time for depiction of emotions they are comically heightened, melodramatized, sensationalized, and, as a result, reduced. Chapter 89 of *Peregrine Pickle*, for instance, is largely concerned with a prank played by Peregrine and accomplices on a gallant. Here the emotional changes are rung frantically:

> The gallant, whose passions were exalted to a pitch of enthusiasm, as susceptible of religious horror as of love, seeing such an apparition, when he was at the point of indulging a criminal appetite, and hearing the dreadful cry, accompanied with the terrible word *damnation*, which Pipes, in his peculiar tone, exclaimed from the alcove, when the animal made its escape; he was seized with consternation and remorse, and falling upon his face, lay in all the agonies of terror, believing himself warned by a particular message from above.[5]

The effect of the over-writing and the pace is comic reduction, which was presumably the intention. The trouble is that Smollett can rarely treat emotion in any other way.

The customary explanations of this stunting of Smollett are these: he was by nature restless and impulsive and 'stuck at nothing'[6] (in the pejorative sense of J. H. Millar's phrase); out of sheer economic necessity he wrote at great speed and carelessly; or, according to Scott, he wrote thus by virtue of 'unlimited confidence in his own powers'.[7] These may be part, but are certainly far from all, of the explanation. Much more important is the fact that Smollett writes as a Scot. His characteristic range and pace relate him to the medieval vision, which endured longer in Scotland than elsewhere, and which was distinguished by its plenitude; and the lack of depth, the disinterest in the individual mind, may be explained likewise. But both these aspects gain further impetus from the post-Union crisis of cultural identity in Scotland. The stylistic *mélange* of Smollett is regarded conventionally as readiness to experiment. It is; but it is also the response of a creative talent that has suffered enforced dislocation from its cultural roots; hence the sudden shifts of tone, the pace, the multiple voices. Similarly, the medieval plenitude of vision, which does nothing to encourage exploration of the individual mind, is reinforced by the post-Union reluctance of the Scot to embark on investigation of identity. Poised thus, Smollett occupies a quite distinctive place in Scottish literature: he looks back to the Makars and beyond, and forwards, via the conflicting notes within Burns and Scott, to that modern alienation which Scotland, severed by the Union from its cultural traditions and denied, or impervious to, the fullest benefits of Romantic idealism, experienced well before the rest of Europe.

Breadth of social vision and stylistic energy are features of earlier Scottish poetry which are present also in Smollett. That primitive vigour of life which informs Dunbar's 'The Dance of the Sevin Deidly Sinnis' is captured by Smollett. In Dunbar, stylistic energy is set to the service of a realistic and comprehensive rendering of community life, as, for instance, in 'The Satire on Edinburgh'. This sense of communal life endures in Fergusson and Burns (e.g. Fergusson's 'Auld Reekie' and 'Leith Races', and Burns's 'The Holy Fair'). It says much for Smollett that he succeeded in communicating this sense in his descriptions, in standard English and in a different genre, of English communal life. Thus Matt Bramble's accounts of social life in Bath and London are more than the conventional unmasking of hypocrisy or revelation of the truth beneath the appearance: they fall within a tradition of the full recording of community life, as it is apprehended by the senses. The obsession with smells and bodily functions is part of Smollett's social realism; the 'man without a skin' (Jery's description of Matt) masks the unflinching social observer. Similarly, the amorous exploits of Smollett's heroes, and the accounts thereof, have a vitality comparable to 'that tremendous principle of life' which John Speirs found exemplified in 'The Twa Mariit Wemen and the Wedo'.[8]

In Smollett, too, there is more than a trace of that coarseness and brutality of humour with which Lyndsay's 'Ane Satyre of the Thrie Estaitis' is imbued. Smollett's farce has an edge to it and involves physical pain to an extent not found in any English writer of the period. In *Roderick Random* the fairly stock farcical exploits (principally of Strap) are prefaced by the physical maltreatment of the young Roderick and the equally physical revenge that is taken on the tyrannical schoolmaster. The farce in *Peregrine Pickle* approximates to the grotesque (e.g. Peregrine's exploit with the chamber-pot), and to the brutal (in pursuit of revenge, Gam and Mr. Sackbut, the curate plan 'to sally upon (Peregrine) when he should be altogether unprovided against such an attack, cut off his ears, and otherwise mutilate him in such a manner, that he should have no cause to be vain of his person for the future'. [*PP*, p. 160]). Even the mellower work of Smollett's later years, *Humphry Clinker*, contains pranks, of which Lismahago is the prime target, and an account of atrocities perpetrated upon the lieutenant and his companion by the American Indians, in a sequence which is almost certainly offered as ironic comment on the vogue of the travel adventure.

There is, then, evidence of a dualism within Smollett's fictional practice: realism and social concern are made to co-exist with a talent, or even a need, for the grotesque and the fantastic. George Kahrl concludes his article, 'Smollett as a Caricaturist', by adducing Martin Foss as follows:

> In times of chaos men return to a magic form of art, using the demoniac aspects of life for their stories and plays: sickness, insanity, death; but they turn them into grotesque means for laughter in order to regain their inner balance . . . The grotesque will always appear and take hold of those ages which are under the strain of disaster, feeling the sinister and chaotic aspects of life, but advanced enough to appease the mind by laughter.[9]

The use of the demoniac and the grotesque was innate within the Scots tradition. How natural, then, that they should be prominent features of Smollett's writing during the crisis of values which Scotland underwent in the decades after the Union.

The expressive force of Smollett's satire is reminiscent of that linguistic energy which is characteristic of so much of earlier Scottish poetry, and of the flyting in particular. Edwin Muir commented:

> Scottish poetry at its best has never run to sweetness or magnificence like English, but to a sort of wild play with imagination and technique, coming from an excess of energy which expends itself both recklessly and surely. It is seen at its most characteristic in Dunbar, the greatest craftsman in Scottish poetry; but it is seen in Burns too, although he was only an apprentice in his craft compared with the older poet.[10]

Smollett was denied, or in part denied himself, the rich and varied linguistic resources that were available to Dunbar or, to a lesser degree, Burns, but in his writing he managed to preserve something of that 'excess of energy which expends itself both recklessly and surely'. Here is Matt Bramble demolishing, with a succession of verbal blows, a distant relative:

> He is not only a sordid miser in his disposition, but his avarice is mingled with a spirit of despotism, which is truly diabolical.— He is a brutal husband, an unnatural parent, a harsh master, an oppressive landlord, a litigious neighbour, and a partial magistrate.—Friends he has none; and in point of hospitality and good breeding, our cousin Burdock is a prince in comparison of this ungracious miscreant, whose house is the lively representation of a gaol. (*HC*, p. 171)

Here there is the expressive force, but little of the humour, of the flyting; and, as often happens, Smollett succumbs to overkill. It is undeniable that he employed such literary energy as a kind of personal therapy: compare the aggressive self-justification of his heroes (e.g. *Roderick Random*, pp. 5–7) with similar passages in his own letters where he directs to personal purposes the vituperation that was part of the convention of the flyting.[11]

But Smollett's concern extended far beyond himself, as is evident from his claim: 'I have such a natural Horror of Cruelty that I cannot without uncommon Warmth relate any Instance of Inhumanity.'[12] Some of his most expressive writing results from the union of that stylistic vitality and his responsiveness to inhumanity. From precisely this the naval scenes in *Roderick Random* derive a force and urgency lacking in the remainder of the book. This is Roderick's account of his first inspection of the sick-bay on the *Thunder*:

> . . . when I followed him with the medicines into the sick berth or hospital, and observed the situation of the patients, I was much less surprised to find people die on board, than astonished to find any body recover.—Here I saw about fifty miserable distempered wretches, suspended in rows, so huddled upon one another, that not more than fourteen inches of space was allotted for each with his bed and bedding; and deprived of the light of the day, as well as of fresh air; breathing nothing but a noisome atmosphere of the morbid steams exhaling from their own excrements and diseased bodies, devoured with vermin hatched in the filth that

surrounded them, and destitute of every convenience necessary for people in that helpless condition. (*RR*, p. 149)

Here realistic observation forms the basis of the forceful expression of outrage, as it does in the accounts of the conduct of the battle, the disposal of the dead, and the effects of the fever epidemic. Like a true child of the Enlightenment, Smollett is committed to the amelioration of the living-conditions of his fellow-men. In *Humphry Clinker*, despite Matt's fulminations against the monster which is mass society (again expressed with similar energy) and his hankering after the social discrimination attendant upon the medieval social hierarchy, by the end he has shed the mask of the irascible valetudinarian and, in guiding Baynard towards the restoration of his farm after the ravages of his wife's vanity, has become practical Enlightenment man (one is reminded of the agricultural interests of Lord Kames, one of the foremost of the *literati*, to whom tributes are paid in the novel). This very real, practical, social concern of Smollett's should not be forgotten, and Matt's vehement denunciations of the lack of hygiene among the *beau monde* should not be dismissed as the rantings of 'Smelfungus'.

Smollett's concern with the physical derives jointly from the medieval plenitude of vision and his Enlightenment social concern. At his best the energetic expression of the former subserves the latter: vigorous rendering of the grotesque subserves social satire. Smollett has the Scot's capacity to discern and render through language the physical in its grotesque extremes. In one of his last letters he wrote:

I am already so dry and emaciated that I may pass for an Egyptian mummy without any other preparation than some pitch and painted linen, unless you think I may deserve the denomination of a curiosity in my own character.[13]

Vivid representation of the physical is part of the earlier Scots tradition. This is an extract from the description of Saturn in Henryson's 'Testament of Cresseid':

His face (fronsit), his lyre was lyke the Leid,
His teith chatterit, and cheverit with the Chin,
His Ene drowpit, how sonkin in his heid,
Out of his Nois the Meldrop fast can rin,
With lippis bla and cheikis leine and thin;

The Iceschoklis that fra his hair doun hang
Was wonder greit, and as ane speir als lang.

With justification G. Gregory Smith remarked of much of the
poetry of the Makars that 'the completed effect of the piling up
of details is one of movement, suggesting the action of a con-
certed dance or the canter of a squadron'.[14] Such writing is not
the product of bland recording of neutral observation. The
mind's purpose directs the eye as to what it will choose to
discern; the mind's expressive capacity invests the rendering of
it with a dynamism of its own. Stevenson described the process
succinctly as that of 'the sentiment assimilating the facts of
natural congruity'.[15] The finest of Smollett has this very quality
suggestive of the momentary arrest of energy, so that, paradoxically, a vividly pictorial impact is achieved without any
diminution of the verbal dynamism. (Again, the analogy is with
a rapid succession of vivid slides, and the method is comparable
to that employed by Burns in 'Tam o' Shanter'.) The great
advantages of a predominantly pictorial method are force of
impact, and economy and range of effect. Thus E. H. Gombrich
could claim that Hogarth's *Marriage à la Mode* 'is equivalent to
at least two volumes of Richardson's novels'. If, as Gombrich
asserts, Hogarth 'accepted the idea of art as a language',[16] the
converse is true of Smollett. In employing language in the
service of visual art, Smollett has to pay the price of sacrificing
depth, as the contrast with Richardson suggests.

Smollett's work, then, falls within a tradition, which endured
longer in Scotland than in England, of that mode of the
picturesque which, as Hazlitt observed, 'depends chiefly on the
principle of discrimination and contrast' and 'runs imper-
ceptibly into the fantastical and the grotesque'.[17] The combination of picturesque strength and freedom of movement
pervades Smollett's novels from misadventures at inns early in
Roderick Random to the Scarborough bathing accident in *Humphry
Clinker*. Smollett's last novel offers acknowledgement of the
mind–body relationship which has been implied in his earlier
novels. Matt Bramble both evinces and admits to a reciprocity
of spirits and health. His acute sensibility, feelingly responsive
to the grotesque and unjust aspects of life, affects his health.
Smollett is close to Matt in this equation of feeling with

71

responsiveness to the grotesque in life. Social concern is allied to the eye of the caricaturist which, as John Butt noted, 'by grossly exaggerating a feature or two converts the human form into a gargoyle'.[18] Discussing the freedom of movement from mood to mood that is a feature of Scottish literature, Gregory Smith commented: 'It takes some people more time than they can spare to see the absolute propriety of a gargoyle's grinning at the elbow of a kneeling saint.'[19]

Smollett offers excellent examples of the deployment of this sense of incongruity in the interests of social satire. In *Peregrine Pickle* a nun, abandoned by her lover, is described thus:

> No tygress robbed of her young was ever exalted to an higher pitch of fury than this nun, when she found herself abandoned by her lover, and insulted in this mortifying explanation. She darted upon her antagonist, like a hawk upon a partridge, and with her nails disfigured that fair face which had defrauded her of her highest expectation. (*PP*, p. 330)

Habitually with Smollett, physical deformity accompanies (or in his descriptions heralds) mental eccentricity. Here is Peregrine's aunt, Mrs. Grizzle:

> Exclusive of a very wan (not to call it a sallow) complexion, which perhaps was the effect of her virginity and mortification, she had a cast in her eyes that was not at all engaging, and such an extent of mouth, as no art or affectation could contract into any proportionable dimension: then her piety was rather peevish than resigned, and did not in the least diminish a certain stateliness in her demeanour and conversation, that delighted in communicating the importance and honour of her family, which, by the bye, was not to be traced two generations back, by all the power of heraldry or tradition. (*PP*, pp. 2–3)

The emphasis on deformity is a feature of the Scots tradition. Noting the differences between Chaucer's 'Troilus and Criseyde' and Henryson's 'Testament of Cresseid', John Speirs says of the latter:

> The moral horror at the 'uncleanness' of the 'fleshly lusts' that have 'changed in filth' Cresseid's 'femininitie' merges into the purely physical horror of the 'uncleanness' of the leprosy that devours her beauty and youth. When the 'Court and Convocation' that inflicts the poetic justice has

> Vanishchit away, than rais scho up and tuik
> Ane poleist glas, and hir schaddow culd luik:
> And quhen scho saw hir face sa deformait
> Gif scho in hart was wa aneuch God wait.

There is no such grim moment in Chaucer.[20]

In precisely such passages are the antecedents for Smollett's concern with grotesque physicality, to which there is nothing comparable in Fielding or in Scott, by whose time this grimness and coarseness had been refined out of much of Scottish literature.

Smollett's caricatures function ·by means of selection and heightening of physical blemish as an index, or mode of access, to character and values. Here, for example, is Mr. Launcelot Crab as he first appears to Roderick:

> This member of the faculty was aged fifty, about five foot high, and ten round the belly; his face was capacious as a full moon, and much of the complexion of a mulberry: his nose resembling a powder-horn, was swelled to an enormous size, and studded all over with carbuncles; and his little grey eyes reflected the rays in such an oblique manner, that while he looked a person full in the face, one would have imagined he was admiring the buckle of his shoe. (*RR*, p. 26)

Under the guise of observation the highly selective use of detail works to produce the desired effect of extravagance. Such caricature aims at uniting the illusion of resemblance with mockery.

Of the figures in Rowlandson's illustrations of Smollett, V. S. Pritchett remarked: 'They are not human beings. They are lumps of animal horror or stupidity.'[21] In earlier Scots poetry— the *Fables* of Henryson, for instance—animals and birds bear resemblance to humans and enact human behaviour. In the manner of the caricaturist Smollett employs extravagant animal analogies to reductive effect in his caricatures.[22] Captain Weazel

> was about five foot and three inches high, sixteen inches of which went to his face and long scraggy neck; his thighs were about six inches in length, his legs resembling spindles or drum-sticks, two feet and an half, and his body, which put me in mind of extension without substance, engrossed the remainder;—so that on the

73

whole, he appeared like a spider or grasshopper erect,—and was almost a *vox et praeterea nihil*. (*RR*, p. 50)

The effect here derives principally from the way in which specificity serves as the basis of imaginative heightening, and from the animal analogies—the former inflating, the latter diminishing. Detailed comparison with animals fulfils this function in almost every one of Smollett's caricatures. Lavement, the apothecary,

> was a little old withered man, with a forehead about an inch high, a nose turned up at the end, large cheek bones that helped to form a pit for his little grey eyes, a great bag of loose skin hanging down on each side in wrinkles, like the alforjas of a baboon; and a mouth so accustomed to that contraction which produces grinning, that he could not pronounce a syllable without discovering the remains of his teeth, which consisted of four yellow fangs, not improperly by anatomists, called *canine*. (*RR*, p. 97)

In *Peregrine Pickle* Trunnion is described habitually in terms of animals. The first account of him is prefaced by this record of the sounds made by him and his companions as they approach Mr. Pickle:

> This composition of notes at first resembled the crying of quails, and croaking of bull-frogs; but, as it approached nearer, he could distinguish articulate sounds pronounced with great violence, in such a cadence as one would expect from a human creature scolding thro' the organs of an ass. It was neither speaking nor braying, but a surprising mixture of both, employed in the utterance of terms absolutely unintelligible to our wondering merchant. . . . (*PP*, pp. 6–7)

Much of the comedy of the early chapters of the book springs from the enforced domestic containment of Trunnion's energy. Here animal analogy is structured by Smollett into a particularly effective sequence: Trunnion is 'like a lion roaring in the toil'; 'was committed to the care of Pipes, by whom he was led about the house like a blind bear growling for prey'; and 'seemed to retire within himself, like a tortoise when attacked, that shrinks within its shell, and silently endure the scourge of her reproaches, without seeming sensible of the smart' (pp. 45–

7). Here the steady subjugation of the Commander in marriage is most tellingly conveyed.

As with Lavement, so with Trunnion and Hatchway, distinctive manner of speech, indicative, as conventionally in caricature, of class, occupation, or nationality, is used in conjunction with physical blemish to achieve the extravagant effect. In one of his earliest caricatures, Lieutenant Bowling, Smollett organizes features into a significant sequence: distinctive physique (with animal analogy), distinctive attire, distinctive behaviour, distinctive speech. In the creation of peculiar personal idioms and distortions of language is one of Smollett's finest accomplishments; and invariably such idiosyncrasy of speech is a component of the caricature. Yet, as James Beattie was to observe less than forty years after Smollett began his career as novelist,

> We smile, when sailors use at land the language of the sea, when learned pedants interlard ordinary discourse with Greek and Latin idioms, when coxcombs bring abroad into the world the dialect and gesticulations of their own club, and, in general, when a man expresses himself on all subjects in figures of speech suggested by what belongs to his own profession only. Now what but habits contracted in a narrow society could produce these particularities? And does not this prove, that ludicrous qualities are incident to men who live detached in a narrow society, and, therefore, that the feudal, or any other, form of government, that tends to keep the different orders of men separate, must be favourable to wit and humour, and to enlarge the sphere of ludicrous writing?[23]

Here is another indication of the pace and the extent of the change which Scottish values underwent in the middle decades of the eighteenth century. Even allowing for individual differences between Smollett and Beattie, this helps to illuminate the extent to which post-Union Scotland was being drawn rapidly away from feudalism and towards the world of mass society. In an irony of which he was probably unaware, Smollett found a source of comedy, and at times mockery, in that kind of limiting individuality which was best fostered in the rigidly structured society whose demise he so lamented.

If Smollett was unaware of this particular tension, it is only right to acknowledge those tensions which are central to his technique as caricaturist and which he brings into equipoise, and those potential contradictions which he resolves into paradox. Indicative of his major achievement as caricaturist are that ambivalence of status with which he invests his caricatures and the ambivalence of response which he is able to elicit towards them. Like many Scottish writers, Smollett both inflates and reduces, celebrates and mocks; and we laugh at such figures, are somewhat in awe of them, and at the same time admire the imaginative and expressive skill of their creator. In, for instance, the description of Crabshaw at the start of *Sir Launcelot Greaves* the range of extravagant detail and analogy is remarkable, and unifying the mass of apparently disparate detail is the mind of the author, intent on identifying, and vigorously rendering or even celebrating, the grotesque in man. This readiness to explore, this imaginative adventurism, is typical of Smollett, and it locates him firmly within the Scottish tradition of dynamic plenitude.

To Scottish literature Smollett left, in his caricatures, a major legacy, with Scott and Galt the most immediate beneficiaries.[24] But in terms of caricature Smollett's most significant bequest may well have been to the English novel and one of its greatest practitioners, Dickens.[25] Smollett's achievements in finding the verbal equivalent to the pictorial, and the exact balance of action and fixity in literary caricature, should not be underrated. E. H. Gombrich notes that in the visual arts

> decorum militated against experimenting with all varieties of human types and emotions. The noble neither laugh nor cry. Thus humorous art was left to be the testing ground of these discoveries.

In the experimentation of this kind attempted in the early novel in English Smollett is arguably more adventurous and 'modern' than Fielding. The verve of Smollett's caricatures almost warrants the application to him of Gombrich's judgement that Picasso's humorous creations 'show that here is a man who has succumbed to the spell of making, unrestrained and unrestrainable by the mere descriptive functions of the image'.[26]

Smollett's characteristic plenitude permits of the coexistence of fact and heightened imaginative vision, social concern and comic or Gothic fantasy. Again, the important aspects of such a fictional method are energy and flux. The opening of *Roderick Random* testifies to this. A paragraph of standard autobiographical introduction in the manner of Defoe rapidly gives way to Roderick's mother's dream in all its remarkable imaginative detail:

> She dreamed, she was delivered of a tennis-ball, which the devil (who to her great surprize, acted the part of a midwife) struck so forcibly with a racket, that it disappeared in an instant; and she was for some time inconsolable for the loss of her off-spring; when all of a sudden, she beheld it return with equal violence, and earth itself beneath her feet, whence immediately sprung up a goodly tree covered with blossoms, the scent of which operated so strongly on her nerves that she awoke. (*RR*, p. 1)

This immediately identifies Smollett's first novel in terms of the traditional propensity of the Scottish literary imagination to the unusual or grotesque.

Each of Smollett's novels is marked in its early stages by just such inspired imaginative flourishes. In *Peregrine Pickle* there are the riotous imaginative fertility of the approach of Trunnion and company to the inn; the splendidly idiosyncratic speech and behaviour of those characters; the bizarre whims of Mrs. Pickle in pregnancy; the absurd prank played upon Trunnion; and, the climax of this opening sequence, the richly comic imaginative representation of Trunnion's ride to his wedding. In the light of such fecundity it is difficult to accept the judgement of Herbert Read, that Smollett 'is at the best but an arranger of the objective facts of existence'.[27] Rather, Smollett's novels reflect his dual role: that of social historian, and fantasist. The union of these qualities in such extreme form is distinctly Scottish. G. Gregory Smith related the coexistence in Scottish literature of the prose of extravagance and the prose of experience to the Scottish character, and commented:

> There is more in the Scottish antithesis of the real and fantastic than is to be explained by the familiar rules of rhetoric. The sudden jostling of contraries seems to preclude any relationship by literary suggestion. The one invades the other without warning. They are the 'polar twins' of the Scottish Muse.[28]

Smollett's prose evinces this notion of antithesis within fictional flux. It has to be stressed that the Union and its cultural effects did not create this duality in the Scottish literary imagination. Rather, it lent strength to the innate tendency within the Scottish imagination to tension, juxtaposition, exaggeration, and reduction (as the flyting, for instance, shows).

Against such a background the concatenation of emotion and farce in Smollett's novels becomes more readily explicable. An emotional reunion between Roderick and Strap takes place as follows:

> At that instant recollecting his face, I flew into his arms, and in the transport of my joy, gave him back one half of the suds he had so lavishly bestowed on my countenance; so that we made a very ludicrous appearance. . . . (*RR*, p. 32)

Indeed Strap serves as a particular embodiment of contraries held in juxtaposition: the journeyman barber with a smattering of Greek rises to a position of some eminence in France only to revert to being Roderick's servant and, latterly, to demonstrate his joy in a manner so exuberant as to be deemed ludicrous. The emotional flux and range of *Roderick Random* is demonstrated in chapter 58: Roderick, 'tortured with jealousy' over Narcissa, vents his fury on Strap by violently pinching his ear, whereupon Strap 'could not help shedding some tears at my unkindness'; this occasions 'unspeakable remorse' which sets all his passions into a ferment:

> . . . I swore horrible oaths without meaning or application, I foamed at the mouth, kicked the chairs about the room, and played abundance of mad pranks, that frightened my friend almost out of his senses.—At length my transport subsided, I became melancholy, and wept insensibly. (*RR*, p. 357)

Roderick is restored to the 'adorable creature', Narcissa, and this emotional high is then undermined by a farcical encounter with Strap, whose presence is betrayed by 'a noise like that of a baboon when he mows and chatters'. For Smollett, truth is contained within these boundaries of the sublime and the ludicrous, and each colours the other by virtue of their juxtaposition. Smollett is detached equally from man at his sublimely emotional and pragmatic extremes. Their juxtaposition is often extremely telling; nowhere more so than when Smollett interplays the physical and intellectual grotesquerie of Narcissa's aunt with the romantic sensibility of Roderick which is blind to all else but the attractions of Narcissa.

For Smollett such emotional self-blinding, and the rapid transition of emotions, are credibly human, and they are comic. The flux of emotions can be so rapid and so extreme as to incapacitate temporarily. Here is the comment in *Peregrine Pickle* on Jolter's response to surviving a squall on the Channel crossing:

> Such a transition from fear to joy, occasioned a violent agitation both in his mind and body; and it was a full quarter of an hour before he recovered the right use of his organs. (*PP*, p. 188)

Man, for Smollett, is the victim of his own emotional extremes which render him comically limited. In Smollett the Augustan satirist's concern with the discrepancy between ideal and actual and with the mind–body relationship is reinforced by a scepticism about the nature of the human condition. This can be traced to his Calvinist background and it relates him to that Scottish tradition of scepticism which arose as an antidote to Calvinism's certitude and which was to culminate in Hume.

Peregrine Pickle is largely concerned with the discrepancy between abstractions and actuality. This is most obviously expressed in the discussions between the Doctor and Pallet (which lead them into a physical duel), at the heart of which is the way in which the Doctor's sublime world of the imagination is invaded by Pallet; and, throughout, Peregrine's vigorous amours provide ironic commentary on this. In *Peregrine Pickle* Smollett depicts man's condition as a battleground between reason and emotions. Of Peregrine he remarks: 'It would have been well for our hero, had he always acted with the same circumspection: but he had his unguarded moments, in which he fell a prey to the unsuspecting integrity of his own heart' (*PP*, p. 612). Central to Smollett's view of life, and to his fictional expression of it, is his belief that the mind is constituted on a principle of energetic contradiction. Peregrine's immediate response to the warrant for his arrest is to beat the bailiff for his insolence, and, on receiving the latter's apology, he 'waked to all the horrors of reflection'. There follows this passage, which is central to Smollett's thought:

> All the glory of his youth was now eclipsed, all the blossoms of his hope were blasted, and he saw himself doomed to the miseries of

a jail, without the least prospect of enlargement, except in the issue of his law-suit, of which he had, for some time past, grown less and less confident every day. What would become of the unfortunate, if the constitution of the mind did not permit them to bring one passion into the field against another? passions that operate in the human breast, like poisons of a different nature, extinguishing each other's effect. (*PP*, p. 678)

For Smollett—and this is a definite legacy of the Scottish background—no emotional note may endure for long without being subject to transition.[29] After his release from the Fleet prison Peregrine feels 'all the extasy that must naturally be produced in a young man of his imagination from such a sudden transition, in point of circumstance' (*PP*, p. 765). The Calvinist Providence ensures such a flux of circumstance as to undermine any emotion that is prolonged beyond the moment. There is a splendid symbolic representation of this in the interruption of the audible progress of Hatchway to an emotional reunion with Peregrine by the breaking of the lieutenant's wooden leg. Here that peculiarly Scottish emphasis on the way in which the providential governance of life reduces it to the farcical-grotesque dimension becomes explicit in Smollett.

These ideas find fuller expression in *Ferdinand Count Fathom*. In his dedication Smollett acknowledges the importance of *Relief*[30] and writes of his attempts 'to subject folly to ridicule, and vice to indignation; to rouse the spirit of mirth, wake the soul of compassion, and touch the secret springs that move the heart' (*FCF*, p. 4). For Smollett there is no incongruity in such composite motivation, since life itself is incongruously complex. Contrast is recognized as the quintessence of life. After the caricature of the aged brothel-keeper Smollett observes:

Yet there was something meritorious in her appearance, as it denoted her an indefatigable minister to the pleasure of mankind; and as it formed an agreeable contrast with the beauty and youth of the fair damsels that wantoned in her train. It resembled those discords in musick, which properly disposed, contribute to the harmony of the whole piece: or those horrible giants who in the world of romance, used to guard the gates of the castle, in which the inchanted damsel was confined. (*FCF*, p. 93)

This acknowledgement that discord is an essential component of the whole is central to Smollett's notion, essentially Scottish, of the inherence of diversity, flux, and contradiction within the total vision.[31] With Smollett the totality of life is in its diversity, and within that totality everything, by virtue of its very presence, is subject to reductive juxtaposition. Thus in such a world the sudden *volte-face* is quite unexceptional. In rapid succession Count Trebasi can express his inveterate hostility to Renaldo by firing at him and removing part of his left eye-brow, and, in an agony of conscience, beg forgiveness for his past treatment of him.

Another manifestation of Smollett's mingling of contraries is his contrasting of manner and matter. In *Roderick Random* this is highly effective as a vehicle of social censure. Roderick's criticism of the society wherein, like Miss Williams, respectable lady can readily degenerate into prostitute is the more forceful by virtue of its expression through Roderick's refined prose; and the same applies to Miss Williams's account of her experiences in Bridewell. But the most striking use of this technique is in Roderick's reports on naval life and his experience of battle, where Roderick's horror is the more forcibly expressed because shockingly realistic details are contained within a carefully modulated prose syntax. In the same novel, however, the contrast of manner and matter is used for the purpose of comic reduction, and in particular those passages in which Roderick appears as romantic lover have an inflation of style which is often undermined by reductive detail.

In *Peregrine Pickle* a clearly identifiable comic-epic manner is employed intermittently. The example of *Tom Jones* possibly influenced Smollett, but his technique should be related also to the Scottish tradition of inflation and reduction. In what Wittig calls the 'dynamic vigour' of Dunbar's poem, 'The Twa Mariit Wemen and the Wedo' and in the mixture of aureate diction, extravagance, and vernacular of 'Colkelbie's Sow' are some of the antecedents of Smollett's comic-epic manner. Wittig notes that the Lowland Scot's 'mistrust of fine senti-ment'[32] is reflected in mock-heroic poems such as the 'Justings' of Dunbar, Lyndsay, and Alexander Scott, and in Mont-gomerie's 'The Cherrie and the Slae'. The following passage, descriptive of Pipes's playing, may be related to that tradition:

This musician accordingly, applied to his mouth the silver instrument that hung at a button-hole of his jacket, by a chain of the same metal, and though not quite so ravishing as the pipe of Hermes, produced a sound so loud and shrill, that the stranger (as it were instinctively) stopped his ears, to preserve his organs of hearing from such a dangerous invasion. The prelude being thus executed, Pipes fixed his eyes upon the egg of an ostrich that depended from the ceiling, and without once moving them from that object, performed the whole cantata in a tone of voice that seemed to be the joint issue of an Irish bagpipe, and a sow-gelder's horn. (*PP*, p. 12)

Hatchway's descriptions of woman in nautical terms, his epitaph on Trunnion, and his letter to Peregrine have all the vitality of the tradition of the mock-heroic;[33] and the courtship of Trunnion by Mrs. Grizzle and the episode of Trunnion's progress to his wedding have the imaginative fertility and attention to comic detail endemic within the same tradition (qualities in the Scots tradition which were to endure in such poems of Burns as 'Tam o' Shanter' and 'The Jolly Beggars').

In *Ferdinand Count Fathom* the mock-heroic mode, and the tone thereof, are crucial to the overall meaning of the book. The narrative tone is established in the first chapter in the claim that 'by that time the reader shall have glanced over the subsequent sheets, I doubt not, but he will bless God, that the adventurer was not his own historian'; and then Ferdinand is described as 'this mirror of modern chivalry' (*FCF*, p. 6). The tone established, Smollett proceeds to make wildly extravagant claims for his method. From the account of Ferdinand's birth in a waggon the comic-epic mode is sustained through the details of his being weaned from the brandy-flask of his mother, his mother's marriage, his progress through infancy, and his mother's participation in warfare and her death. Throughout, the comedy derives from the application of heroic formulae and the high style to low matter; from the undermining of that manner by telling linguistic detail; and from the reductive juxtaposition of world and individual, history and personal experience, which prefigures the use of such a stratagem by Burns and Galt.[34]

The effect of the irony is to distance author from subject and to identify Smollett's attitude to his material as one of realism of assessment. Thus when Fathom feigns the romantic lover to

Wilhelmina Smollett undermines his effusions by skilful use of detailed observation. The 'lover's' protestation is succeeded by the statement, 'So saying, he threw himself upon his knees, and seizing her plump hand, pressed it to his lips with all the violence of real transport' (*FCF*, p. 47). 'Plump hand' establishes beyond doubt the comic tone which informs the subsequent 'heroic' account of the courtship:

> the nymph's . . . heart began to thaw, and her face to hang out the flag of capitulation, which was no sooner perceived by our hero, than he renewed his attack with redoubled fervour. . . .

Smollett distances himself as the ironic observer of human weaknesses and pretensions, and the comic-epic manner is instrumental in depicting the gap between illusion and actuality. The reflections of Fathom on his first day in England are described thus:

> On this very first day of his arrival, he perceived between the English and the people among whom he had hitherto lived, such essential difference in customs, appearance, and way of living, as inspired him with high notions of that British freedom, opulence, and convenience on which he had often heard his mother expatiate. On the road he feasted his eye-sight with the verdant hills covered with flocks of sheep, the fruitful vales parcelled out into cultivated inclosures; the very cattle seemed to profit by the wealth of their masters, being large, sturdy and sleek, and every peasant breathed the insolence of liberty and independance. In a word, he viewed the wide extended plains of Kent, with a lover's eye, and his ambition becoming romantic, could not help fancying himself another conqueror of the isle. (*FCF*, p. 129)

Such illusions are, it is stressed, rare for Fathom:

> He was not, however, long amused by these vain chimeras, which soon vanished before other reflections of more importance and solidity. His imagination, it must be owned, was at all times too chaste, to admit those overweening hopes, which often mislead the mind of a projector. He had studied mankind with incredible diligence, and knew perfectly well how far he could depend on the passions and foibles of human nature. (p. 129)

The following chapter opens with an emphatic reminder of the actuality of human nature, at least in its English version:

> Those who had taken places for the coach, understanding the sixth seat was engaged by a foreigner, determined to profit by his ignorance; and with that politeness which is peculiar to this happy island, fixed themselves in the vehicle, in such a manner, before he had the least intimation of their design, that he found it barely practicable to insinuate himself sidelong between a corpulent quaker and a fat Wapping-landlady, in which attitude he stuck fast, like a thin quarto between two voluminous dictionaries on a bookseller's shelf: and as if the pain and inconvenience of such compression, was not sufficient matter of chagrin, the greatest part of the company entertained themselves with laughing at his ludicrous station. (p. 130)

After the heroic description of the altercation between the 'gentleman' and the 'gentlewoman', the narrator sets the seal on this instance of the divergence of ideal and actual with the comment:

> Such a redundancy of epithets and variety of metaphors, tropes and figures were uttered between these well-matched opponents, that an epic bard would have found his account in listening to the contest, which, in all probability, would not have been confined to words. . . . (pp. 131–32)

In the compound of values which Smollett's work evinces the predominant note is ultimately that of a rationalist realism. Smollett proffers forceful endorsement of reason and sounds warnings against fancy, imagination, and romance. The Preface to *Roderick Random* includes the claim that 'Romance, no doubt, owes its origin to ignorance, vanity, and superstition' (*RR*, p. xliii). The misfortunes of Miss Williams originate in her 'having more imagination than judgement' (*RR*, p. 118). In his youth Peregrine was 'a distinguished character, not only for his acuteness of apprehension, but also for that mischievous fertility of fancy . . .' (*PP*, p. 81); and in his early manhood Peregrine, influenced by the young bucks whose company he keeps, frequents 'a certain tavern, which might be properly stiled the temple of excess, where they left the choice of their fare to the discretion of the landlord, that they might save themselves the pains of exercising their own reason' (p. 582). (Significantly, here, and elsewhere, Smollett notes that Peregrine did not relish such riotous excess, indicating that he may

84

yet be saved for the side of reason which could then direct his 'acuteness of apprehension' to good effect.)

Habitually Smollett's rationalist sense manifests itself in the investigation of the reality beneath appearances, or in the confrontation of innocence and experience. Rifle, the highwayman of whom Roderick, Strap, and others have been terrified, is captured, and Roderick comments: 'I was amazed to see what a pitiful dejected fellow he now appeared, who had but a few hours ago, filled me with such terror and confusion' (*RR*, p. 42); Captain Weazel is soon to be more farcically unmasked; and in the interval the landlord to whom Roderick warms because of his classical learning has proved himself an uncompromising opportunist. Smollett employs virtually as a formula the encounter between his hero and the group of characters—be it *beau monde* or fellow-prisoners—where no-one is as he seems; and Jery Melford discovers that learned and fashionable society is informed by irony and paradox.

All of this might be regarded as conventional Augustan satire but for an edge to the censure which is characteristic of Smollett and which relates him to the Scottish tradition of sceptical rationalism typified in Hume and given imaginative expression in Burns's fondness for the unmasking of hypocrites. This sharpness is present, for instance, in Smollett's effective juxtaposition in *Ferdinand Count Fathom* of London life and that of the lunatic asylum and the prison: in Chapter 31 the Tyroleze, Ratchkali, tells Ferdinand that 'this metropolis is a vast masquerade, in which a man of stratagem may wear a thousand different disguises, without danger of detection' (*FCF*, p. 146), and, fortified by this information, Ferdinand dismisses Ellenor who, distraught as a result, is 'conveyed into the hospital of Bethlem; where we shall leave her for the present, happily bereft of her reason' (p. 147). Himself committed to prison a little later, Ferdinand encounters other victims of the masquerade which is life in mass society, including Minikin, Macleaver, and Theodore, King of Corsica. Significantly, the same novel contains a little later the most unequivocal statement of Smollett's scepticism regarding human nature and achievement. A discourse on the fact that a lucky miscarriage has promoted Fathom's medical reputation leads to the following forthright admission:

Success raised upon such a foundation, would, by a disciple of Plato, and some modern moralists, be ascribed to the innate virtue and generosity of the human heart, which naturally espouses the cause that needs protection: but I, whose notions of human excellence are not quite so sublime, am apt to believe it is owing to that spirit of self-conceit and contradiction, which is, at least, as universal, if not as natural, as the moral sense so warmly contended for by those ideal philosophers. (p. 263)

Here Smollett dissociates himself from Shaftesbury's belief that man is naturally predisposed to good (and, Damian Grant has suggested, from Fielding's fictional expression of this view),[35] and adopts a position that is close to Humean scepticism. On the relationship between reputation and moral worth Smollett has no misgivings: 'The most infamous wretch often finds his account in these principles of malevolence and self-love.'

Like all good writers, Smollett exemplifies a congruence of values and technique. His rationalism finds expression by means of reductive devices and modes, and in this he typifies that innate propensity of Scots and Scottish literature towards diminution. In his report of his visit to the French court Roderick unwittingly undermines by reductive detail the pretension of himself and the whole company:

Thus equipt, I put on the gentleman of figure, and attended by my honest friend, who was contented with the station of my valet, visited the Louvre, examined the gallery of Luxemburgh, and appeared at Versailles, where I had the honour of seeing his Most Christian Majesty eat a considerable quantity of olives. (*RR*, p. 256)

In prison a discussion of European politics among Theodore, King of Corsica, Fathom, Macleaver, and Minikin, founders thus:

While they were busy in trimming the balance of power on the other side of the Alps, their deliberations were interrupted by the arrival of a scullion, who came to receive their orders touching the bill of fare for dinner, and his majesty found much more difficulty in settling this important concern than in compromising all the differences between the emperor and the queen of Spain. (*FCF*, pp. 188–89)

On one particularly comic occasion the progress of Peregrine's

amours is thwarted by the entry to his apartment of Pallet on a
reluctant ass. In the midst of Win Jenkins's account of her visit
to London is the following:

> And I have seen the Park, and the paleass of Saint Gimses, and
> the king's and the queen's magisterial pursing, and the sweet
> young princes, and the hillyfents, and the pyebald ass, and all the
> rest of the royal family. (*HC*, p. 108)

Keats is quite right: Smollett does 'pull down and level what
other Men would continue Romance'. He does so, in the
manner he does, at least partly because he is a Scot. Such
trenchant comic reduction can be found in Scottish literature
from the Makars to Burns.

The Scottish characteristic of diminution is a direct legacy of
the Calvinist emphasis on the omnipotence of Providence: if all
is predetermined can illusions be cherished about the significance of the individual, the value of his actions, or the scope of
his understanding? For Smollett all depends on 'the tossing up
of a halfpenny'.[36] The world of his novels, where the fortunate
last-ditch encounter habitually saves the beleaguered hero,
would seem to be a fictional demonstration of Hume's thoughts
on how 'the cause of events is concealed from us'.[37]

Herein too lies at least part of the explanation for the nature
of Smollett's characterization; and here he is again representative in that until Hogg no Scottish novelist really engaged with
individual characters in a way that was other than reductive.
From Smollett's first novel to his last more is promised than is
ever fulfilled by way of character development. The effect of
Miss Williams's tale on Roderick is to induce a pause for
self-examination and an uncharacteristic consideration of the
situation of another. This would seem to imply the onset of a
significant stage in Roderick's development, and the humanitarian sentiments which he voices in the naval sequence would
appear to endorse this; but thereafter any suggestion of growth
in personality or values is dropped. When, later, in the company of Miss Snapper Roderick meets his beloved Narcissa,
love banishes instantly the opportunism which he has so vigorously practised. It is plainly providential, and there is not a hint
of self-awareness or self-examination. There is no need: Fortune
has smiled, and it continues to smile on Roderick to the last.

Here is the one major contradiction in Smollett which is never resolved (and, arguably, never could be): the Calvinist determinism runs counter to the satirist's humanitarian concern. Even in *Humphry Clinker* there is the same problem. The theme of understanding developing out of experience is broached but not convincingly treated: it is suggested that greater mutual understanding has arisen between Jery and Matt but Jery, significantly, remains to the end a spectator at life's farce.

In Smollett's world, then, individuality is flattened out as being of no inherent interest. Should individuality persevere, against the grain as it were, it is necessarily driven to grotesquely idiosyncratic extremes. Thus V. S. Pritchett writes of Trunnion as 'a fantastic and maimed character'.[38] The Calvinist background casts light on Smollett's reductive treatment of subjectivity and individual ways of seeing: these are but examples of human limitation. As the language of his caricatures shows, for Smollett individuality both characterizes and limits in a way that is often comic. Smollett exemplifies that 'radical and violent subjectivity of vision'[39] which Francis Russell Hart, adducing Wittig, sees as distinctly Scottish; but, for all the energy, the subjectivity is ultimately a manifestation of limitation. Thus Smollett delights in stark and sudden juxtaposition of individual responses: contrast the respective letters of Peregrine and Trunnion, as indicative of character and values, on the occasion of the opposition of the commodore and his wife to Peregrine's interest in Emilia. *Sir Launcelot Greaves*, following the experiences of a cross-section of society on the move, is concerned with the limiting effects of subjectivity and anticipates the fuller treatment of this in *Humphry Clinker*, where the very form implies in-depth investigation of individual limitation.

The epistolary mode of fiction is naturally conducive to ironic self-revelation. Smollett had already achieved this effect by means of first-person narration in *Roderick Random*. For instance, Roderick warns Strap against being duped, by the pregnant widow, into marriage, only to proceed to pursue his own interest in Melinda. The irony is heightened here by virtue of Roderick's conviction, evident in his account of his subsequent rebuff by Melinda, that he is more worldly-wise and self-aware than Strap (for example, he speaks of the success of the 'finesse' of his 'affected passion' (*RR*, p. 296)). Similarly, after the encounter with Strutwell, Roderick feigns melancholy to disguise his joy and so affect Strap the more; Roderick, attempting to fool Strap, is much more seriously duped by Strutwell.

Such ironic self-revelation is central to *Humphry Clinker*. Matt betrays his values in his first letter—the obsession with health, the veneer of irascibility, and the embarrassed generosity. 'What business have people to get children to plague their neighbours?' (*HC*, p. 5) he exclaims; and, in his penultimate letter and well after the revelation of his paternity of Humphry, he can remark of the latter's projected marriage:

> I would have wished that Mr. Clinker had kept out of this scrape; but as the nymph's happiness is at stake, and she has had already some fits in the way of despondence, I, in order to prevent any tragical catastrophe, have given him leave to play the fool, in imitation of his betters; and I suppose we shall in time have a whole litter of his progeny at Brambleton-hall. (p. 345)

Underlining the irony here is the fact that, prior to this discourse on matrimony, Matt had referred to his natural son as 'Mr. Clinker Loyd'. Matt's unwitting disclosure of contradiction within himself is achieved in masterly fashion. The fact that a doctor has offered a diagnosis of his condition which he finds unacceptable leads to his raging 'I wish those impertinent fellows, with their ricketty understandings, would keep their advice for those that ask it', and the same letter to Dr. Lewis ends with the postscript, 'I forgot to tell you, that my right ancle pits, a symptom, as I take it, of its being oedematous, not leucophlegmatic' (pp. 24–5). A lengthy harangue on the fashionable ball at Bath culminates in a heated denunciation of the odours of polite society; his storm at last over, Matt then remarks: 'But few words are best: I have taken my resolution' (p. 66).[40]

Each of the characters is subjected to ironic self-revelation. For instance, Tabitha's first letter displays her characteristics of vanity, meanness, and repressed physicality. Tabitha attempts to present herself as the devout religious convert; the reality is that of the repressed sexuality of the spinster—as the nature of her errors in vocabulary so often indicates—venting itself in such niggardliness as:

> You will do well to keep a watchfull eye over the hind Villiams,

who is one of his (Dr. Lewis's) amissories, and, I believe, no better than he should be at bottom. God forbid that I should lack christian charity; but charity begins at huom, and sure nothing can be a more charitable work than to rid the family of such vermine. (p. 156)

Here surely is one of the ancestors of 'Ye high, exalted, virtuous dames/Tied up in godly laces' of Burns's 'Address to the Unco Guid'; and James Beattie might have written 'Mean sentiments, or expressions, in the mouth of those who assume airs of dignity, have the effect . . . of laughter'[41] with Tabitha in mind.

Ironic self-revelation is a feature of Scottish literature. Wittig rightly discerns it in Dunbar's 'Testament of Mr. Andro Kennedy',[42] and Burns was to employ it to great effect in 'Holy Willie's Prayer'. In fiction, Smollett's use of the technique almost certainly influenced Galt: *The Ayrshire Legatees* adopts the format of *Humphry Clinker*, and *Annals of the Parish* and *The Provost* are masterpieces of self-revelation. Writing of *Humphry Clinker*, Scott praised

> the finished and elaborate manner in which Smollett has, in the first place, identified his characters, and then fitted them with language, sentiments, and powers of observation, in exact correspondence with their talents, temper, condition, and disposition.[43]

Precisely such a capacity ought to have produced fine drama. The evidence of *The Regicide* and *The Reprisal* proves, regrettably, that it was late in his career that Smollett reached this peak of ability in imaginative delineation of character, while still commonly subjecting his characters to reductive (here self-reductive) treatment.

Multiple voices are characteristic of Scottish literature, and in this Smollett is no exception. Amongst the considerable range of moods and voices he adopts—those of sensibility, the sentimental, the melodramatic, the Gothic, the embryo Romantic—that of the rationalist is ultimately predominant. Diverse notes are sounded and have a temporary, and sometimes forcefully affective, validity, but in the end they are subordinated to Smollett's reductive rationalism. In designating it 'the rationalizing and sentimentalizing Enlightenment'[44] Morse Peckham has, rightly, identified the interfusion of elements within that complex intellectual movement. These elements coexist in Smollett, but the former has the upper hand. His first hero, Roderick, can display readily the sensibility of the man of feeling. When Miss Williams swoons in response to his concern for her wretched condition, he comments:

> Such extremity of distress must have waked the most obdurate heart to sympathy and compassion: What effect, then, must it have on mine, that was naturally prone to every tender passion? (*RR*, p. 116)

Here Roderick seems to anticipate Mackenzie's Harley, or Diderot, who wrote: 'If Nature ever made a sensitive soul, that soul, and you know it, was mine.'[45] It is undeniable, as a letter praising Richardson shows, that Smollett appreciated the values of the tender heart, but he does not allow sensibility to exist in isolation: it is, like everything else, subject to the flux of experience. The overwrought prose in which Roderick's encounters with Narcissa are presented is clear evidence of the distance at which Smollett stands from his hero's conduct. Smollett's fiction substantiates Wittig's observation that 'when confronted by a parade of feeling that an Englishman might be tempted to handle somewhat cavalierly, it gives the Scot a malicious satisfaction to take it down by apparently taking it seriously'.[46] In *Peregrine Pickle* in particular there is considerable satire of the romantic effusion: the letters of Gam Pickle and of Mrs. Hornback contrast with the love-letters of Peregrine, and there is the splendid irony wherein Emilia receives the *reductio ad absurdum* of this mode in the 'fustian' effusion in the name of Peregrine but revised by the clerk-schoolmaster (p. 105). Again, Smollett has taken care to distance himself from his hero when he notes of the earlier meeting with Emilia that Peregrine

> laid hold of the proper opportunities to express his admiration of her charms, had recourse to the silent rhetoric of tender looks, breathed divers insidious sighs, and attached himself wholly to her during the remaining part of the entertainment. (p. 95)

When he is later and understandably spurned by Emilia, he gives way to 'a violent fit of distraction, during which he raved like a Bedlamite, and acted a thousand extravagances which convinced the people of the house (a certain bagnio) that he had actually lost his wits' (p. 409).

The behaviour of Peregrine exemplifies a central tenet of Smollett's thought, which in this novel is expressed in the discovery made by Cadwallader Crabtree that

> when the passions are concerned, howsoever cool, cautious and deliberate, the disposition may otherwise be, there is nothing so idle, frivolous, or absurd, to which they will not apply for gratification. (p. 564)

And in so doing they run the risk of absurdity. For Smollett, when the single passion is indulged to the neglect of all others the result is inevitably comic. Such is the bias of Peregrine's passion that when he mistakenly believes that Emilia's heart has been won by a young officer his jealousy manifests itself in violently physical form that culminates in his fainting. The prospect of the ultimate fruition of such an all-consuming passion evokes a complex response from Emilia: Smollett records that 'Peregrine's heart was fired with inexpressible ardour and impatience; while the transports of the bride were mingled with a dash of diffidence and apprehension' (p. 777). Similarly, in *Ferdinand Count Fathom* Renaldo 'entered the apartment, and like a lion rushing on his prey, approached the nuptial bed where Serafina, surrounded by all the graces of beauty, softness, sentiment, and truth, lay trembling as a victim at the altar' (*FCF*, p. 351). The consummation of the single emotion gives rise to this remarkable concatenation of beauty and truth with the instinctive or animal passions.

It is important to consider the place of Smollett in the movement of emphasis in European literature in the eighteenth century towards the eliciting and the manifestation of emotion. This embraced emotion in both its sentimental and Gothic forms, and the Scottish contribution was not inconsiderable. Now it is undeniable that there are episodes in Smollett which prefigure the vogues of benevolism and sentimentality (e.g. the meeting between Peregrine and Gauntlet in the Fleet (*PP*, p. 751); the effect of Emilia's 'sympathizing regard' on Peregrine (*PP*, p. 758); the occasion when Monimia, being taken away by Ferdinand, meets Renaldo's dog (*FCF*, p. 221); Tom Clarke's sobbing and weeping plenteously 'from pure affection' (*LG*, p. 17); and the encounter at the smithy with the grief-stricken widow who believes Clinker is her husband restored to her, an incident described as 'too pathetic to occasion mirth' (*HC*, p. 186).

It must be repeated, however, that to Smollett's eyes intense or extreme emotion exists—quite validly—as part of an emotional complex, and hence in a situation of flux; if it is prolonged or indulged this is unnatural and becomes comic or grotesque and fit matter for reduction. This is precisely what Scott missed or chose to ignore when he wrote of Smollett's soaring 'far above [Fielding] in his powers of exciting terror' and commented further:

> Upon many other occasions Smollett's descriptions ascend to the sublime; and, in general, there is an air of romance in his writings, which raises his narratives above the level and easy course of ordinary life. He was, like a pre-eminent poet of our own day (Byron), a searcher of dark bosoms, and loves to paint characters under the strong agitation of fierce and stormy passions.[47]

In the half century which separates Scott from Smollett the taste of Europe had ensured that Gothicism and sentimentality were able to elude the control of reason. Scotland, in the course of the post-Union crisis of identity, experienced deep nostalgia for a remote Scottish past which had never existed. The creation of that past happened to meet the European need for Gothic romance, sentimentality, and natural, 'benevolent' man. This is a coincidence from which Scottish culture has never recovered.

A letter of Smollett's gives some indication of his place in this movement of values. He wrote of Nice: 'Here is no Learning, nor Taste of any kind. All is gothic pride, Ignorance, and Superstition.'[48] In his novels, with the qualified exception of *Ferdinand Count Fathom*, horror, fear, and superstition, as well as sentiment, are elicited, played upon, and almost invariably undermined rapidly (e.g. the encounter of Roderick and Strap with the raven and the 'ghost'; the suspicion of witchcraft that is maintained against the wise and kind Mrs. Sagely; the bizarre prank with the speaking-trumpet and the whitings which exploits Trunnion's fear of the supernatural (such a union of the fear of the supernatural and the comic prefigures Burns and is distinctly Scottish); Crabtree's assuming the part of magician and his exploits as fortune-teller continue the satire on superstition; and Win Jenkins's experience in 'the land of congyration' (*HC*, p. 261), and the episode of the 'ghost' who turns out to be Lismahago, do likewise).

In *Ferdinand Count Fathom*, though such emotions and subjects are undermined ultimately and participate in a total context in which their significance is only relative, this is not done nearly as rapidly as in the other novels. Here the Gothic and sentimental elements are afforded much more forceful and sustained expression, though in the context of the whole novel they still fall beneath the aegis of Smollett's reductive rationalism. This has to be recognized, and when Damian Grant claims that 'what is original in *Fathom* is Smollett's willingness to accept the experience of terror without ironic reserve'[49] he is overlooking both those occasions when the 'terrors' are reduced and the nature of the conclusion. The experience of terror is 'genuine' for its—limited—duration, but it is only one of various emotional chords in what is for Smollett the compound and flux of experience.

What is significant in *Ferdinand Count Fathom* is the relationship which Smollett establishes thus between fear and his alleged didactic aim:

> Yet the same principle by which we rejoice at the remuneration of merit, will teach us to relish the disgrace and discomfiture of vice, which is always an example of extensive use and influence, because it leaves a deep impression of terror upon the minds of those who were not confirmed in the pursuit of morality and virtue, and while the balance wavers, enables the right scale to preponderate. (p. 3)

Furthermore, he claims, 'the impulses of fear which is the most violent and interesting of all the passions, remain longer than any other upon the memory'. This helps clarify the rationale of the 'Gothic interlude' in Chapters 20 and 21 (which Grant suggests may be 'partly the result of inadvertence, a casting about for something different, or simply something next, to do').[50] In fact, in this episode Smollett firmly and clearly relates the Gothic to the fantasizing power of the imagination:

> the darkness of the night, the silence and solitude of the place, the indistinct images of the trees that appeared on every side, 'stretching their extravagant arms athwart the gloom', conspired

with the dejection of spirits occasioned by his loss to disturb his fancy, and raise strange phantoms in his imagination. Although he was not naturally superstitious, his mind began to be invaded with an awful horror, that gradually prevailed over all the consolations of reason and philosophy: nor was his heart free from the terrors of assassination. (p. 83)

The fancy positively induces an increased receptivity to fear: after the sighing of the trees and the roar of the thunderstorm, Ferdinand 'had well nigh lost the use of his reflection, and was actually invaded to the skin' (p. 84). As generally in Smollett, the correlation of mental and physical is important: in the course of his struggle through the forest 'his skin suffered in a grievous manner, while every nerve quivered with eagerness of dismay' (pp. 84–5).

The point of this episode is to demonstrate that Ferdinand, for all the success of his rational opportunism, is subject, like any other human being, to fear, and in particular to that co-operation of the mind with circumstances in the creation of fear. Thus the episode follows the pattern of alternation between Gothic horror and reductive observation, and between Ferdinand's terror and his opportunism. In the house of the old woman who offers him shelter he finds 'the dead body of a man, still warm, who had been lately stabbed, and concealed beneath several bundles of straw' (p. 86). The terror which this induces is vividly described in terms, first of physical effect, then of its stimulus to his conscience. When the robbers return to finish off their victim Ferdinand 'remained in a trance that, in all probability, contributed to his safety; for, had he retained the use of his senses, he might have been discovered by the transports of his fear' (p. 86). His first use of his 'retrieved recollection' is to note the open door as a means of escape, but, ever the opportunist, Fathom stops long enough to rob the corpse. The fluctuation between terror and practicality corresponds with a game of cat and mouse, with the roles changing, between Fathom and the old woman who, seeing the departing Fathom, 'accustomed as she was to the trade of blood . . . did not behold this apparition without giving signs of infinite terror and astonishment, believing it was no other than the spirit of her second guest who had been murdered' (p. 87).

The episode is an accomplished ironic study of human limitation as manifested in the mind's capacity to induce fear. Again traversing the wood, with 'every whisper of the wind . . . swelled into hoarse menaces of murder . . . [Fathom] felt what was infinitely more tormenting than the stab of a real dagger'. Smollett's point is that the effects of the imagination are far worse than any actuality (precisely the point made and exploited by Burns in 'Tam o' Shanter'). The episode ends with a splendidly ironic sequence. Now safe, Fathom

> earnestly exhorted her to quit such an atrocious course of life, and attone for her past crimes, by sacrificing her associates to the demands of justice. She did not fail to vow a perfect reformation, and to prostrate herself before him, for the favour she had found; then she betook herself to her habitation, with full purpose of advising her fellow-murderers to repair with all dispatch to the village, and impeach our hero, who wisely distrusting her professions, staid no longer in the place. . . . (p. 89)

After the interlude of horrors, devious scepticism had resumed its ascendancy.

It is once more indicative of what was to happen to Scottish values in the ensuing half-century that Scott's judgement of this episode should miss the counterpointing that is at the heart of Smollett's method and instead concentrate on his attainment to the sublime. For Scott,

> The horrible adventure in the hut of the robbers, is a tale of natural terror which rises into the sublime; and, though often imitated, has never yet been surpassed or perhaps equalled.[51]

In fact, Smollett's achievement here is an instance of that identifiably Scottish strain which Hugh MacDiarmid described as 'tremendously idiosyncratic, full of a wild humour which blends the actual and the apocalyptic in an incalculable fashion';[52] and Gregory Smith found a connection between the 'double mood' inherent in much of Scottish literature and 'the easy passing . . . between the natural and the supernatural, as if in challenge to the traditional exclusiveness of certain subjects, each within its own caste'.[53]

There is a tradition of interest in the demonic in Scottish writers such as Dunbar, Burns, Hogg, and Stevenson. Plainly Smollett can be included here, but the passing between the natural and the supernatural, between the actual and the apocalyptic, is subsumed within his reductive vision. Fathom is a vividly realized individual (as Scott recognized, contrasting him as 'a living and existing miscreant' with Jonathan Wild, 'a cold personification of the abstract principle of evil').[54] However the novel contains suggestions that Fathom is a demon-figure. Fathom's diabolism resides in his ability to identify life in terms of its flux and interfusion of values and to capitalize upon this by role-playing.

The extent to which seventeenth- and eighteenth-century Scotsmen were concerned with the opposition between the instincts and the rational will has been recognized.[55] It is precisely this opposition that Fathom appears to resolve by uniting instincts and rational will in the common cause of self-interest. At the outset Smollett identifies Ferdinand's 'insidious principle of self-love' (p. 20); and his early plotting establishes that equation of intimacy and self-advancement that characterizes him. His first experience in the demonic role is farcical: Wilhelmina believes that Fathom is the devil come on earth as her lover, and 'while her imagination teemed with those horrible ideas' he emerges soot-covered from his chimney hiding-place and is mistaken 'for Satan *in propria persona*' (p. 52). With the mother he adopts the postures of pathos and romantic love for self-advancement. A succession of roles follows thereafter, with Fathom appearing as a one-eyed fiddler, the Young Pretender, and a philosopher armed with a full confutation of Newton's philosophy. Such petty deception is prelude to the more sinister diabolism of his encounter with Celinda. Here Fathom's demonic qualities reach their height. Fathom wants 'to banquet his vicious appetite with the spoils of her beauty' (p. 158). Recognizing her 'superstitious fear', he plays upon 'such sensibility': by means of music he soothes her sense of hearing 'even to a degree of ravishment, so as to extort from her an exclamation, importing, that he was surely something super-natural' (pp. 158–59). The subtle modulation of the prose shows how Fathom interplays emotion, senses, music, and the supernatural in the interests of his diabolic purposes: by his virtuosity on the Aeolian harp Fathom pours forth 'a stream of melody more ravishingly delightful than the song of Philomel, the warbling brook, and all the concert of the wood' which introduces 'a succession of melodies in the same pathetic style'. All this achieves the desired effect on the sensations of Celinda which 'naturally acute, were whetted to a most painful keenness, by her apprehension' (p. 161). In the manner of the Satanic tempter Fathom orchestrates her emotions and in particular he plays upon her fear and superstition, with the result that

> In her paroxysms of dismay, he did not forget to breathe the soft inspirations of his passion, to which she listened with more pleasure, as they diverted the gloomy ideas of her fear; and by this time his extraordinary accomplishments had made a conquest of her heart. (p. 163)

After Fathom's triumph, Smollett, in a most effective juxtaposition, transports him to Bristol where he 'formed the nucleus or kernel of the beau monde' (p. 165): the significance is clear—at the heart of society is the man of demonic accomplishments. This theme is maintained in his claim 'that fire was the sole vivifying principle that pervaded all nature', and in his high medical reputation 'though the death of every patient had given the lie to his pretensions' (pp. 166–67). Having raised Fathom's status to this peak of diabolism, Smollett then proceeds to reduce it and to restore him to the level of the merely and patently human. In chapter 38 'the biter is bit'; at the encounter with Renaldo, what the latter believes to be tears of love, gratitude, and joy in fact 'proceeded from conscious perfidy and fear' (p. 196); confronted by Monimia's pledge of vengeance, 'he was not so much affected by his bodily danger, as awestruck at the manner of her address, and the appearance of her aspect, which seemed to shine with something supernatural, and actually disordered his whole faculties' (p. 237) (a splendidly ironic reversal of roles).

It is significant that it is just after Smollett's unequivocal statement of his realistic attitude to the human condition that Ferdinand's 'diabolism' is finally subsumed within Smollett's reductive realism by its being made to degenerate into its first condition—that of farce:

> Then was his chariot overturned with a hideous crash, and his face so much wounded with the shivers of the glass, which went to pieces in the fall, that he appeared in the coffee-house with half

> a dozen black patches upon his countenance, gave a most
> circumstantial detail of the risque he had run, and declared, that
> he did not believe that he should ever hazard himself again in any
> sort of wheel carriage. (p. 268)

Likewise, his grandiloquent repentance is undermined most
effectively by the acknowledgement of the circumstances of its
origin. In this there are obvious affinities with Burns's reduction of the Devil to the level of the human in 'Address to the
Deil', and of Death in 'Death and Dr. Hornbook' and 'Tam o'
Shanter', where he is 'tousie tyke, black, grim, and large'—
fearsome but also familiar. But the point of difference is that
Smollett has first to inflate, to create his 'devil', before reducing.
By the conclusion the Satan-substitute has been restored to the
dimension of flawed human being. Any attempt to relate
Ferdinand Count Fathom directly to Romantic Satanism must of
necessity overlook this distinctly Scottish reductive trait.

If Fathom is treated thus, at the same time Smollett establishes a comparable distance between himself and Renaldo, the
melancholic and sentimental lover. Through the experiences of
Renaldo Smollett reveals the often-grotesque effects upon the
emotional compound that result from the pursuit and the
indulgence of the single emotion. He exploits to the full the
potential pathos of Renaldo's situation, but the nature and the
sequence of the author's prose indicates that his own attitude is
far from being unrelievedly pathetic. The effects on Renaldo of
the loss of Monimia are presented first in terms of physical
detail, and then Smollett offers an account of the effect of his
condition on his mother and sister. It is a situation fraught with
paradox: their joy on witnessing his apparent recovery is
merely, for Renaldo, a protraction of his misery. His melancholy is nourished by attempts to counter it. Melancholy,
revenge, love, and physical beauty are all interfused, and the
recollection of Monimia in sensuous pastoral terms induces
what is termed his 'pleasing anguish'. The midnight pilgrimage
to Monimia's tomb displays sentiment overbalancing into the
grotesque:

> As they approached this capital, Renaldo's grief seemed to
> regurgitate with redoubled violence. His memory was waked to
> the most minute and painful exertion of its faculties; his imagina-

tion teemed with the most afflicting images, and his impatience became so ardent, that never lover panted more eagerly for the consummation of his wishes, than Melvile for an opportunity of stretching himself upon the grave of the lost Monimia. (p. 315)

The Gothic accompaniment is appropriate to Renaldo's extreme version of the sentimental lover, in which

the soul of Melvile was wound up to the highest pitch of enthusiastic sorrow. The uncommon darkness of the night, the solemn silence, and the lonely situation of the place, conspired with the occasion of his coming, and the dismal images of his fancy, to produce a real rapture of gloomy expectation, which the whole world would not have persuaded him to disappoint. (p. 317)

Such terms would seem to identify Smollett as one of the harbingers of the belief that painful emotions can be relished for their own sake and can be pleasurable. Yet, like everything else in Smollett, such passages cannot be extracted from context and considered apart from the total composite meaning of the book, a meaning which does nothing to suggest that Smollett's attitude is one of unequivocal endorsement of the joys of anguish. Renaldo's speech delivered prostrate on Monimia's tomb is deliberately over-wrought (on Smollett's part), and the recognition of the therapeutic effects of such an effusion is at least partly reductive:

[Renaldo] frankly owned, that his mind was now more at ease than he had ever found it, since he first received the fatal intimation of his loss; that a few such feasts would entirely moderate the keen appetite of his sorrow, which he would afterwards feed with less precipitation. (p. 319)

Far from this being so, he 'renews the rites of sorrow, and is entranced'. The reunion with Monimia, stage-managed by his 'friends . . . in consequence of his enthusiastic sorrow' (p. 327), allows Smollett to introduce most of the trappings of Gothicism, but once again the prose account of Renaldo's response becomes extravagant and self-deriding:

In the midst of these ejaculations, he ravished a banquet from her glowing lips, that kindled in his heart a flame, which rushed thro' every vein, and glided to his marrow: this was a privilege he

had never claimed before, and now permitted as a recompence
for all the penance he had suffered. (p. 326)

As habitually in Smollett, such emotional extremes accompany
(and in some cases are prompted or reinforced by) awareness of
the pleasurably sensuous.

Towards the end of *Ferdinand Count Fathom* the theme of the
pleasures of benevolism gains importance, but here again
Smollett's attitude is far from being entirely unironical. Serafina
pleads on behalf of Fathom, claiming to Renaldo: 'his present
wretchedness . . . will move your compassion, as it hath already
excited mine' (p. 341). In time Renaldo agrees to visit Fathom,
'not with a view to exult over his misery, but in order to
contemplate the catastrophe of such a wicked life, that the
moral might be the more deeply engraved on his remem-
brance', and, on entering, 'they beheld the wretched hero of
these adventures stretched almost naked upon straw, insensible,
convulsed, and seemingly in the grasp of death' (p. 353).
Fathom writes that he wishes to 'excite the compassion of the
humane count de Melvile', and his confession, he hopes, 'may
be a warning for him to avoid henceforth, a smiling villain, like
the execrable Fathom' (p. 354). Fathom's situation may have
evoked compassion in the reader, but this is qualified by the
element of grovelling in his appeals. However the self-approving
joy of Renaldo is then subjected to comparable qualification.
Fathom's suitably overwrought plea ('ah murthered innocence!
wilt thou 'not intercede for thy betrayer at the throne of grace?'
[p. 359]) is interrupted by a lecture from Renaldo on the subject
of Providence, the tone and nature of which are such as to
suggest that Renaldo regards the benevolent as the Elect. Even
more disturbing is the mixture of motives claimed in the
comment of the narrator:

> . . . the strange occurrence of the day . . . seemed to have been
> concerted by supernatural prescience, in order to satisfy the
> vengeance, and afford matter of triumph to the generosity of
> those who had been so grievously injured by the guilty Fathom.
> (p. 359)

Renaldo proceeds to relish the 'luxurious enjoyment of communicating happiness to his fellow creatures in distress'
(p. 360), the first instalment of which in an annuity of £60 per

annum and a promise of more if Fathom's behaviour warrants it.

For Sterne, 'there is nothing unmixed in this world'.[56] In Smollett too nothing—not benevolism, sentiment, or sensibility—remains unmixed. As Matt Bramble and his party travel further into the Highlands the use of such terms as 'romantic', 'picturesque', and 'sublime' increases, and this might be regarded as a forerunner of the Romantics' concern with such qualities. Jery notes that the country and the people are 'more wild and savage the further we advance' (*HC*, p. 238), and he goes on to enthuse over the antiquarian spirit and the Ossian poems. Such romanticizing over tartanry is then undermined in the fine comic detail of the laird's 'invincible antipathy to the sound of the Highland bagpipe' (p. 241), and his unavailing attempt to dispense with the ritual morning recital thereon.

Perhaps the greatest reason for the neglect of Smollett by his countrymen now becomes plain. Sentiment and rationality coexist in Smollett's vision, but the latter holds the supremacy. Smollett's values were formed before the Scottish dissociation of sensibility could have an effect on them. Underlying the diverse manifestations of his vision is a unity which derives from his reductive rationalism. By Burns's day, and certainly by Scott's, feeling had become polarized as sentiment and existed virtually independently of reason. Thus a nation whose taste dictated that they separate quite rigidly Burns's satiric voice from his sentimental could have little interest in a writer in whom these and many other voices intermingle. In this Smollett exemplifies the older Scottish literary tradition.

NOTES

1. *The Letters of John Keats*, ed. Maurice Buxton Forman (London, 1947), pp. 76–7.
2. Here the following observations of Edwin Muir are invaluable: 'There were not many genteel Scottish writers before Scott; there have not been many ungenteel ones since. His gentility can be seen in his *Border Minstrelsy* which he loved and yet could not but Bowdlerize. But the difference he introduced into Scottish poetry can be seen most clearly by

comparing his own poems in the ballad form with the old ballads themselves. It is pretty nearly the difference between

> I lighted down my sword to draw,
> I hacked him in pieces sma',

and

> 'Charge, Chester, charge! On, Stanley, on!'
> Were the last words of Marmion,

the difference between a writer fully conscious that he is dealing with dreadful things and one who must make even carnage pleasing and picturesque' ('Scott and Tradition', *The Modern Scot*, ed. J. H. Whyte [London, 1935], p. 120).

3. *The Lives of the Novelists* (London and New York, 1910), p. 112.

4. 'On Humour', Lectures (1818), *Complete Works of Coleridge*, ed. W. G. T. Shedd (New York, 1853), IV, 277. V. S. Pritchett made almost the same point with reference to Smollett himself, claiming: 'Something is arrested in the growth of his robust mind; as a novelist he remains the portrayer of the outside, rarely able to get away from physical externals or to develop from that starting-point into anything but physical caricature' (*The Living Novel* [London, 1966], pp. 20–1).

5. *The Adventures of Peregrine Pickle*, ed. with an introduction by James L. Clifford (London, 1964), pp. 541–42. Editions used are those of the Oxford University Press, i.e. the above and *The Adventures of Roderick Random*, ed. with an introduction by Paul-Gabriel Boucé (Oxford, 1979); *The Adventures of Ferdinand Count Fathom*, ed. with an introduction by Damian Grant (London, 1971); *The Life and Adventures of Sir Launcelot Greaves*, ed. with an introduction by David Evans (London, 1973); *The Expedition of Humphry Clinker*, ed. with an introduction by Lewis M. Knapp (London, 1966).

6. *A Literary History of Scotland* (London, 1903), p. 561.

7. *Lives*, p. 110.

8. *The Scots Literary Tradition* (London, 1962), p. 68.

9. Martin Foss, *Symbol and Metaphor in Human Experience*, p. 143; cited George Kahrl, 'Smollett as Caricaturist', *Tobias Smollett: Bicentennial Essays presented to Lewis M. Knapp*, ed. G. S. Rousseau and P-G. Boucé (New York, 1971), p. 200.

10. Review of *To Circumjack Cencrastus*, *Criterion*, X (April, 1931), 518.

11. Compare Burns, whose scathing epigrams on the Earl of Galloway served a therapeutic end.

12. *The Letters of Tobias Smollett*, ed. Lewis M. Knapp (Oxford, 1970), p. 69.

13. *Letters*, ed. Knapp, p. 140.

14. *Scottish Literature: Character and Influence* (London, 1919), p. 15.

15. Cited Gregory Smith, *Scottish Literature*, p. 18.

16. *Art and Illusion: A Study in the Psychology of Pictorial Representation* (London, 1959), pp. 286, 296.

17. *Table Talk* (London, 1819), pp. 448–49.

18. 'Smollett's Achievement as a Novelist', *Tobias Smollett*, ed. Rousseau and Boucé, p. 11.
19. *Scottish Literature*, p. 35.
20. *The Scots Literary Tradition*, p. 47.
21. *The Living Novel*, p. 19.
22. See further Gombrich, *Art and Illusion*, p. 290, for the origins of this practice in the work of the brothers Carracci. This is not to diminish the significance of animal imagery in earlier Scottish literature and the likely influence on Smollett.
23. 'On Laughter and Ludicrous Composition', *Essays* (London, 1779), pp. 431–32.
24. As John Butt noted, 'in Micklewhimmen he has drawn the first of a type of Scotch lawyer in whom Scott was later to specialize' (*Tobias Smollett*, ed. Rousseau and Boucé, p. 20). In the dancing-master and his pupil in *HC* may be the inspiration for Galt's MacSkipnish in *Annals of the Parish*.
25. Amongst a gallery of characters with affinities with those of Smollett one thinks of Mr. Turveydrop and Prince in relation to the same dancing-master; and the *ménage* of Wemmick and the aged parent in *Great Expectations* may owe something to Trunnion.
26. *Art and Illusion*, pp. 295, 301.
27. *Reason and Romanticism* (London, 1926), p. 191.
28. *Scottish Literature*, p. 20.
29. The following comment of Hugh MacDiarmid is apposite: 'I have always agreed with him [John Davidson] too, that if one has a healthy mind it is wholesome to go from extreme to extreme, just as a hardy Russian plunges out of a boiling bath into the snow' ('John Davidson: Influences and Influence'), *Selected Essays* (London, 1969), p. 202.
30. See also Matt Bramble's admiration of *chiaro oscuro* (*HC*, p. 76).
31. Wittig writes of Dunbar: 'The beautiful and the grotesque dwell side by side in his breast. Both form part of the same undivided world' (*The Scottish Tradition in Literature*, p. 73, Edinburgh, 1958).
32. *The Scottish Tradition*, pp. 73, 121.
33. Compare the use of similar imagery to scurrilous effect with reference to the future William IV in Burns's 'A Dream', stanza 13.
34. See Galt, *Annals of the Parish*, ed. James Kinsley (London, 1967), pp. 1, 13, 15 and 21; Burns, 'Elegy on the Departed Year 1788'.
35. *FF*, ed. Grant, p. 263 n. 3.
36. *Letters*, ed. Knapp, p. 98.
37. Cited Paul Hazard, *European Thought in the Eighteenth Century* (Harmondsworth, 1965), p. 319.
38. *The Living Novel*, p. 20.
39. *The Scottish Novel: A Critical Survey* (London, 1978), p. 15.
40. Similarly, a lengthy attack on London life subsides into 'my letter would swell into a treatise, were I to particularize every cause of offence that fills up the measure of my aversion to this, and every other crowded city' (*HC*, p. 123).
41. *Essays*, p. 354.
42. *The Scottish Tradition*, p. 74.

43. *Lives*, p. 99; and see also Lord Woodhouselee, cited Scott, p. 85. For examples see letters by Jery (p. 8) and Lydia (p. 27).
44. *The Triumph of Romanticism* (Columbia, S. Carolina, 1970), p. 27.
45. Cited Hazard, *European Thought in the Eighteenth Century*, p. 409.
46. *The Scottish Tradition*, p. 121.
47. *Lives*, p. 109.
48. *Letters*, ed. Knapp, p. 124.
49. *FF*, ed. Grant, p. xviii.
50. *FF*, ed. Grant, p. xiv.
51. *Lives*, p. 84.
52. C. M. Grieve, *Albyn, or Scotland and the Future* (London, 1927), p. 22.
53. *Scottish Literature*, pp. 36–7.
54. *Lives*, p. 110.
55. See, for instance, Thomas Crawford, *Burns* (Edinburgh and London, 1960), p. 41.
56. *A Sentimental Journey through France and Italy*, ed. Graham Petrie with an introduction by A. Alvarez (Harmondsworth, 1967), p. 112.

4

The Note of Protest in Smollett's Novels

by TOM SCOTT

I believe it was that fine critic V. S. Pritchett who, many years ago, described Smollett as 'a sanitary inspector of genius with a skin too few'. More prosaically, that means he was a writer of genius who had a vocation for examining the physical and mental hygiene of his society, or the lack of it, to which he brought not only a robust intellect but a hypersensitive (in his last years febrile) sensibility. He felt as a slap what ordinary men would feel as a mild pat. Smollett himself puts it even better through Jerry Melford in his second letter to Phillips in *Humphry Clinker*:

> I was once apt to believe him [Bramble-Smollett] a complete cynic . . . I am now of another opinion. I think his peevishness arises partly from bodily pain, and partly from a natural excess of mental sensibility; for, I suppose, the mind as well as the body is in some cases endued with a morbid excess of sensation.

Whether morbid or not (and like D. H. Lawrence he died of T.B.), his genius rises from the yoking of a restless extravert intellect with an abnormally acute, also mainly extravert, sensibility. This is what makes him by far the best social, though not psychological, critic among novelists of his time.

This genius was shaped by his medical training and studies, which made him keenly aware of the nervous system and the interaction between mind and body, the effects of psychological processes on the body and vice versa. He was much influenced by the Glasgow school of medicine, being a Clydesider, such men as John Gordon, John Moore, William Hunter and John Armstrong, some of whom were close personal friends. It was a basically materialist school. But Smollett was also interested in philosophy and was friendly also with David Hume. He was well read in and aware of the intellectual currents of his time and the revolutionary unrest of feudalism giving way to capitalism, a rural economy to the industrial revolution: the one exploding mainly in France, the other pioneered in the U.K. He translated Voltaire as well as Le Sage and Cervantes. All these influences made for rationalism, the enthronement of reason as God. The irrationality of contemporary life impinged on him as a chronic outrage of both sense and sensibility. The god of reason is a perfectionist in a world the real God made very 'imperfect'.

It is from such an intellectual world-view interacting with his nervous hypersensitivity that the note of protest in Smollett's novels (though by no means only in his novels) rises. At the centre of it is a protest against the human condition as such, almost a quarrel with God, with reality, the imprisonment of the human soul in the human body: in Yeats' phrase, the soul 'tied to a dying animal', the perfectible trapped in the imperfect, the mortal. Instances of this abound and will emerge later in this comment. The protest reaches out from this root and centre through human sensations, feelings, emotions, conflicts, physical and emotional disturbances to society, the world. It is a protest that begins in the self, reaches out to the circumference of his experience, and returns to the self. From this psychophysical constitution stem his acute sense of the grotesque, of outrage, his overreaction (and that of so many of his characters), his scorn, his ridicule of humbug, of the incongruous, his hatred of injustice, exploitation, cruelty, class pretensions, snobbery, arrogance, his contempt for 'authority', his scunner at dirt, poverty, misery, hypocrisy, ignorance, bad taste, false values, his Swiftlike disgust and spiritual nausea at the crude state of human society and its mores not only in England but the continent, his revulsion from the ugliness surrounding his fine, discriminating senses. He is intolerant of war, both naval and military, of prison barbarity, the horrors of prostitution, abuse of women and abuses by women, of the innate thrawnness of things, of life's vulnerability to chance and accident, of social evil and crass inadequacies, of the system of mental and physical torture of children miscalled education, of (and here is his essential Scottishness) 'man's inhumanity to man' which makes countless millions mourn. It is not nature but people who make this Earth a vale of tears. Smollett was a medical man because he was one of the brotherhood of pain, those who are pulled by suffering beneath the surface of life and so impelled to try to do something about it, to ameliorate suffering. In this the writer and the physician are one, two means to the same end. He was not so much a stoic as a hedonist: never indifferent to pleasure and pain but all too responsive to them, an aesthete, an epicurian. He was too honest to try to escape into stoical indifference.

Given such a nature, conflict with things as they are inevitably follows. Each of the eponymous characters of these five novels is in some sense a social misfit, born to collide with things as they are but ought not to be. Thus Roderick Random, whose mother dreamed before his birth that 'she was delivered of a tennis-ball which the devil struck so forcibly with a racket that it disappeared in an instant', is disinherited with his father by his tyrannical grandfather. He is born in such outcast circumstances that his mother dies as a result, deserted by his distracted father, farmed out on a nurse by his grandfather from whom he is further estranged by scheming relatives, and brutally abused by a sadistic schoolmaster whose birch seems to play the part of the devil's tennis racket in the dream. His mother's brother Tom Bowling, outraged by the schoolmaster, pays him out by flogging him with a cat-o-nine-tails: an act of poetic justice by no means common in Smollett. Peregrine Pickle is not quite such an outcast of fortune, but he too is born to collide with society: his inhuman mother douses him every morning in icy water, his aunt sticks pins in him, his father is too lazy to take any interest in him, his mother sees to it he is flogged daily by way of 'education' so mercilessly that he becomes shocked into dull withdrawal. This leads to his being sent to an even worse fate, a boarding school where he is subjected to such neglect and contempt that he is reduced to tears, melancholy, loss of appetite and solitary brooding: a nervous breakdown. Nevertheless, like Random, and most of Smollett's heroes, he has such natural gifts that even he comes through—but as a clever rogue, the unscrupulous product of his upbringing. He is befriended by Trunnion, one of the best of a number of seamen in these novels whose nautical language applied as a sustained metaphor to non-nautical life is an incomparable prose poetry, and his companion Tom Pipes, but little appreciates the old commander's real love and kindness to him. Ferdinand, Count Fathom, is an even greater rogue from the most appalling background of all (Smollett sees them as products of their backgrounds), his birth 'without running the risk of being claimed by any earthly father' might have entitled him to 'have laid claim to divine extraction' like some mythical hero. His mother is a military camp-follower who, like financiers, arms manufacturers and warmongers in general, profits from both sides of battles by slaying the wounded and robbing them of any valuables. She is eventually killed by one of her victims, leaving Ferdinand, aged nine to live by his considerable wits, a dis-placed person born between two countries, belonging to neither.

Wit, brains, parts, all three had aplenty and in common. Smollett makes the point that such men of guile, lies, fraud, unscrupulous self-seeking in luckier circumstances would have made statesmen and politicians, operating inside the laws instead of outside, honoured instead of condemned. Smollett uses them as mirrors of the corrupt society, the embodiment of his protest against it. He might have anticipated Auden's 'Those to whom evil is done/Do evil in return.' The central pill of this unsmiling, outraged protest is of course coated with a surrounding sugar of rumbustious comedy: the sugar soon melts, the medicine remains to change the consciousness of the good reader. Smollett has more than a little in common with another great Scottish writer, William Dunbar, not only in his sense of scunner at social injustice but in his sheer linguistic exuberance. Like Dunbar, and yet another great Scottish writer Thomas Urquhart, he 'langage had at large', as David Lyndsay, another relevant ancestor, put it. In this the Scot is unsurpassed by any contemporary English novelist.

So far a declension into roguery: deeper than Fathom he could not go, so he soars to the other extreme in Sir Launcelot Greaves. Greaves is born with the silver spoon in his mouth and the aristocracy of his breeding is matched by an aristocracy of soul of high ideal and values. He is the positive statement of the idealism at the heart of Smollett's negative satire, the standards by which society is judged and condemned. He is Smollett at the core without the humour, the protective irony, the defensive mockery. He is the perennial do-gooder, humourless and cranky, but noble and admirable. He is also as much a misfit in society as the rogue is, but for the opposite reasons. These secular (or clerical) saints are the salt of the earth, though they tend to be, inevitably, ineffectual against the status quo, against which the individual protest can avail but little. The Christian allusion is apt, for such people, Greaves among them, tend to be Christlike in their lesser ways.

Humphry Clinker is by no means a rogue, nor is he a saner version of Don Quixote like Greaves, but in his poverty, his outcast state, his bastardy, he is closer to the first three than to Greaves: and like them all he is a social misfit. But the real 'hero' of this novel is not Clinker but Matthew Bramble, who takes on the destitute young Clinker as his servant, discovering later that Clinker is his own illegitimate son. Bramble is as near to being Smollett himself in later years as can be, for most of the novel, and it is in him that the note of protest reaches its most perfect, comprehensive, mature and articulate utterance. When Clinker is taken on as postillion to ·Bramble's health-seeking pilgrims, about quarter way through the book, he is in rags, 'a poor Wiltshire lad' who offends Mrs. Tabby (and delights Win Jenkins the maid) with a sight of his bare backside through his rags. Bramble questions him about his plight, hears he was brought up a bastard in a workhouse, and is much touched by the tale of his woes. 'Heark ye, Clinker,' Bramble says, 'you are a most notorious offender. You stand convicted of sickness, hunger, wretchedness and want.' He tempers justice with compassion by giving Clinker a guinea to clothe himself with: an example lost on our judges.

Behind all these characters of course, the eponymous ones, is the tradition of the *picaro*—by definition a social misfit. Smollett is no slavish imitator of Scarron or Le Sage, but without them his novels could not have been written. His range of social reference, of human character, is larger than and unequalled by any of his contemporaries. We are nearer to the medieval-Renaissance amplitude, the wealth of Boccaccio and of Chaucer of whom

110

Dryden said 'here surely is God's plenty'. Smollett is not that great, but he comes nearer than any of his contemporaries, who are more corsetted, the beginning of a bad, genteel censorship of life as it is. In what other writer of the period is homosexuality, for example, not only mentioned but manifested in such characters as Smollett's Captain Whiffle (Random) and Earl Strutwell and their friends? Indeed much of the prissiness of early critics is precisely aimed at making a vice of this virtue: the rot had already set in, the writers being blinkered like carthorses. Smollett the Scot is closer to the catholic Europe of the great continental novelists than the Englishmen are: despite his Calvinist background. He is less insular, more European in outlook though the note of his protest sounds even louder in France and Italy than it does in England. His psychological range, from the nadir of Fathom to the zenith of Greaves, though less acute in some reaches than that of Richardson or Sterne, is unparalleled: and at all levels he is alertly critical. All his experience comes before the court of his values and standards for scrutiny and balanced judgement, no cow being favoured for its sacredness. The pretensions and impostures of lying 'authority' come under the lash of his scorn, including the classical Rome in whose literature he was himself so well versed. Stature apart, his satiric vision differs from that of his great Renaissance predecessors such as Boccaccio, Chaucer and Rabelais, in that they laugh with a large catholic tolerance of human comedy whereas Smollett is intolerant and condemnatory. But tolerance can stem also from blunt senses rather than any charitable virtue. 'He jests at scars who never felt a wound.'

The ferocity of his scorn first reaches major utterance in his treatment of the British navy at Cartagena in *Random*. Smollett's own experience as a ship's surgeon at Cartagena is here used through the mask of Random, who has been pressed into service. The brutality he endured, the cramped, filthy, dark and stinking quarters, the vile food, insanitary conditions, tyranny of rank, slavish labour, above all the moronic incompetence, all add up to a claustrophobic hell. The great naval tradition was founded on the press gang, tyranny, sodomy, rum and the lash, not to say keelhauling. It has been alleged that Nelson's last words were not 'kiss me, Hardy' but 'two hundred and fifty lashes'. As for the sick berth where fifty men lay packed like sardines 'deprived of the light of day as well as of fresh air', their wounds crawling with vermin, it bludgeons the imagination. His description of the wretches attending surgery with their various horrible afflictions makes one wonder how a sensitive soul like Smollett was able to bear it at all: there is a sinewy toughness in him too. Not only were some of the poor sufferers forced back to work, where they died, but Random and others have difficulty preventing the surgeon 'curing' their friend's broken leg by amputation: what if his head had been broken? Spite and malice among the officers adds an unnecessary burden to the general misery: the phenomenon has been observed in tightly confined rats. The vicious spite of Mackshane against Random, Morgan and Thompson leads to their being imprisoned as suspected spies, and ultimately to Thompson's suicide: he jumps overboard.

The Cartagena episode itself is dealt with in the guise of the daft wee laddie whose innocence excuses what would be offensive in one more sophisticated: Smollett went to school with Swift. Random tells us, deadpan, the story, and then brings the obvious charges against it in 'they-say' form, but loyally defends his superiors from them in such a way as underlines their force and brings out the idiocy of the authorities. Thus, when the British ships, having sailed along the north coast of Colombia, anchor for ten idle days off Cartagena, Random dismisses the charge of criminal waste of time with 'I would ascribe this delay to the generosity of our chiefs who scorned to take any advantage that fortune might give them even over an enemy.' The idiocy of landing marines near the harbour mouth and camping them on the beach to be battered by the enemy guns he defends as 'practised, I presume, with a view of accustoming our soldiers to stand fire'. The fact that they were raw recruits sent on such a mission while veterans lay idle at home he defends as

> they were loth to risk their best troops on such desperate service; or, the colonels . . . who . . . enjoyed their commissions as sinecures . . . refused to embark in such a dangerous . . . undertaking; for which refusal no doubt they are much to be commended.

He goes on in similar vein to give an ironic account of the battle, or at least his own ship's part in it. Even the simple Jack Rattlin is able to tell Random what ought to have been done, and the sheer madness of openly challenging the whole might of the enemy on his own ground: he asserts that three out of four of 'our' shots were wasted by unskilled men; and so on. But the criminal folly of the English attackers was matched by similar incompetence on the Spanish side so that the English have some successes: an advantage they throw away by further idiocies. Random defends this as 'our heroes disdained as a barbarous insult over the enemy's distress, and gave them all the respite they could desire . . . to recollect themselves.' The upshot is a retreat and the survival of 1,500 men out of 8,000. Ships were loaded with wounded, with men handless, legless, eyeless, their horrible wounds neglected, filthy and rotting and crawling with millions of maggots, due to the absence of surgeons. Random defends his chiefs from the charge that plenty of surgeons were at hand to cope with this emergency by saying

> perhaps the general was too much of a gentleman to ask a favour of this kind from his fellow chief (the admiral) who, on the other hand, would not derogate so much from his own dignity as to offer such assistance unasked . . . for . . . the Demon of Discord . . . had breathed her influence upon our counsels.

He goes on in the same blistering vein about the appalling human suffering and agonizing death thus occasioned by the petty vanities of forces commanders. Swift himself is rarely more flaying in his icy passionate contempt. He heaps up the evidence against the admiral and then turns it on the government at home who exonerated instead of hanging him. Then even more than now the ruling class misruled Britain as a gentleman's club, interlocking clubs, rather, in which they made and unmade the rules as they went along: quangos might be our nearest term. The corpses of the poor wretches thus victimized were unceremoniously, unchristianly, thrown overboard to the sharks.

The above incident is followed by his description of the ship being taken over by Captain Whiffle, an exhibitionist homosexual, and his friend Mr. Simper: we are treated to some camp, pansy scenes at which Smollett is not laughing with us—he is outraged.

A similar, though milder irreverence for authority and the Establishment is Lismahago's great deflation of the Treaty of

Union and its results, not to say all things English even to their abuse of their own language, which Scots honour with a truer care for its virtues, values and proprieties. The speech on the Union I will refer to later: it is one of the truest statements on the subject ever written, as true today as when it was penned, and should be required reading not only for all Scots but all English. He is particularly good on the massive benefits accruing to England at the expense of the Scots, and in it the mask of Lismahago slips to reveal our author as potentially a great political leader of Scots.

Returning to *Random,* he also flays the French aristocracy in the episode with the brain-washed soldier of King Louis: Smollett would not have been surprised by the events of 1789. And in *Pickle,* in the scene where the physician gives a feast in the manner of the ancient Romans, he ridicules the 'authority' of the classics. I regret that my writ precludes comment on his fine poem 'The Tears of Scotland' on the horrors Butcher Cumberland, symptomatic of the panic Charles Edward roused in the mediocre hearts of the Hanoverians, after Culloden, except to say that Smollett could have been a great verse satirist, had he not chosen, or been chosen by, the novel. Certainly he was a poet, a fact evident in his feeling for words and cadence, his sense of style and rhetoric, his imagery, his lyrical descriptive passages and his actual verse in and outwith the novels.

Protest and reform, the twin principles of the Reformation, are particularly evident in his prison scenes in each novel: though York prison is seen as somewhat exemplary in Clinker. These homes of the damned are full of squalor, filth, monstrous cruelty, crime, injustice, lawlessness and disorder. Most of the inmates are guilty of little but bad luck, victims of a society that blames its victims instead of itself: and some are 'cured' by a change in luck, a stroke of good fortune. The horrors of Bridewell in the Miss Williams episode in Random are the more so because done to a wretched girl who has been by degrees drawn into prostitution by a series of misfortunes and betrayals. She is set tasks in the workhouse far beyond her strength and, failing to manage them, is mercilessly flogged by the jailer who sets them: 'I was often whipped into a swoon and lashed out of it': and while being flogged her fellow-prisoners rob her of the clothes she has been stripped of. Allan Ramsay refers to such floggings of women's bottoms in correction-houses in 'Lucky Spence's Last Advice':

There's ae sair cross attends the craft   [prostitution]
That curst correction-house, where aft
Wild Hangy's tawse ye're riggings saft   [rig-ends, bottom]
   Maks black and blae,
Enough to put a body daft;
   But what'll ye say?

Nane gaithers gear withouten care,
Ilk pleasure has o pain a share;
Suppose then they should tirle ye bare   [flog you naked]
   And gar ye sike,   [sob]
E'en learn to thole . . .   [endure]

Smollett does not exaggerate. Miss Williams reaches such depths of pain and despair that she tries to kill herself, fails, and for that is given thirty stripes (presumably with the cat on her back) which drives her out of her mind for several days. She is eventually freed when the man who really committed the crime she was alleged to have committed is caught and confesses: no compensation of course.

Smollett's hatred of injustice and cruelty inform almost everything he wrote, though at times the demands of his comedy—usually kept so grotesque as to distance from sentient reality—seem to invite us to laugh at suffering. The prison scenes seem to me to have symbolic force: prison is an ironic comment on the 'free' society (as it is in our own time), and at another level it symbolizes the real nature of that society—a barbarous caricature of civilization, its freedom illusory, merely the freedom to exploit, rob and defraud, all the usual crimes dignified by the names of commerce, trade, business, in capitalist society. We find a similar symbolism in Scott's *Heart of Midlothian*: the heart is the Tolbooth prison, symbol of captive Scotland, and to get any semblance of justice Jeanie has to take the road to Whitehall and the court. The bars of the prison are capitalist war against the wage-slave class, gross inequality of income and maldistribution of wealth, the few having the bulk of national wealth, the many the residue, organized crime protected by evil laws, a legal system which protects the major

criminals who make the laws and persecutes the minor criminals
who live outwith them; and for the Scots, no government: then
as today. Smollett is our contemporary, his analysis only
different in degree, not kind. We still live in the eighteenth
century as far as economics and politics are concerned, our
system obsolete. In some ways we have progressed: in others we
have worsened. Prisoners are better treated, we no longer flog
and hang them, nor soldiers nor sailors, such barbarity linger-
ing on only against children who are still legally assaulted in
school and in home. Since Smollett's time the whip, the rope
and the birch, except in such anachronisms as the Isle of (sub)
Man, for prisoners, soldiers and sailors have been abolished
without the prisons exploding into anarchy, the army running
wild, the navy erupting in mutiny: but it is still argued that this
would happen in our schools but for the tawse and the cane:
such are our educators. We no longer imprison people for petty
debt, but in Scotland we still poynd and sell poor people's goods
for a tithe their value: only a few years ago an ex-lord provost of
Edinburgh and his young bride committed suicide after such
treatment, but the evil is still with us. We must never read
Smollett (nor anybody else of worth) the way the academics
would have us read him: as divorced from real life here and now:
that is wicked subversion of the function of literature in creating
reform. Smollett stood at all the frontiers of progress in his time,
and in spirit stands at the frontiers of progress today. His
demand for constant social improvement stems from his belief
that people are the product of their social environment, and to
change them you must change it. There are exceptions who
prove the rule—is Greaves perhaps one of them? Or is he too
entirely accountable for in terms of his background? In any case
he is largely motivated by sexual frustration and sexual fulfilment humanizes him, ending the pathos and futility of a purely
individual bucking of the system.

At the heart of Smollett's indignation and protest is an
immense compassion, a sympathy with suffering which literally
involves him in the pain he witnesses and forces him to action,
even if only literary action. This compassion is perhaps most
explicit in *Sir Launcelot Greaves*, especially the incident of the two
small boys whom the young Greaves finds picking hips and
haws on his father's estate. He questions them, finds they are

only six and five years old respectively, that their widowed mother was robbed of the two cows she depended on to feed them and their sister: the old squire's bailiff had seized the cows in lieu of arrears of rent. The widow is ill as a result, the sister crying with hunger, so the boys are gathering berries for food. Young Greaves is outraged, his face scarlet with anger and shame. He takes the boys by the hands and confronts his father with this infamy, accusing him of oppressing the weak and fatherless of his own tenants. He is so vehement in his protest that his father is reduced to tears and immediately upbraids the bailiff. He gives orders that two of his own best cows be given the woman at once, better than her own, and on discovering she is the widow of his own late gamekeeper, gives her life-free rental, further undertaking to provide for the children out of his own pocket. Greaves is so pleased by this he kisses his father's hand. We see here not only Smollett's intense compassion and hatred of villainy but his affirmation of a loving society. Seeing the old squire as society, society should right its own wrongs by love and care for the wronged, the relief of suffering, not aggravation of it. At a spiritual level this is real Christianity: at the material it is real socialism: neither of course yet tried in any country. In a society like ours, founded on selfish greed and rapacity, you don't punish people for being unable to meet your inordinate demands: you provide them with the wherewithal to meet your more modest demands. Here is a true ethos underlying and pervading all his work.

Instances of this ethical compassion abound in the novels. To mention a few, there is Random's befriending of Miss Williams; Matthew Bramble giving secretly £20 (a large sum in those days) to the poor woman; Trunnion's sustained kindness to Pickle. It is from this compassion the note of protest springs and it is at the core of his bitterest satire, such as the Cartagena episode mentioned above. It is probably what guided the young Smollett into medicine, a desire to relieve suffering, not only of others but the pain his own sympathy brought him, his open-eyed, open-nerved approach to life. He was not in any priggish sense a moralist, but a profound ethos of love and care is at the heart of his indignation at the contradiction of society as it is and as it ought to be. His vision of the good society implicit in his protest against the bad is Christian in affinity if not in origin:

117

a vision of the New Jerusalem, the Kingdom of God on Earth. Indeed, much of it is the Sermon on the Mount in eighteenth-century prose. Would that we could see it in twentieth-century prose also.

At the beginning of this essay I quote Pritchett's acute remark that Smollett was a 'sanitary inspector of genius'. We must take that in the psychological as well as the physical sense: in fact I have so taken it above. They are head and tail of the same coin. The sanitary inspector is nowhere more evident in these novels than in *Humphry Clinker,* and in no character than Matthew Bramble. Bramble's ill-health makes him particularly sensitive and vulnerable to the social ills his journey in search of recovery exposes him to, and they in turn make him worse not better in mind and body. He is obsessed with his own malaise and that of all around him: this shows even in the fact that his letters are all to his doctor friend, Lewis, for only to a physician could he pour out his obsession. The note is struck in the opening sentence of his first letter: 'The pills are good for nothing.' He then goes on to complain about his constipation, demands a better prescription, complains about his tormented body, his distress of mind, his sister's plaguy children, his niece Liddy, his gout, his neighbour at home: an all-in gripe. But he also orders that Morgan's widow be given a cow and £2 to clothe her children—to be done secretly. He is as kind as he is prickly. In his second letter the good man is outraged by God and nature: he got soaked while out riding and has been in bed for a fortnight as a result. This borders on the insane: you can change society, or try to, but you cannot change reality, though you can adapt to it. He goes on griping about the people round him, every least thing irritates him and must be relayed to the doctor (why Smollett uses the doctor of course), yet underlying it all is the central compassion, an unhealable divine wound. In Smollett heaven and hell contend, with no purgatory in between: his Calvinist background rejects purgatory in favour of an either-or, election or damnation. But people are neither elect nor damned, neither angels nor devils, and purgatory is where people live in real life. His Calvinist legacy creates a split, a dissociation of personality (not, as is popularly thought, schizophrenia) which is typical of the Scots character: the Jekyll-Hyde syndrome. Fathom is the Hyde of Smollett's nature,

Greaves his Dr. Jekyll: and Bramble the uneasy interaction of the two in Smollett himself.

In his third letter Bramble turns from the environs of self to social ones. He is exposed to the 'dirt, the stench, the chilling blasts and perpetual rains that render this place to me intolerable'. There is something almost valedictory in that, overtones of 'this place' meaning Earth itself. In his next letter, from Bath, he apologizes to Dr. Lewis for his grizzling correspondence which, he says, might be called 'the lamentations of Matthew Bramble': but he goes on wailing all the more and even turns on the doctor himself 'whose province it is to remove those disorders that occasion it'. The first sign of the deification of the 'doctor'?— and that by one who ought to know better, and indeed he pulls himself up with 'it is no small alleviation of my grievances that I have a sensible friend to whom I can communicate my crusty humours.' He then launches into the first of his tirades against Bath, though admitting his invalid state may be jaundicing his visions: Bath 'is become the very centre of racket and dissipation' instead of the health resort of peace and calm it is supposed to be. He inveighs against the noise, the oppressive ceremonial; it is a national hospital where 'none but lunatics are admitted', and he will become one himself if he stays much longer. He describes the city layout, the dirty, dangerous, mean and twisted streets, he flytes the architecture and such, the state of the chairs for invalids and much else, then pinpoints the chief cause: 'All these absurdities arise from a general tide of luxury which hath overspread the nation.' There follows a tremendous catalogue (that favourite resource of Scottish writers) of those responsible: colonial exploiters of natives and their lands, all sorts of vampires on the people's blood, usurers, brokers, 'jobbers of every kind', *nouveaux riches,* a mob of tasteless philistines who flock to Bath for no other reason than to mix with the idle ruling class to which these rascals aspire. The diatribe stops in its crescendo because his fingers are too cramped to scribble more.

In his next letter we get the sanitary inspector *pur sang.* He was about to enter the King's Bath when he saw 'a child full of scrophulous ulcers carried in the arms of one of the guides, under the very noses of the bathers'. He is so shocked and outraged that he leaves at once. This makes him think of all the other matter from sores which must be leaked into the water, 'what sort of matter we may thus imbibe'. This is an eloquent example of Smollett's being far in advance of his time, which took such filth as quite normal. He is the early voice of a revolution which has led to the hospital of today almost pathologically obsessed with antiseptic cleanliness. In this, as in so much else, Smollett's sensibility is pioneering the future, he is a frontiersman extending human consciousness, his aches are labour-pains of a better society. Still in sanitary inspector garb he goes on to tell Lewis of how he enquired into the construction of the pump and cistern, concluding that the patients actually drink the filthy water he has just condemned as unfit for bathing, 'the scourings of the bathers'. He enlarges, almost masochistically, on this 'delicate beverage' of abominations drunk as medicinal waters. Nauseated, he seeks a spring fit to drink, but the one he thinks above suspicion he discovers drains the site of an old Roman burial ground and that 'we swallow the strainings of rotten bones and carcasses'. This leads on to musings about the hoggish drinks in general daily consumed in England. He is so scunnered by all this that he becomes more misanthropic every day:

> snares are laid for our lives in every thing we eat or drink: the very air we breathe is loaded with contagion. We cannot even sleep without risque of infection.

His musing then leads him to consider consumption, the disease Smollett himself was by then suffering from and died of—a socially conditioned disease, we now know. His fears and suspicions are astute and well-grounded in truth; but he was far ahead of his time. Were he alive today his pen would thunder on such subjects as nuclear fall-out, pollution of land, sea and air, the general poisoning of the Earth, the threat of global suicide, the third world and other poverty, the insanity of the capitalist system, the inhumanity of Russianism disguised as socialism, overpopulation faced by reactionary priesthoods, commercialism, conservation—everything that exercises the antennae of our own time. Bramble goes on to say he is leaving Bath as soon as possible and meantime further lambasts its high prices, filth and luxury, snobbery and vulgar flaunting of wickedly gotten riches. He has swooned at some particularly overpowering rush of abominable smells operating 'upon nerves of uncommon sensibility', a

> compound of villainous smells . . . mingled odours arising from putrid gums, imposthumated lungs, sour flatulences, rank armpits, sweating feet, running sores and issues, plaisters, ointments and embrocations, Hungary-waters, spirit of lavender, asafoetida drops, musk, hartshorn, and sal volatile: besides a thousand frowzy steams *which I could not analyse.* (My italics)

He then leaves for London, en route for Scotland.

London too of course provides grist for his protestant mill. He foresees its coming monstrous growth, praises the improved street lighting but little else, inveighs against the rural spoliation, both human and agricultural going on, the ubiquitous corruption and luxury of a commercial society knowing the price of everything and the value of nothing. He hates the levelling of classes into one characterless mush he thinks he sees (not economic classes anyway) the 'demons of profligacy and licentiousness'. Ranelagh and Vauxhall are hammered, and he longs to return to the good air of his Welsh mountains: as well he might. Even the British Museum is criticized for not being in one large saloon, and its library should be more comprehensive (as it in fact became). He has been to court, to the Royal Exchange, everywhere: 'and everywhere we find food for spleen and subject for ridicule.' He contrasts the idyllic country-life he has at home with the hell of London where even the water is nauseous,

> the mawkish contents of an open aqueduct exposed to all manner of defilement; or swallow that whch come from the river Thames, impregnate with all the filth of London and Westminster. Human excrement is the least offensive part of the concrete, which is composed of all the drugs, minerals and poisons used in mechanics and manufacture, enriched with the putrifying carcases of beasts and men, and mixed with the scourings of all the wash-tubs, kennels and common sewers. . . .

The wine too is poisonous, the bread rubbish, the veal as wersh as it is cruelly killed. He grouses on through all the various foods, meats, fish, vegetables. He admits that Covent Garden has some good fruit for the rich who can afford it, but our sanitary inspector condemns it for a whole catalogue of abominations he has found there, an itemized list of complaints as full as one could imagine: he then ends the letter with 'my letter would swell into a treatise were I to particularize every cause of offence that fills up the measure of my aversion to this and every other crowded city'. Just so.

On the road north, every place they come to is inspected, dissected and damned, except for a few villages and small towns, till they come to Tweedmouth. Bramble's first impressions of Scotland beyond Berwick are of a dreary moor intended by nature to be 'a barrier between two hostile nations'. But he is soon impressed by the fields of wheat, and after Dunbar, the pleasant country seats of his own gentry class: for even in his rebellion Smollett is still middle-class, a Scots laird whose class was the backbone of the social revolution which goes by the religious name of The Reformation. He is a bairn of Johnny Knox. It is no mere whim that makes Bramble a country gentleman: he is a Smollett *alter ego*. This may account for the fact that when Bramble criticizes Lesley for the fanaticism which caused the Scots, as at Flodden, to give up their vantage-point in the field and descend to meet Cromwell, with disastrous results, there is an underlying note of pride in their action. Smollett is himself rather fanatical in his rationalism.

A curious change comes when he reaches Edinburgh. True, the sanitary inspector cannot but gird at gardyloo, at the ludicrous height of some of the lands (tenements) and the consequent fire risk to life: here he has a practical solution, that all the houses (flats) should have access to each other as fire-escapes. Here he anticipates Patrick Geddes in town planning, as did the creators of the New Town. But he is uncharacteristically restrained and objective from here on, almost protective of Edinburgh. He speaks highly of the hospitality of the people, though noting that to an Englishman nearly everything compares unfavourably with England. In view of what we have heard of England up to this point we might expect the most excoriating satire of the whole book: but the contrary is what we get. From here on the note of protest is muted, even suppressed, and we get whitewash. The sanitary inspector modulates into a patriotic Scot defending his country capital from English attack. Was much of Smollett's prickly sensitivity largely due to an unconscious homesickness for the Clydeside of his youth, for

Scotland? It is interesting that Bramble in his search for health gravitates north: more so that he seems to find it in Scotland, for now the mask of the Welsh squire falls off to reveal the real Smollett. The rest is completely out of character for Bramble. True, Bramble finds a resemblance between Clydeside and Wales, both essentially British (Smollett is no Gael): but this is not enough to account for the transformation, for even Wales had denied him health. Glasgow is described as 'one of the prettiest towns in Europe', everywhere in Scotland is praised, the sanitary inspector with the hawk eye for the least blemish now shuts that eye and seeks only what he can praise. His own native Leven so moves him that he bursts into verse, the poet he always was under the surface now breaking through, in praise of Leven Water. Nothing is more astounding in this transformation from the note of protest than Bramble's opening words to Dr. Lewis in a letter from Cameron: 'If I were disposed to be critical . . .'. If a prophet were disposed to be prophetic! He goes on to speak of 'this Scottish paradise'. The note of protest is not heard again and we even have him writing to Lewis that he has 'laid in a considerable stock of health' in Scotland and looks forward to wild-fowling with his Scottish brother-in-law, the veteran warrior Lismahago who joined them at Durham and marries Bramble's sister Tabitha. It is an astonishing transformation.

The reality of Scotland was if anything even worse than that of England in most respects, bereft of even a government to better itself through. One need not dwell on the lashings, lug-nailings, hanging of men, women and children for paltry offences, often stemming from desperate need, which were the common staple of everyday life in Edinburgh and elsewhere, the misery of the poor whether the urban poor or the peasantry. One may refer to Ramsay's poem 'Lucky Spence's Last Advice' quoted above, to the appalling fate of Robert Fergusson in 'this Scottish paradise', a fate which led to a psychiatric revolution through Andrew Duncan in treatment of the indigent (for it was only his poverty led to Fergusson's death in Bedlam) insane. Smollett himself, far from finding health, died within a few months of *Clinker*'s publication. The patriotic Scot has taken over from the ferocious social critic and, knowing the low opinion his English audience have of the Scots, he leaps to the defence. The figure of Lismahago begins to fill the canvas here. This shadowy old warrior, scalped in his Amerindian wars, comes into the book like a grotesque apparition at Durham and gradually takes over Bramble, like a truer self. With his coming Bramble begins to recover his true self, the Scot from whom he has been too long estranged by his émigré life in London. Lismahago is Random, Fathom, Pickle, and even part of Greaves (Bramble is nearer Greaves) in one, an older synthesis of. He is Bramble's 'brother' (he becomes so by marriage to Tabby), with his coming the novel becomes one of integration, the parts of Bramble-Smollett's psyche coming together in marriage and friendship: Lismahago the Scots self; Tabby his sister, his own femininity; Clinker his lost son restored to his father; Liddy, the daughter-figure, marries her beau. It is in this context that the astonishing description of Scotland as 'paradise' has meaning: paradise is where we are whole, the wholeness we once had and lost through the Fall. Lismahago also is the hero in Smollett in his battles in life in alien lands. Therefore the big speech of Lismahago mentioned above takes on new significance, and it is with a quotation from it I leave that great Scotsman and great writer, Tobias Smollett:

Great and manifold are the advantages which England derives from the union (said Lismahago in a solemn tone). First and foremost, the settlement of the protestant succession, a point which the English ministry drove with such eagerness that no stone was left unturned to cajole and bribe a few leading men, to cram the union down the throats of the Scottish nation, who were surprisingly averse to the expedient. They gained by it a considerable addition of territory, extending their dominion to the sea on all sides of the island, thereby shutting up all back-doors against the enterprises of their enemies. They got an accession of above a million of useful subjects, constituting a never-failing nursery of seamen, soldiers, labourers and mechanics; a most valuable acquisition to a trading country exposed to foreign wars and obliged to maintain a number of settlements in all four quarters of the globe. In the course of seven years during the last war, Scotland furnished the English army and navy with seventy thousand men, over and above those who migrated to their colonies or mingled with them at home in the civil departments of life. This was a very considerable and seasonable supply to a nation whose people had been for many years decreasing in number, and whose lands and manufactures were actually suffering for want of hands. I need not remind you of the hackneyed maxim that, to a nation in such circumstances, a supply of industrious people is a supply of wealth; nor repeat an observation which is now received as an eternal truth, even among the English themselves that the Scots ... are sober, orderly, and industrious.

Part Two:

THE NOVELS IN PARTICULAR

5

Roderick Random: Language as Projectile

by DAMIAN GRANT

1

The first thing to remember about *Roderick Random* is that it is a young man's novel. Defoe was fifty-nine when he wrote *Robinson Crusoe*, Richardson fifty-one when he wrote *Pamela*, Sterne forty-six when he began *Tristram Shandy*. Even Fielding was thirty-five (and had written almost that number of plays) when he turned his hand to fiction in *Joseph Andrews*. Smollett by contrast was a raw young man of twenty-six when he wrote *Random*, during the space of only eight months in 1747 (the novel was published in January of the next year).

Not only a raw but an angry young man. As a Scotsman he shared the sense of grievance against a Whig, Hanoverian England (or 'South Britain') that had betrayed Scottish interests both before and after the Act of Union in 1707; he had even given courageous expression to this feeling in his poem 'The Tears of Scotland', which he had published in London (against the advice of his friends) the previous year, in sympathy for the failure of the Scottish cause in the rising of 1745 and in protest against the atrocities committed by the English after Culloden. He felt a personal grievance, too, at the way his play *The Regicide* had been handled by the theatre managers, and at the generally complicated circumstances that found him at this time trying to set up as a surgeon in London.[1]

129

So *Random* is not the fruit of long experience and mature reflection: Roderick's adventures are flavoured instead with the 'berries harsh and crude' of Smollett's early, undigested encounters with a mostly abrasive and intractable reality. The fictional world we are introduced to here has little or nothing of Fielding's Augustan harmony[2]; it is more remarkable for its physical shocks than the psychological trials that provided Richardson with his subject. It is a world which is vulnerable to reality, to what a poet of our own time has called 'The incalculable malice of the everyday'[3]; a world which will not suffer interpretation through a dominant metaphor (as happens even in Defoe's fiction) or suffer the kind of imaginative transformation worked by the structures of Sterne. What we have here, as Arnold Kettle perceived, is the result of Smollett's compulsive need to 'get life on to the page'[4]; a need exorcized with a directness and power that earned him, from one perceptive nineteenth-century critic, the title of 'the greatest realist in our language'.[5]

2

Smollett's novel has an urgency and passion which make it very readable; qualities which are evident from the very first paragraph.

> I was born in the northern part of this united kingdom in the house of my grandfather, a gentleman of considerable fortune and influence, who had on many occasions signalized himself in behalf of his country; and was remarkable for his abilities in the law, which he exercised with great success, in quality of a judge, particularly against beggars, for whom he had a singular aversion. . . . (p. 1)[6]

The sentence is pitched immediately towards extremes: 'considerable . . . many . . . remarkable . . . great . . . particularly . . . singular'; the adjectives and adverbs give the narrative 'lift-off', and establish a verbal trajectory which is to be maintained throughout the novel. Roderick, it is clear, will never be offered the moderate consolations of the 'middle State' of life proposed to Crusoe by his father; that condition in which men may go 'silently and smoothly thro' the World, and comfortably out of it'[7]: Smollett's language discounts in advance the possibility of such an alternative.

This formidable grandfather introduces us to Smollett's world of arbitrary power and moral anarchy, detonating in his own example that violence of feeling and extravagance of behaviour that echo through the novel. Both parents fall 'miserable victims to his rigour and inhumanity' in the first, short chapter; his mother dying as a direct result of being turned out of the house three days after Roderick's birth, and his father (who has no recourse but 'the most dreadful imprecations' against this treatment) disappearing, a presumed suicide 'in a fit of despair' (pp. 3–4).

The characteristic violence of Roderick's world may best be indicated by a recapitulation of the physical restraints and assaults he both endures and inflicts in the adventures that follow. This is of course the most material level of the narrative; but Smollett presents us continually with bodies and surfaces in collisions of the most material kind—collisions which may be understood as the reverberations in the novel of Newton's physics and Locke's empirical philosophy.

Because Roderick has had the imprudence to write to his grandfather, his schoolmaster 'caused a board to be made with five holes in it, through which he thrust the fingers and thumb of my right hand, and fastened it by whip-cord to my waist, in such a manner, that I was effectively debarr'd the use of my pen' (p. 5). Roderick makes aggressive use, however, of this primitive instrument: a fellow pupil 'taking upon him to insult my poverty, I was so incensed at this ungenerous reproach, that with one stroke of my machine, I cut him to the skull' (p. 6). Of course Roderick is 'severely punished' in consequence.

There follows a summary of Roderick's ill-treatment at school which, in its very schematization, forces physical reality into the realms of the grotesque and absurd:

> I was often inhumanly scourged for crimes I did not commit, because having the character of a vagabond in the village, every piece of mischief whose author lay unknown, was charged upon me.—I have been found guilty of robbing orchards I never entered, of killing cats I never hurted, of stealing gingerbread I never touched, and of abusing old women I never saw.—Nay, a stammering carpenter had eloquence enough to persuade my

master, that I fired a pistol loaded with small shot, into his window; though my landlady and the whole family bore witness, that I was a-bed fast asleep at the time when this outrage was committed.—I was flogged for having narrowly escaped drowning, by the sinking of a ferry-boat in which I was passenger.—Another time for having recovered of a bruise occasioned by a horse and cart running over me.—A third time, for being bit by a baker's dog.—In short, whether I was guilty or unfortunate, the vengeance and sympathy of this arbitrary pedagogue were the same.

This passage (with the comically superfluous detail of the 'pistol loaded with small shot') *is* absurd, as Roderick's most spontaneous actions (avoiding drowning) and even the necessary operations of his organism (recovering of a bruise) meet with punishment. But it is also terrifying, in that the physical precariousness of his condition, and the moral arbitrariness he endures here, are to be seen as a true measure of his later experience. David Copperfield's treatment at school seems mild by comparison.

Out of school, Roderick is hunted by his cousin—literally, as an animal: 'This young Acteon, who inherited his grandfather's antipathy to every thing in distress, never set eyes on me, without uncoupling his beagles, and hunting me into some cottage or other, whither I generally fled for shelter' (p. 7). On one such occasion, Roderick aims a stone at his tutor, 'which struck out four of his foreteeth' (p. 8): the first of three sets to be demolished during the novel. Roderick's revenge on the schoolmaster is painfully administered (with his uncle's assistance) in Chapter 5, and in the next he empties a chamberpot over three ruffians who have been hired to beat him up, 'which did great execution upon them' (p. 21).

Roderick soon resolves to head south in search of his fortune, accompanied by his friend and follower Hugh Strap. On the road south to London, they are pursued and shot at by a highwayman (p. 38), Strap is provoked to fight by the *braggadocio* Captain Weazel, 'who swore he must either fight him, or he would instantly put him to death' (p. 54), and the pair attacked in their bed by a 'monstrous overgrown raven' (p. 60). Once they have arrived in London things predictably get worse. They are spattered with mud by a 'dexterous' coachman on arrival,

and forced to fight in an alehouse where they go to dry themselves (pp. 62–3). Roderick is nearly suffocated in a cheap
eating-house in a cellar (p. 65), and shortly afterwards Strap
has a chamberpot emptied over him in the traditional manner:
the reader has some sympathy with his complaint to Roderick,
that 'We have been jeered, reproached, buffeted, pissed upon,
and at last stript of our money; and I suppose by and by we shall
be stript of our skins' (p. 72).

A few chapters later, Roderick is 'stretch'd . . . senseless on
the ground' by a blow from a rival for a lady's affections; his
revenge for this attack is subsequently administered with nettles
(pp. 104, 106). The woman in question later spits in his face
(p. 113). Attempting to rescue a friend from a gang of footpads,
Roderick receives 'a blow on the eye . . . that had well nigh
deprived me of the use of that organ' (p. 110). Deliverance from
the hazards of life in London is only achieved when he is
assaulted and carried off by the Press Gang (p. 139).

Who is it that can say he is at the worst? On board the
pressing tender Roderick is spat upon through the hatch with a
quid of tobacco, and having been transferred to the *Thunder* he is
immediately abused, assaulted, and put in irons by the demonic
midshipman Crampley (who must surely have served as a
model for Claggart in Melville's *Billy Budd:* p. 142). He eventually fights with Crampley, by whom he is pursued with 'implacable animosity' (p. 155); enduring persecution at the same
time by his superior doctor Mackshane and Captain Oakum.
On the captain's orders Roderick is manacled to the deck,
'being exposed in this miserable condition to the scorching heat
of the sun by day, and the unwholesome damp by night, during
the space of twelve days' (p. 166).

This systematic persecution is over and above the traditional
terrors of a storm at sea (pp. 162–63); the nightmare experience
of an engagement during Roderick's captivity (when 'the head
of the officer of Marines, who stood near me, being shot off,
bounced from the deck athwart my face, leaving me well-nigh
blinded with brains': pp. 167–68); the 'most infernal scene of
slaughter, fire, smoak, and uproar' at the cannonading of a land
battery (p. 184); and the horror of the hospital ships, where the
'wounds and stumps' of the wounded 'contracted filth and
putrefaction, and millions of maggots were hatched amid the

corruption of their sores' (p. 187). Roderick also has to put up with the inevitable (but still extreme) discomforts of cramped quarters, disgusting food, and the constant attention of lice. It is not surprising that he contracts a near-fatal fever, and is almost given up for lost (pp. 190–92).

Back in England, Roderick is stripped and robbed after having been assaulted by Crampley and his gang (p. 210), and spurned by the villagers to whom he crawls for assistance (p. 213); he cudgels a rival who attacks him with a sword (p. 229), and whilst attempting to avoid the expected retribution is carried off once more, this time by a gang of smugglers; robbed yet again, and deposited in France (pp. 231–32). With few alternatives he joins the French army, and promptly fights two duels with a fellow soldier before engaging in the Battle of Dettingen, against the English (pp. 247–48).

Only through the intervention of Strap does Roderick secure his release from the French army and return to London; where however his fortunes work out scarcely better than before. Here the violence takes a grotesque sexual turn, as Roderick is first molested by a lustful old woman (who 'flew upon me like a tygeress, and pressed her skinny lips to mine' before belching garlic all over him: p. 305), and then 'hugged and kissed' by the homosexual Earl Strutwell (p. 309) on the way to a further disappointment. Roderick has another duel to fight (p. 365) before being carried to the Marshalsea prison for debt (p. 373); and another fever to endure, after he meets his father in Jamaica (p. 414) before coming home to play his part in the perfunctory happy ending.

In sum: after the savage introduction of his schooldays, Roderick has seven violent fights or duels, is assaulted five times, abducted twice, spat upon twice; put in irons, stapled to the deck of a ship, and imprisoned; endures two near-fatal fevers, and takes part in battles by land and sea. This is a record only of the physical violence, and takes no account of the times he is robbed, cheated, snubbed, deceived, disappointed, misinformed, misdirected, terrified and humiliated in dozens of different ways; nor of the violence of Roderick's own emotional response to these (and other) experiences.

It will afford particular insight into Smollett's method to consider the register of Roderick's response. At different stages of the novel he describes himself as: 'incensed', 'inured to adversity' (p. 6), 'alarmed' (p. 19), 'in a transport of rage and sorrow' (p. 23), 'extremely mortified' (p. 24), 'deserted to all the horrors of extreme want' (p. 25), 'terribly startled', 'under dreadful apprehensions' (p. 28), 'in the utmost perplexity' (p. 29), 'very much disconcerted' (p. 37), 'in an agony of consternation' (p. 43), 'petrified with fear' (p. 61), 'in an agony of despair' (p. 72), 'much elevated' (p. 89), 'much lightened' (p. 92), prey to 'the horrors of jealousy and disappointment' (p. 102), 'in utter confusion' (p. 109), 'fired with resentment and disdain' (p. 112), 'in a much more deplorable condition than ever' (p. 114), 'filled with astonishment and horror' (p. 143), 'bereft of all discretion' (p. 168), 'quite beside myself with the desire of revenge' (p. 205), 'penetrated with grief' (p. 208), 'in the extasy of despair' (p. 210), 'transported with grief, anger, and disdain' (p. 243), 'struck with horror and astonishment' (p. 316), 'in a rapture of joy' (p. 318), 'a flood of joy' (p. 340), 'in a kind of apoplexy of drunkenness' (p. 350), 'enraged at his presumption' (p. 355), 'in the condition of a frantic Bedlamite' (p. 356), 'tortured . . . into madness' (p. 359), 'in a transport of fury' (p. 365), 'full of desperate resolution' (p. 370), 'ready to despair' (p. 377), 'utterly confounded' (p. 398), and finally, when his 'inordinate sallies of desire' have been satisfied by Narcissa, 'distracted with joy' (p. 430). From these phrases we can clearly perceive how the narrative is pitched well beyond the normal emotional register; the violence is confessedly within as well as without, as Roderick magnifies every variation in his fortunes.[8]

We can readily agree, then, with the recent critic who advances the thesis that 'the Smollett world' is violent, and Smollett's art is equally 'peremptory'. Angus Ross contrasts the 'Punch and Judy Show' violence of *Lazarillo de Tormes* and the 'literary stylization' of violence in Fielding's work, with the violent action in Smollett, which is 'of vastly more importance': 'It would seem that the deepest and most instinctive of Smollett's reactions to the injustices of social cruelty as he conceived it took the form of imagining emblematic violent scenes.'[9] In the course of an excellent article on the oppressive moral atmosphere of Smollett's novels, linking their violent physicality to determinist materialist forces in general, David

Punter asks, 'by what standards are we to compare the humane and forgiving world of Fielding with the wilderness in which Smollett's characters roam and prey?'[10] And elsewhere in this volume, David Daiches observes, 'A generation which is interested in the nature of violence and in the relation of violence to moral feeling might well find Smollett's novels, in one of their favourite words, extremely "relevant".'[11]

It is a remarkable confirmation of the implicit materialism of Smollett's outlook how often, in detailing the response of his central character to the coarse stuff of his experience, Smollett specifies the actual sense by which Roderick receives his impressions. This is particularly true of the chapters dealing with life at sea (24 to 37: pp. 138–210), when Roderick's senses are more than usually exercised. But even when relating the consummation of his marriage, with some enthusiasm, Roderick risks the epistemological remark: 'I could not believe the evidence of my senses' (p. 430). It is almost as if Smollett is adopting as a programme the empirical belief that all knowledge must be derived from sensation. Of course Smollett's training and practice as a doctor would have helped to stimulate (and even provide a vocabulary for) this scientific registration of experience on Roderick's sensory mechanism. Roderick's eyes are continually 'amazed', his nose offended, his taste disgusted, his ears alarmed, 'invaded' and assaulted by a hundred different sounds (and voices); his sense of touch (as we have seen) communicates distressful sensations in a variety of ways.[12]

But if it is Roderick's senses that withstand the myriad shocks in the novel, it is Smollett's language after all that registers this experience for the reader. And this is the really remarkable thing about *Random*, the real reason why we enjoy reading and re-reading the work: the fact that Smollett's language is adequate to convey, to precipitate in all their rapid sequence and alarming detail, the extravagance of Roderick's adventures. Conrad described writing as 'the conversion of nervous force into phrases',[13] and Smollett is able to convert his own forces with maximum efficiency on Roderick's behalf. Substantives assume a jagged actuality; verbs gesticulate, adverbs intensify, adjectives pitch towards the superlative as Smollett galvanizes his language to generate a sense of continuous, distracted activity. Things happen 'suddenly', characters react 'without hesitation', consequences ensue 'immediately', and new situations develop 'in an instant', imparting a curious, almost dreamlike simultaneity to much of the action. The syntax, too, is fluent, supple, and permissive, providing the perfect medium for the headlong narrative.

Any chapter, almost any paragraph of the novel provides examples of this supercharged style; it will not be necessary to select them here. I would however like to state my own belief that what I have called the 'verbal trajectory' of *Random* is unique, and never quite regained by Smollett in his later fiction. *Peregrine Pickle, Ferdinand Count Fathom*, and *Launcelot Greaves* all contain memorable, characteristic and brilliant things; but they are also compounded with more clay than this first novel, which does seem to have been written from sheer passion (of different kinds) and creative exuberance. Of course, *Humphry Clinker* is another case; more complex and more organized, and not to be described in terms of a single movement or level of response.

3

We can take a relevant 'section' of Smollett's style, his address to reality in *Random*, by considering the way characters in the novel address each other; and this is what I intend to offer as the main exercise of this essay, concentrating on Smollett's presentation of direct and indirect speech, speech indicators and accompanying gestures: which, taken together, are a determining feature of the novel, and account for much of its stylistic vigour.

Because if it is true that many blows are given and received in *Random*, many appalling sights and disgusting smells endured, one could still argue that the most dangerous weapon used in the novel is the tongue; the organ most frequently assaulted is the ear; the ammunition most freely fired off is words. Tristram tells us that Uncle Toby's life was put in jeopardy by words: in a rather different way, Smollett's characters exhibit their aggression against each other (and even their frustration at the inanimate world) most consistently in the accusations, condemnations, and reproaches, the startling oaths, threats, and general invective terms that decorate their vocabulary.

It is not only that words often lead to blows, as when the apothecaries Crab and Potion 'chancing to meet at a christening, disagreed about precedence, proceeded from invective to blows' (p. 26), or when Roderick retorts in kind to the French soldier's taunt: 'To this inuendo I made no reply but by a kick on the breech, which overturned him in an instant' (p. 249). Very often the antagonism is restricted to impressive threats (recalling the valour of Ben Jonson's Captain Bobadil) that never materialize in anything more terrifying than the words themselves. The highwayman Rifle exclaims ' "I'll send them all to hell in an instant" ' on being disturbed by Roderick, Strap, and a pedlar in the next room, rides off 'venting a thousand execrations, and vowing to murder the pedlar' when the latter sneaks away, and later challenges Roderick and Strap 'with a volley of oaths and threats' (pp. 34–8). The formidable Captain Weazel exclaims (much to Strap's terror) ' "That Scotchman who carries the knapsack shall not breathe this vital air another day" ', and swears 'he must either fight him, or he would instantly put him to death' (pp. 53–4). Strap is again the object of a gentleman's rage, who on being cut by the barber ' "swore a deadly oath, and was going to horsewhip me" ' (p. 84). A recruiting sergeant actually terrifies Roderick and Strap by uttering threats compulsively in his sleep (p. 43), and a justice who has mistakenly threatened Roderick's friend with hanging explains 'it was always his way to terrify young people, when they came before him, that his threats might make a strong impression on their minds' (p. 92). The parson to whom Roderick is carried for help after being dumped on shore 'fell into a mighty passion, and threatned to excommunicate him who sent as well as those who brought me' (p. 213). Irritated by a lawyer in the coach to Bath, a loudmouth captain 'threatened to cut the lawyer's ears out of his head' (p. 332). Enraged by his misfortunes in London, Roderick himself tells Strap he 'would, without hesitation put him to death', and repeats this threat to an impertinent messenger a few pages later (pp. 358, 361).

These threats are sufficient. Words themselves are weapons; language itself becomes projectile material in the mouths of the passionate, impatient, antagonistic characters that collide in Smollett's densely populated, dangerous, and arbitrary world.

Sometimes of course the threats are returned, and here we still find that words themselves provide quite adequate materials for carrying through the most hostile of encounters, without the need for physical demonstration. The words *enact* the conflict in every sense. A good example of this occurs in Roderick's response to a challenge from a coachman, whose cook-wench mistress he has 'unwittingly made a conquest of':

> ... he accordingly, with many opprobrious invectives, bid me defiance, and offered to box with me for twenty guineas.—I told him, that although I believed myself a match for him, even at that work, I would not descend so far below the dignity of a gentleman, as to fight like a porter; but if he had any thing to say to me, I was his man at blunderbuss, musket, pistol, sword, hatchet, spit, cleaver, fork or needle;—'nay more, that if he gave his tongue any more saucy liberties at my expence, I would crop his ears without any ceremony.—This rhodomontade delivered with a stern countenance, and resolute tone, had the desired effect upon my antagonist, who, with some confusion, sneaked off, and gave his friend an account of his reception. (p. 227)

The coachman is beaten not in a fair fight but by Roderick's superior nerve and articulateness. His own 'opprobrious invectives' (which we are not given, for once) are no match for Roderick's intimidating enumeration of nine possible weapons— which is made more decisive by the omission of any article between them; the device of asyndeton having the relevant effect of allowing the items so listed to achieve a greater mass and specificity.

Roderick is himself shown to be conscious of the 'rhodo-montade' involved here, and we may attribute this verbal confidence on his part to an earlier study of how to handle the irascible temper of his master Crab: that is, by determined contradiction (p. 28). The theory and practice of aggressive dispute learned here serves Roderick in good stead for the rest of the novel. There is an excellent demonstration of this in a dramatic encounter Roderick has at the gaming tables during his second period in London:

> As I marched out with my prize, I happened to tread upon the toes of a tall raw-boned fellow, with a hooked nose, fierce eyes, black thick eyebrows, a pig-tail wig of the same colour, and a

formidable hat pulled over his forehead, who stood gnawing his fingers in the crowd, and no sooner felt the application of my shoe-heel, than he roared out in a tremendous voice, 'Blood and wounds! you son of a whore, what's that for?'—I asked pardon with a great deal of submission, and protested I had no intention of hurting him; but the more I humbled myself the more he stormed, and insisted upon gentlemanly satisfaction, at the same time provoking me with scandalous names that I could not put up with; so that I gave a loose to my passion, returned his Billingsgate, and challenged him to follow me down to the piazzas.—His indignation cooling as mine warmed, he refused my invitation, saying, he would chuse his own time, and returned towards the table muttering threats, which I neither dreaded nor distinctly heard; but descending with great deliberation, received my sword from the door-keeper, whom I gratified with a guinea according to the custom of the place, and went home in a rapture of joy. (pp. 317–18)

This paragraph has often been quoted as a quintessentially Smollettian 'episode', Roderick's 'raw-boned' antagonist starting from nowhere and returning again immediately afterwards into the crowded but anonymous background of the novel. It is so, but the mechanisms (physical, verbal, and psychological) are totally characteristic of encounters in the rest of the work. The figure from the crowd speaks exactly as we would expect him to speak; the descriptive heightening of the caricature and the dramatic heightening of the dialogue work together to create the sudden, obtrusive presence of this fantastic individual. And that the rest of the exchange should be in indirect speech is perfectly well judged; we only need to have the idiom announced (like a key signature) to be able to interpret the rest in like terms. It is as if we are hearing the voice itself and the report of the voice simultaneously.

Roderick is by no means always a participant in these verbal duels. His uncle Bowling gets very much the better of Roderick's grandfather and cousins in the early chapters, with the help of his expressive naval jargon: ' "Lookee, you lubberly son of a w——e, if you come athwart me, 'ware your gingerbread-work—I'll be foul of your quarter, d—n me" ' (p. 9). The Welsh surgeon Morgan defends himself by sheer accumulation of phrases against orders from his superior: ' "Got pless my soul! does he think, or conceive, or imagine, that I am a horse, or an ass, or a goat, to trudge backwards and forwards, and upwards and downwards, and by sea and by land, at his will and pleasures?" ' (p. 146). Roderick's friend Banter has warned him of the gifts of Miss Snapper in this regard (' "the little deformed urchin joined her mother with such virulence and volubility of tongue, that I was fain to make my retreat, after having been honoured with a great many scandalous epithets" ': p. 323) and the young lady certainly lives up to her reputation when she takes on the swearing soldier in the coach to Bath:

> We continued a good while as mute as before, till at length, the gentleman of the sword, impatient of longer silence, made a second effort, by swearing, he had got into a meeting of quakers.—'I believe so too, (said a shrill female voice, at my left hand) for the spirit of folly begins to move.'—'Out with it then, madam,' (replied the soldier.)—'You seem to have no occasion for a midwife,' (cried the lady.)—'D—n my blood! (exclaimed the other) a man can't talk to a woman, but she immediately thinks of a midwife.'—'True, Sir, (said she) I long to be delivered.'—'What! of a mouse, madam?' (said he.)—'No, Sir, (said she) of a fool.'—'Are you far gone with fool?' (said he.)—'Little more than two miles,' (said she.)—'By Gad, you're a wit, madam!' (cried the officer)—'I wish I could with any justice return the compliment,' (said the lady.)—'Zounds! I have done,' (said he.)—'Your bolt is soon shot, according to the proverb,' (said she.)—The warrior's powder was quite spent, the lawyer advised him to drop the prosecution, and a grave matron, who sat on the left hand of the victorious wit, told her, she must not let her tongue run so fast among strangers. (pp. 323–24)

But the most memorable of all the verbal encounters in *Random* is that which blows up between Captain Weazel and Miss Jenny when the passengers of the waggon are assembled in the kitchen of the inn. Jenny obstructs Weazel's wish that he and his wife should dine by themselves:

> At this, the captain put on a martial frown and looked very big, without speaking; while his yoke-fellow, with a disdainful toss of her nose, muttered something about 'Creature;'—which miss Jenny overhearing, stept up to her, saying, 'None of your names, good Mrs. Abigail;—creature quotha,—I'll assure you,—No such creature as you neither—no ten pound sneaker—no quality coupler.'—Here the captain interposed with a 'Damme, madam,

what d'ye mean by that?'—'Damn you, sir, who are you? (replied miss Jenny) who made you a captain, you pitiful, trencher-scraping, pimping curler?—'Sdeath! the army is come to a fine pass, when such fellows as you get commissions.— What, I suppose you think I don't know you?—By G—d, you and your helpmate are well met,—a cast-off mistress, and a bald *valet de chambre* are well yoked together.' 'Blood and wounds! (cried Weazel) d'ye question the honour of my wife, madam?—Hell and damnation! No man in England durst say so much.—I would flea him, carbonado him! Fury and destruction! I would have his liver for my supper.'—So saying, he drew his sword, and flourished with it, to the great terror of Strap: while miss Jenny snapping her fingers, told him, she did not value his resentment a f—t. (p. 51)

Weazel has just been described in caricature as '*vox & preterea nihil*', and this is all he needs to be for Smollett's purposes—and for Jenny's convenience. No character in the novel threatens more and does less; he is the quintessence of verbal valour, which is exclusively exercised in the undemanding linguistic space of the future tense and the conditional mood. Miss Jenny's strategy is different, more direct and yet equally gratuitous. Her recognition of Weazel and his wife is pure fantasy, and the destructive epithets ('you pitiful, trencher-scraping, pimping curler') are affixed to him groundlessly in the time-honoured tradition of 'flyting' and festive abuse, which has its sources and perennial strength in the language and symbolism of the body.

Mikhail Bakhtin has said of such abuse (in his study of Rabelais, much of which is relevant to Smollett) that it is 'grammatically and semantically isolated from context and is regarded as a complete unit, something like a proverb'.[14] Such an idea certainly applies here, where there is no question of consequence or development from the exchange; it is pure demonstration. Bakhtin's suggestion possibly reminds us of T. S. Eliot's metaphor for Ben Jonson's satire, that it works not negatively but creatively, projecting 'a new world in a new orbit',[15] and the parallel has its own appositeness, since Ben Jonson is one of the masters of such comic invective in English literature (this passage from Smollett has something in common with the argument that opens *The Alchemist*).

Smollett apologized to the 'delicate reader' in his Preface for the 'unmeaning oaths which proceed from the mouths of some characters in these memoirs', pleading that 'nothing could more effectually expose the absurdities of such miserable expletives, than a natural and verbal representation of the discourse with which they are commonly interlarded' (p. xlvi). But it is clear that Smollett actually enjoys exploiting the blustering oaths of Weazel here, as he does the heavily 'interlarded' boasting of the captain in the Bath coach later (Ch. 53, pp. 324–25). The reader too is entertained and refreshed by these displays of verbal virtuosity that are the reverse of 'miserable'. What Bakhtin has to say on the subject, again, goes some way to providing an explanation for 'the attraction which these expressions still exercise': 'A vague memory of past carnival liberties and carnival truth still slumbers in these modern forms of abuse. The problem of their irrepressible linguistic vitality has as yet not been seriously posed.'[16] If the 'problem' of this vitality has not been considered, the source of it (fortunately) remains available; and Smollett's novel draws on it with great inventiveness.[17]

Language as projectile. The air of *Random* is thick with these verbal missiles, 'sounds' (we might almost say, as readers) 'that give delight, and hurt not'. Even where the actual terms are not (or not completely) provided, in the dialogue, Smollett uses a number of summarizing nouns and phrases to indicate the kind of weapon being employed: declaration, invective, parley, admonition, clamour, altercation, ejaculation, acclamation, exclamation, dispute, insinuation, inuendo [*sic*], appellation, imprecation, repartee, harangue, remonstrance, conjuration, rhodomontade, billingsgate. These nouns are often galvanized by a relevant adjective, such as great, hideous, sudden, startling, smart, unexpected, dreadful, lamentable, opprobrious.

Smollett himself has frequently made the ballistic metaphor explicit: as with Rifle's 'volley of oaths and threats' (p. 38), Weazel's 'volley of oaths' (p. 52), and the 'volley of execrations' uttered by the scalded soldier in the ordinary (p. 65). Metaphors of venting, discharging, assailing, and assaulting are also part of the projectile system. We have both together in Medlar's furious response to Banter's fabrications: 'he discharged his indignation in a volley of oaths' (p. 288). Where, as also

143

happens, a character is 'loaded with curses' (p. 9) or 'loaded with execrations' (p. 52), we have the suggestion instead of the punitive weight of the words, like chains or manacles—as when Roderick is literally 'loaded with irons' (p. 166) on the deck of the *Thunder*; a no less effective image of hostility.

But if we have attended to the missiles themselves, the oaths, curses, 'miserable expletives' and 'opprobrious epithets', we should not neglect to notice the extraordinary and effective range of verbs Smollett uses to launch them towards their target—or simply out into the atmosphere. These indispensable synonyms for 'said' are, after all, the peculiar contribution of the novelist, who (unlike the playwright) must use them to describe, identify, and contextualize his dialogue. Here we find Smollett at his most verbally resourceful. (I do not claim that the sixty-six verbs listed here are a complete inventory.) Besides the staple said, answered, replied, returned, observed, and the mild explained, asked, began, continued, told (me), we have the comic stuttered, stammered, mumbled, muttered, and mumped; the emphatic verbs cried (out), called (out), shouted, uttered, complained, avouched, interposed, pronounced, affirmed, declared, proclaimed, assured, advised, demanded, applauded, maintained, begged, prayed, protested, exclaimed, groaned, lamented, growled, jawed (together), implored, held forth; moving on to the aggressive: challenged, rebuked, swore, cursed, abused, accosted, inveighed, vowed, threatned [*sic*], jeered, reproached, refused, upbraided, interrupted, ordered, reprimanded, harangued; and finally the abandoned: 'set up their throats', 'vented' (bitter imprecations), broke forth, bellowed (out), thundered (out), raved, ranted, roared.

Often these verbs are purposefully grouped together at moments of special stress. When young Rory's tyrannical teacher is punished by Bowling, 'he roared like a mad bull, danced, cursed, blasphemed, and acted to the life, the part of a frantick bedlamite' (p. 18). Roderick is assured by Mr. Concordance that 'boys will hoot at me as I pass along; and the cinder wenches belch forth reproaches wafted in a gale impregnated with gin' (p. 115). Stapled to the deck during an engagement, Roderick 'began to bellow with all the strength of my lungs' and 'vented my rage in oaths and execrations' (p. 168).

Morgan is prepared to 'affirm, and avouch, and maintain' that captain Whiffle has unfairly maligned him. Donald Davie quotes Fenollosa: 'The great strength of our language lies in its splendid array of transitive verbs. . . . A study of Shakespeare's verbs should underlie all exercises in style.'[18] Smollett knew his Shakespeare; and a study of Smollett's verbs leads us to the source of his stylistic energy as well.

4

This, then, is Smollett's first novel: savage, funny, sinister, comic, violent, sentimental, extravagant; satire, romance, realistic adventure; a curious, contradictory narrative. And under all these qualities, an exploding magazine of words. Peter Porter recently wrote of the *Satyricon*, 'It seems to me to be a novel as novels ought to be—full of surface brilliance, sharply drawn characters, fizzing language and that final taste of mystery, which is usually the province of poetry or drama.'[19] This prescription certainly fits *Random*, and reminds us at the same time of the relevant tradition of grotesque, word-eating fictions to which (if to any) it belongs: the tradition of Apuleius and Lucian, Rabelais and Swift, Dickens and Joyce.

When Roderick relates his adventures (so far) to Strap when they meet in France, he describes Strap's reaction: 'He started with surprise, glowed with indignation, gaped with curiosity, smiled with pleasure, trembled with fear, and wept with sorrow, as the vicissitudes of my life inspired these different passions' (p. 253). Laughter is incongruously omitted (no doubt because Strap himself occasions a good deal of it) but perhaps there is a hint here as to how the novel should be read. Certainly, if his own description of pedants at work is anything to go by, Smollett would have had little patience with scholarly navigation through those critical quicksands where works of literature (and their readers?) vanish without a trace. The reader of *Random* need not be concerned as to whether the novel is properly picaresque, and if so of what kind; as to where its unity lies, or what convenient moral it encourages us to draw. Behind such questions one hears the echo of the conversation between a group of virtuosi in *Peregrine Pickle*, about the weather: 'which was investigated in a very philosophical manner by one of the company, who seemed to have consulted all the barometers and thermometers that ever were invented, before he would venture to affirm that it was a chill morning'.[20] This is a novel as novels ought to be—or ought to be allowed to be. Launched 250 years ago, *Roderick Random* is still clearly visible in its distinctive if somewhat elliptical orbit.

NOTES

1. For an account of the composition of *Random*, see the Introduction to the edition of the novel by P.-G. Boucé (London, 1979). This edition also contains a Select Bibliography of twentieth-century criticism of the novel. To this should be added: Roseann Runte 'Gil Blas and Roderick Random: Food for Thought', *The French Review* (Journal of the American Association of Teachers of French), 50 (1977), 698–705; K. G. Simpson, 'Roderick Random and the Tory Dilemma', *Scottish Literary Journal*, 2 (1978), 5–17.
2. Qualified, no doubt; see C. J. Rawson, *Henry Fielding and the Augustan Ideal under Stress* (London, 1972); but still available to Fielding as a point of reference, and used as an organizing principle in *Tom Jones*.
3. Sylvia Plath 'Three Women', *Winter Trees* (London, 1971), p. 49.
4. *An Introduction to the English Novel*, 2 vols. (London, 1951), I, 20.
5. Preface to *The Works of Tobias Smollett* (Edinburgh, 1870), I, 22.
6. All page references to *Random* are to the edition by P.-G. Boucé (London, 1979).
7. *Robinson Crusoe*, ed. J. Donald Crowley (London, 1972), pp. 4–5.
8. *Humphry Clinker* is of course the novel in which Smollett most fully exploits the subjective and relativist view of experience; but it is frequently identified in the earlier novels as well—especially in the individual's tendency to exaggeration. When Strap is terrified by the raven, Roderick reports that 'his fears had magnified the creature to the bigness of a horse, and the sound of small morris bells to the clanking of chains' (p. 61).
9. 'The Show of Violence in Smollett's Novels', *Yearbook of English Studies*, 77 (1972), 118–29.
10. 'Smollett and the Logic of Domination', *Literature and History*, 1 (1975), 60–83.
11. P. 46.
12. For a fuller account of how Smollett exploits the evidence of the senses in his fiction, see my *Tobias Smollett: A Study in Style* (Manchester, 1977), pp. 122–26.
13. Letter to H. G. Wells, 30 November 1903; *Life and Letters*, ed. G. Jean-Aubry (New York, 1957), I, 321.

14. *Rabelais and His World,* trans. Helene Iswolsky (Cambridge, Mass., 1968), p. 16.
15. *Selected Essays* (London, 1951), p. 159.
16. *Rabelais and His World,* p. 28.
17. *Peregrine Pickle* also furnishes excellent examples of articulated antagonism; as in Pickle's adventures with the 'Nymph of the Road' (Ch. 95), whose 'natural genius for altercation' (p. 598) is fully dramatized; and the College of Authors (Ch. 101), whose arguments, fomented by Pickle, proceed from words to blows (p. 642). References are to the edition by James L. Clifford (London, 1964).
18. *Articulate Energy* (London, 1955), p. 49; quoting Fenollosa's 'Ars Poetica' as prepared for the press by Ezra Pound.
19. T.L.S., 29 May 1981, p. 603.
20. P. 662.

6

'With Dignity and Importance': Peregrine Pickle as Country Gentleman

by IAN CAMPBELL ROSS

'[S]o notorious is the discouragement of all those who presume to live independent of court-favour and connexions', we read in Chapter XLIV of *Peregrine Pickle*,

> that one of the gentlemen, whose friendship Peregrine cultivated, frankly owned he was in possession of a most romantic place in one of the provinces, and deeply enamoured of a country life; and yet he durst not reside upon his own estate, lest by slackening in his attendance upon the great, who honoured him with their protection, he should fall a prey to some rapacious intendant.[1]

Smollett is here writing of France and few features of French life escape his censure entirely—'I am but a week returned from having made a Tour thro' part of France, Flanders and Holland, which has only served to Endear my own Country to me the more',[2] he wrote to Alexander Carlyle in 1749—but on this occasion the criticism implied is central to the values of his second novel. Forming part of an extended episode in Peregrine's political education in which, as the chapter heading asserts, he 'acquires a distinct Idea of the French Government', the story anticipates dangers the hero himself will later face and which, unresisted, will lead to financial and moral bankruptcy. To the reader, the incident gestures towards the damaging effects of political dependence on the individual and nation alike. It is the climax of Peregrine's moral and social regeneration when, having once more aspired to 'a state of independency', he is 're-established in that station of life which . . . he could fill with dignity and importance' (p. 768). In thus asserting the value of independence, Smollett gives fictional expression to one of the most powerful and persistent political ideals of eighteenth-century Britain and in Peregrine Pickle creates not simply an individual but a representative figure of his age — the independent country gentleman.

In this respect, Smollett's novel appears as a late (though by no means the last) imaginative expression of a political ideology which had dominated the politics of opposition, inside and outside of parliament, for the previous thirty years. The country party philosophy suggested that in place of the old party divisions of the period before and immediately after 1688, the real political split was between court and country. Lord Bolingbroke, principal ideologue of the country party, put it like this:

> nothing can be more ridiculous than to preserve the nominal division of whig and tory parties, which subsisted before the revolution, when the difference of principles, that could alone make the distinction real, exists no longer; so nothing can be more reasonable than to admit the nominal division of constitutionalists and anti-constitutionalists, or of a court and a country-party, at this time, when an avowed difference of principles makes this distinction real.[3]

This was far from being the objectively descriptive account Bolingbroke alleged, but the division was a widely proposed one, especially during the ministry of Robert Walpole from 1721 to 1742. Briefly, the opposition argument was that Walpole maintained his own power by corrupt means, undermining the independence of ministers, members of parliament, and voters alike by an extensive system of patronage and bribery. In so doing, he had cemented the relationship between a court aristocracy and the financial interests of the City of London, which had existed since the 1690s, to the detriment of the nation in general and independent country landowners in particular. Ministerial corruption, it was said, encouraged the spread of corruption throughout the nation fostering not only venality but a general laxity of morals. Bolingbroke, for instance, writing in *On the Policy of the Athenians*, compared his own society to the Athens of Pericles who, he asserted:

> by the licentious distribution of bribes and bounties amongst the people, soon extinguished all sentiments of their former honesty and love of their country . . . [even among] the best families in Athens, and soon made them so necessitous, that forgetting their ancient honors and the dignity of their birth, they were not ashamed to become the known pensioners of Pericles, living in as abject a dependence upon him as the meanest of the people.

Thus was universal corruption spread over the whole state.[4]

Smollett was to write in similar vein throughout his life; in *The Present State of all Nations*, for instance, he argued that:

> The constitution of England, though said to be as perfect as human wisdom could suggest, and human frailty permit, yet, nevertheless, contains in itself the seeds of its own dissolution. While individuals are corruptible, and the means of corruption so copiously abound, it will always be in the power of an artful and ambitious prince to sap the foundations of English liberty.[5]

To resist the moral degeneracy of the age, ran the country philosophy, it was necessary to break the alliance of court aristocracy and monied men and return power once more to the hands of an independent landed gentry.

This theme was not confined to political or historical writing only; it figures importantly in the work of, for example, Swift, Gay, and Pope. Nor was it a characteristic only of those authors who had themselves been closely associated with political life in the reign of Queen Anne; younger writers—most notably, perhaps, Fielding and Johnson—produced, early in their careers, works which consciously invited comparison with the achievement of their older contemporaries, especially Pope, the most admired literary figure of the age. Such works not only testified to the literary ambitions of their authors but frequently endorsed the moral, social, and political values of their models. When Pope died in 1744, he left no obvious successor of comparable eminence and it was not altogether surprising that the twenty-five-year-old Smollett, ambitious for literary renown, should have cast two of his earliest works—the verse satires *Advice* and *Reproof,* published in 1746 and 1747 respectively—into a form which recalled Pope's *Imitations of the Satires of Horace* or the *Epilogue to the Satires*.[6] In these two dialogue poems, and despite the fact that Walpole had lost power in 1742 and had died three years later, Smollett attacked with equal indignation and relish many of the politicians who had been Walpole's closest associates and who had been the targets of Pope's own satires. More generally, he hit out in his verse against a corrupt political system, a venal aristocracy, and a widespread confusion of moral values, urging instead the need for independence as the only means of retaining personal integrity.

Peregrine Pickle, then, was not the first (nor would it be the last) work in which Smollett asserted the importance of independence but it is the work in which the moral and social dangers of dependence—especially the dependence of the country gentleman on a court aristocracy—are delineated most vividly and at greatest length.[7] In examining the position of the country gentleman, Smollett considers his hero's social role by means of three sets of relationships—between Peregrine and the nobility, his social peers, and his dependents—which are of structural and thematic importance to his novel. Already in *Roderick Random,* Smollett had described the protracted but finally successful attempt of an apparently declassed young man to resist the social and economic pressures which seem to force him against his will into the middle classes or below, as tradesman or servant, and to retain the rank of gentleman to which, as Roderick himself asserts, he was entitled 'by birth and education'.[8] In *Peregrine Pickle,* Smollett portrayed another young man of the same social rank as Roderick who is led by inordinate pride and excessive ambition into a state of dependency on a corrupt nobility which nearly results in a loss of status even more dramatic than his predecessor's.

In the opening chapters of his novel, Smollett puts into perspective the hero's exaggerated sense of his own pre-eminence by means of an unusually detailed account of Peregrine's parentage. Though his aunt delights in communicating the importance and honour of her family, that family 'was not to be traced two generations back, by all the power of heraldry or

151

tradition' (p. 3). Peregrine's grandfather is revealed as a successful London merchant who acquired the estate, one hundred miles from London, to which Peregrine's father—Gamaliel—retires and which provides the hero's own boyhood environment. Peregrine's aunt, we find, has 'renounced all the ideas she had acquired before her father served the office of sheriff; and the æra which regulated the dates of all her observations, was the mayoralty of her papa' (p. 3). This minor detail is more than a satiric aside on Mrs. Grizzle's social pretensions, for as Smollett would observe with scrupulous precision in *The Present State*, mayors were one of the groups entitled by virtue of their office to the appellation of esquire or gentleman.[9] Finally, and in order to ensure the preservation of the family name, Mrs. Grizzle arranges a marriage between her brother and Miss Sally Appleby, daughter of a neighbouring gentleman who had '(to use his own phrase) replenished their veins with some of the best blood in the county' (p. 13), and it is of this union that Peregrine is born. Gamaliel Pickle's total withdrawal from trade to the landed estate and his marriage to a member of the landed gentry are important. Despite an increasing tendency in the eighteenth century for cadet members of the landed gentry to earn their livings not merely in the professions but in trade also, Smollett everywhere—in his fictional, historical, and economic writings—refuses to acknowledge the claims to gentility of those wholly engaged in domestic trade. While Samuel Johnson could assert that ' "An English Merchant is a new species of Gentleman",'[10] Smollett would certainly have agreed with his compatriot, the more conservative Boswell, in his dissent ('The general sense of mankind cries out with irresistible force, "*Un gentilhomme est toujours gentilhomme*" '),[11] for in *The Present State* he ranked 'merchants and traders' below freeholders and copyholders among 'plebeians'[12] and denominated them with a condescension that many must have found offensive as 'a better kind of vulgar'.[13] The hero of Smollett's second novel is, therefore, born a gentleman and heir to a landed estate, but his origins are—at no great distance—plebeian. His duty, as the first generation of his family to enjoy his position, is to come to terms with the obligations of his rank as well as with its privileges.

Peregrine has very different ideas. Unlike Roderick Random,

who must fight to assert his right to the rank of gentleman and to its privileges—the respect of his peers and the deference of his inferiors—Peregrine enjoys his status unchallenged. He benefits from a liberal education at Winchester and Oxford, makes a continental tour, and when Trunnion's death leaves him in possession of an independent fortune achieves, just halfway through the novel, the independence Roderick attains only in the closing pages of Smollett's first novel. As a result, Peregrine's social aspirations, prompted by his pride, are not to the consolidation of his position but to uniting his interests to those of the nobility.

The moral character of the hero is directly described by the narrator at an early stage in the novel:

> His pride rose in proportion to his power, and . . . he contracted a large proportion of insolence, which a series of misfortunes that happened to him in the sequel could scarce effectually tame. Nevertheless there was a fund of good nature and generosity in his composition. (pp. 56–7)

This formulation, emphasizing the mixture of admirable and censurable qualities in Peregrine's character, is repeated elsewhere in the novel and there is evidence to suggest that Smollett intended his hero to embody both the best and worst features of his own society. He later wrote of Great Britain in 1751, the year in which *Peregrine Pickle* was published, that 'the kingdom exhibited a most amazing jumble of virtue and vice, honour and infamy, compassion and obduracy, sentiment and brutality'.[14] In the course of the novel, Peregrine must learn to balance the conflicting elements in his character and, without losing, must temper his pride to suit his situation.

At Oxford, as previously at school, Peregrine's behaviour swings wildly from one extreme to the other, his intelligence and intellectual curiosity offset by his arrogance and the frivolity that manifests itself in drunkenness, gaming, and sexual debauchery. Already, the hero would appear to stand as a representative of his class as Smollett saw them and as he would describe them in *The Present State* where, after outlining their virtues, he concludes: 'On the reverse of their character, we likewise observe a disposition to gaming, riot, and excessive insolence of pride, and a strong propensity to contemptuous ridicule.'[15] Peregrine's love of ridicule is apparent from his earliest childhood, manifesting itself especially in the practical jokes he plays on his brandy-loving aunt and her husband, the boastful Hawser Trunnion. At Oxford, such escapades have a more direct thematic relevance as when, for example, he resents the behaviour of his tutor, Mr. Jumble. Judging an exercise to paraphrase two appropriate lines of Virgil to be 'a piece of unmannerly abuse levelled against his own conduct [and] also as a retrospective insult on the memory of his grandfather, who (as he had been informed) was in his life-time more noted for his cunning than candour in trade' (p. 117), Peregrine revenges himself by means of a satirical poem on Jumble's lowly origins as the son of a bricklayer and a pie-maker. Jumble's own unwise social pretensions make Peregrine's punishment comically appropriate but the hero's exaggerated sense of superiority is already evident and will shortly be seen in a more damaging light.

George M. Kahrl has called the continental section of *Peregrine Pickle* 'one great, sustained prose satire on the Grand Tour, every detail of which can be fully substantiated from contemporary books on Continental travel',[16] and Peregrine's role as principal traveller certainly reinforces his importance as a representative figure. Given the paradoxical nature of the hero's character (the opportunity to travel gratified 'his thirst after knowledge' and 'flattered his vanity and ambition'), Peregrine can suggest both those intelligent and receptive enough to profit from making the Tour and those who abdicate their moral and social responsibilities, those 'raw boys, whom Britain seemed to have poured forth on purpose to bring her national character into contempt: ignorant, petulant, rash, and profligate',[17] as Smollett was later to write. Of the four epithets Smollett applies to British tourists only the first is inapplicable to Peregrine for if he reveals, in his satirical manipulation of the ignorant painter and pedantic doctor, that he lacks neither intelligence nor judgement, then he is certainly petulant, rash, and profligate to an unwelcome degree.

All of these failings may be directly attributed to Peregrine's pride and to the exaggerated sense of his own importance that he unfailingly displays. Immediately on arrival in Calais, his 'natural haughtiness of disposition' leads him into conflict with the French customs and his exaggeratedly offensive precautions against theft lose him the personal respect he has previously inspired with ease. He is, it is true, soon 'ashamed of his own petulance' but he will shortly be troubled not at all by reflections of this kind. When in Paris, Peregrine makes the acquaintance of a nobleman who introduces him to 'persons of fashion', and who, recognizing the hero's social aspirations, 'let slip no opportunity of gratifying his ambition' (p. 209). As a result, Peregrine is entertained by the best families of France and joins in all their amusements, enjoying his 'honourable connexions' until such time as he can no longer afford to sustain the gambling losses he suffers among them. In part, Smollett is here describing (as he would do elsewhere[18]) what he regarded as a particularly French trait, but the episode also serves as Peregrine's introduction to the venality of the nobility which will eventually help to ruin him in England. During the remainder of the Tour, Peregrine is successively taken prisoner by the Paris City-guard, quarrels and later fights with a Mousquetaire, elopes with the wife of a fellow-traveller, is imprisoned in the Bastille (from which he is set free only with the aid of the British Ambassador) and obliged to leave France; he also engages in numerous sexual intrigues. For the eighteenth-century gentleman, the Grand Tour was not, of course, merely recreational; it was the culmination of his education and a preparation for adult life. The abuse of the opportunities it offered consequently became a target for moralists and satirists alike. Peregrine does not waste his time entirely—his character is too mixed for him to become a Smollettian version of the traveller Pope castigates in Book IV of *The Dunciad* or those who might, as Fielding wrote, 'have been sent as profitably to Norway and Greenland'[19] as to France or Italy—but he has certainly not profited as he should have done and for him the Tour acts not as a preparation for the life of a country gentleman but as a prelude to his immersion in the aristocratic world he has come so intensely to admire.

'Sorry am I,' says the narrator in his most direct comment on the hero,

> that the task I have undertaken, lays me under the necessity of divulging this degeneracy in the sentiments of our imperious

155

youth, who was now in the heyday of his blood, flushed with the consciousness of his own qualifications, vain of his fortune, and elated on the wings of imaginary expectation. (p. 353)

Making use of letters of introduction he has received in France, Peregrine presents himself to some noblemen by whom, the narrator informs us, he

> was not only graciously received, but even loaded with caresses and proffers of service, because they understood he was a young gentleman of fortune, who, far from standing in need of their countenance or assistance, would make an useful and creditable addition to the number of their adherents. (p. 354)

The hero's dependence has truly begun, and lest the reader believe the mercenary values of the Parisian aristocracy are merely the attributes of the peculiarly immoral French, Smollett informs us that his hero finds a special welcome from the ladies, 'to whom he was particularly agreeable, on account of his person, address, and bleeding freely at play' (p. 354).

It is at this juncture in Peregrine's career that he most obviously has the possibility of choosing between modest independence and pursuing his social ambitions, for on Trunnion's death he inherits the Garrison and a fortune of £30,000. Just halfway through the novel, therefore, and with little effort on his part, Peregrine has attained the position to which his predecessor, Roderick Random, aspires throughout the whole course of his adventures and the achievement of which forms the conclusion to Smollett's first novel. The contentment with which Roderick accompanies his father to assume his rightful place on the landed estate is, however, the fruit of much bitter experience and is quite alien to Peregrine. 'The possession of such a fortune,' the narrator declares,

> of which he was absolute master, did not at all contribute to the humiliation of his spirit, but inspired him with new ideas of grandeur and magnificence, and elevated his hope to the highest pinnacle of expectation. (p. 395)

Immediately leaving the country for London, Peregrine makes an ostentatious appearance in the beau monde, even preferring to live up to exaggerated accounts of his fortune rather than admit its true extent. He also gives renewed evidence of his ambition, now coupled with the venality characteristic of the aristocratic circles he aspires to join:

> He thought he should have it in his power, at any time, to make prize of a rich heiress, or opulent widow; his ambition had already aspired to the heart of a young handsome duchess dowager, to whose acquaintance had had found means to be introduced: or, should matrimony chance to be unsuitable to his inclinations, he never doubted, that by the interest he might acquire among the nobility, he should be favoured with some lucrative post, that would amply recompense him for the liberality of his disposition. (p. 397)

Ambition, venality, and corruption here go hand in hand and the moral and social dangers of dependence are detailed at length. Though he hears the story of Lady V—— (whose thematic relevance in detailing the immorality of aristocratic life justifies its inclusion if not its length), Peregrine

> still continued to maintain his appearance in the beau monde; and as his expence far exceeded his income, strove to contract intimacies with people of interest and power: he shewed himself regularly at court, paid his respects to them in all places of public diversion, and frequently entered into their parties, either of pleasure or cards. (pp. 571-72)

Peregrine's voluntary surrender of his independence is followed by the loss of that intelligent discrimination which has previously helped in some measure to redeem his behaviour. Turning poet and patron, for instance, Peregrine finds himself dependent on the interested flattery of the poetasters he gathers around him. If his reason forces him to despise those who offer such mercenary adulation, vanity still prompts him to reward his sycophants liberally, with the eventual result that 'he began to think himself, in good earnest, that superior genius which their flattery had described' (p. 576). His ambition, meanwhile, prompts Peregrine to join a set of young noblemen 'who had denounced war against temperance, œconomy, and common sense, and were indeed the devoted sons of tumult, waste, and prodigality' (p. 581), until such time as he has become 'insensibly accustomed to licentious riot' (p. 582). Loss of discrimination, operating with the hero's still strong ambitions, prompts an even greater recklessness, and Peregrine is persuaded to

157

gamble at horse-racing by a 'Newmarket Nobleman' who befriends him for his own purposes. 'A spirit of gaming', Smollett was later to write, 'runs riot with such violence at a horse-race, that one would imagine all the spectators were actually possessed',[20] and though Peregrine loses first £3,000 and then £6,000, he continues to believe his fortune will change, and in this mistaken confidence he abandons all ideas of financial prudence in favour of a renewed prodigality. As gambling is one supposed resource for Peregrine, so (ironically, given his origins and the social direction in which he believes himself to be moving) commerce becomes another. While his previous praise of trade (Chapter LXXX)—delivered cynically to Emilia's uncle as part of an attempt at her seduction—was entirely hypocritical, Peregrine is now 'seized with the desire of amassing' and he risks much of his greatly reduced fortune on bottomry, in the hope of profiting by the excessive premiums.

Peregrine's career thus far has already exhibited the venality and licentiousness Smollett suggests to be characteristic of the aristocracy; in its final stages it takes on an overt social dimension which emphasizes the intimate and reciprocal connection between individual and national corruption. When the 'Great Man',[21] his patron, suggests that he stand for Parliament, Peregrine throws himself wholeheartedly into the project, 'intoxicated with the ideas of pride and ambition' (p. 614). Peregrine's political talents, those 'qualifications in which he thought himself superior', are detailed at some length:

> He made balls for the ladies, visited the matrons of the corporation, adapted himself to their various humours with surprising facility, drank with those who loved a cherishing cup in private, made love to the amorous, prayed with the religious, gossiped with those who delighted in scandal, and with great sagacity contrived agreeable presents to them all. This was the most effectual method of engaging such electors as were under the influence of their wives; and as for the rest, he assailed them in their own way, setting whole hogsheads of beer and wine abroach, for the benefit of all comers; and into those sordid hearts that liquor would not open, he found means to convey himself by the help of a golden key. (p. 615)

Having once encumbered himself with a heavy debt in his attempt to buy victory in the election, however, Peregrine finds himself the victim of an arrangement between the Duke, whose borough he is contesting, and the ministry; the hero is ordered to withdraw under pain of his patron's and the minister's displeasure, and finds 'all the vanity of his ambitious hope humbled in the dust' (p. 615).

Smollett is here not simply moralizing about excessive ambition but is making a specific social criticism. At no time does Peregrine give any thought to his responsibilities as a landowner or as a potential member of the House of Commons. His sole aims in seeking election are social advancement and financial advantage, and as he has assiduously bought the votes of the electors so he hopes in turn to sell his vote to the ministry in return for a lucrative sinecure. Implicit in this entire episode are the sentiments Smollett later made explicit in the *Continuation of the Complete History of England* when, writing of the 1750s, he declared that

> The scenes of corruption, perjury, riot, and intemperance, which every election for a member of parliament had lately produced, were now grown so infamously open and intolerable . . . that the fundamentals of the constitution seemed to shake, and the very essence of parliaments to be in danger.[22]

The danger Smollett fears is that loss of individual liberty, resulting from corruption, will result in loss of national liberty and that the country will once more find itself under the arbitrary rule of an absolute monarch.[23] Peregrine himself, venal and ambitious, corrupt and corrupting, is a figure familiar in the rhetoric of the country party, and can stand at this stage of the novel for all those whom Bolingbroke attacked in *On the Idea of a Patriot King*, those concerned with 'the acquisition of wealth to satisfy avarice and of titles and ribands to satisfy vanity'.[24]

Smollett is advocating in *Peregrine Pickle*, as many had done before him, the need for independence, not least in the legislature, and to whom could Britain look for such independency? Not to the court aristocracy, nor to the monied interest on whom they depended; only the country gentleman, Smollett argued, could, by his independence, maintain both his own personal integrity and the constitution. Thus Matthew Bramble, Smollett's fictional portrayal of the ideal country gentleman, asserts proudly in *Humphry Clinker* that 'Whilst I sat in parliament, I never voted with the ministry but three times, when my conscience told me they were in the right.'[25] Peregrine, of course, has no such ideas and in any case soon finds to what extent he may depend on ministerial patronage.[26] Ordered to withdraw from one election and continually fobbed off with unfulfilled promises of election elsewhere, he 'curs'd the whole chain of his court connexions, [and] inveighed with great animosity against the rascally scheme of politicks, to which he was sacrificed' (p. 615), but there is little he can do. He commences 'Minister's Dependent' and 'laboured in the wheel of dependance, with all that mortification which a youth of his pride and sensibility may be supposed to feel from such a disagreeable necessity' (p. 619).[27] The remainder of the novel from this point has two principal concerns: the narrative describes Peregrine's social decline to the nadir of his fortunes in the Marshalsea (to which his rapid rise to a renewed independency forms a brief coda); thematically, the novel concerns itself with the hero's belated recognition of the value of independence and his growing awareness of the moral and social responsibilities attendant on his rank as gentleman.

The responsibilities of Peregrine's rank are closely related to its privileges—the respect of peers, the deference of inferiors. Within the novel, these responsibilities are primarily indicated by the hero's developing relationships with two characters: Emilia Gauntlet and Tom Pipes. Peregrine falls in love with Emilia at first sight, but though the sight of her 'rivetted the chains of his slavery beyond the power of accident to unbind' (p. 96), his mistaken sense of social superiority causes a breach between them which can be healed only by Peregrine's eventual recognition of their social equality. Immediately on meeting Emilia, Peregrine finds her to be the orphan daughter of a field officer, in modest circumstances, and the discovery 'alarmed his pride; for his warm imagination had exaggerated all his own prospects; and he began to fear, that his passion for Emilia might be thought to derogate from the dignity of his situation' (p. 97). Subsequently, Emilia's mother pointedly stresses that her daughter is 'no upstart, without friends or education, but a young lady as well bred, and better born, than most private gentlewomen in the kingdom' (p. 421), but Peregrine is unable to recognize the truth of this assertion and his relationship with Emilia continues to be characterized by a misguided subordination of his love to social ambition.

The hero's extreme self-consciousness concerning his social position intrudes into all his sexual intrigues. Despite the 'vows of eternal fidelity' he makes on leaving for France, Peregrine gets no further than Calais before attempting the seduction of Mrs. Hornbeck, wife of a fellow-traveller. Though Mrs. Hornbeck had been an oyster-wench before her marriage, the narrator insists that Peregrine would not have imagined that her education was different from that of other ladies of fashion, yet he attempts to seduce her directly, 'on the presumption, that a lady of her breeding was not to be addressed with the tedious forms that must be observed in one's advances to a person of birth and genteel education' (p. 199). In this case, the narrator suggests, Peregrine is probably correct but the hero's egotism is not always similarly justified. When he mistakes the natural frankness of a *traiteur*'s wife for a sexual invitation, he ends up in a brawl with her husband and his resultant injury confines him to his room for a week. More damagingly still, Peregrine is equally direct in attempting to seduce the wife of a French gentleman whom he encounters en route to Flanders. Gaining access to her by bribing the Capuchin friar who accompanies her, Peregrine openly declares his love and 'though by a man of a less sanguine disposition, her particular complaisance would have been deemed equivocal' (p. 283), Peregrine believes it a tribute to his personal charms and proceeds eventually, though unsuccessfully, to attempt rape.

In Paris, Peregrine does not doubt that 'his person would attract the notice of some distinguished inamorata, and was vain enough to believe that few female hearts were able to resist the artillery of his accomplishments' (p. 207). Events do not, in fact, bear out his opinion of his abilities and his failure to take an aristocratic mistress obliges him to pay for the favours of a 'Fille de joye' at a monthly cost of twenty Louis. Far from tempering his social aspirations, however, Peregrine's stay in Paris encourages them still further and he neglects a letter from Emilia because

> his imagination was engrossed by conquests that more agreeably flattered his ambition . . . and his vanity had, by this time,

disapproved of the engagement he had contracted in the rawness and inexperience of youth; suggesting, that he was born to make such an important figure in life, as ought to raise his ideas above the consideration of any such middling connections, and fix his attention upon objects of the most sublime attraction. (pp. 217–18)

The confusion of love, sexual desire, and hope of social advancement becomes one of the novel's most persistent themes; of Peregrine on his return from the Continent, the narrator declares that

> Tho' he was deeply enamoured of miss Gauntlet, he was far from proposing her heart as the ultimate aim of his gallantry, which (he did not doubt) would triumph o'er the most illustrious females of the land, and at once regale his appetite and ambition. (p. 353)[28]

When he settles in London after Trunnion's death, Peregrine compounds his confusion of values still further by adding venality to his motives. It is now that he aims to 'make prize' of a wealthy heiress or widow and that he aspires even to a young duchess dowager. The duchess, however, is no more impressed by Peregrine's social pretensions than were the Parisian nobility, and assured by a friend that Peregrine could not possibly entertain more than 'respectful sentiments' towards her, replies:

> 'Respectful sentiments! . . . if I thought the fellow had assurance enough to think of me in any shape, I protest I would forbid him my house. Upon my honour, such instances of audacity should induce persons of quality to keep your small gentry at a greater distance; for they are very apt to grow impudent, upon the least countenance or encouragement.' (p. 428)

Peregrine's always sensitive pride is hurt, but the duchess's view of the hero's social position is closely analogous to the erroneous view Peregrine has of Emilia's rank. By this time, in fact, Peregrine's ambition has already led him to disregard entirely the respect he owes Emilia as his social equal. Taking her, under false pretences, to a *bagnio*, he attempts Emilia's seduction and when, in an effort to forestall him, she mentions marriage Peregrine dismisses it as 'vulgar fetters' and offers her in its place banknotes to the value of two thousand pounds. The episode, following on Peregrine's failure to seduce Emilia by any other means, reveals not merely the hero's belief (not unreasonable in the light of his previous experience) that money will buy anything but acts as a structual counterpart to his failure in Paris to profit sexually by his intimacy with the French aristocracy, for which he consoles himself by purchasing the services of the 'Fille de joye'.[29] While the relationship Peregrine proposes would make him Emilia's protector, he attempts to placate her by offering her his entire fortune—'you shall be mistress of my whole estate, and I shall think myself happy in living dependent on your bounty!' (p. 407). Dependency is at the heart of the arrangement Peregrine desires, and whether conceived of in a real or specious form indicates how far Peregrine is from recognizing the social equality that exists between himself and Emilia.

The episode also marks the low point of the hero's moral decline. Almost immediately he recognizes Emilia's conduct to be 'so commendable, spirited, and noble, that he deemed her an object of sufficient dignity to merit his honourable addresses, even though his duty had not been concerned in the decision' (p. 420). Not only does Peregrine consider Emilia other than in relation to her fortune or her friends, but by reference to honour and duty indicates two qualities of his own rank more important than the material attributes to which he has previously restricted his notions of gentility. The hero's pride, still so evident in the arrogance of his formulation, nevertheless prevents any rapid change and only when his social decline is complete does Peregrine have the desire and opportunity of manifesting a genuine disinterestedness, by refusing to 'interfere with the interests of Emilia' when he is unable to match her fortune—a difficulty quickly obviated when he inherits his father's fortune and the family estate.

Peregrine's relationship with Emilia enables the hero, at last, to recognize how he should behave towards his social peers, and thus helps define for him what it means to be a gentleman. The hero's relationship with Tom Pipes helps complete that definition by indicating the ideal nature of the relationship between a gentleman and his dependents. Socially, the distance between Peregrine and Pipes is marked and unequivocal; Pipes is always the 'faithful valet', the 'trusty squire', or the 'faithful adherent' (fidelity and subservience characterize him), while Peregrine remains the 'young master'. Nevertheless, it is Pipes rather than Peregrine who most clearly perceives the nature of the relationship that, ideally, should bind them. From Peregrine's boyhood, Pipes's attachment stems from affection as well as duty, and it is at his own request that he becomes footman to Peregrine when the hero leaves the Garrison for school. When he departs for France, however, Peregrine deems Pipes unfit for his needs, dismisses him, and hires instead a Swiss *valet de chambre*. Only when Pipes opportunely reappears to save the ship on which Peregrine is crossing the Channel does the hero again take him into his service, 'from which', he declares, 'he should never be dismissed, except by his own desire' (p. 187). Despite this promise, and Pipes's faithful service, Peregrine again peremptorily dismisses Tom in France, this time for an insult to a Chevalier, and refuses, despite the entreaties of Jolter, Pallet, the physician, and the Chevalier himself, to reinstate him. Reappearing a second time to save Peregrine— on this occasion from an enraged husband the hero has cuckolded—Pipes is again taken into service, with Peregrine assuring Tom (in words which read particularly ironically) that 'it should be his own fault if ever they should part again' (pp. 317–18).

The double dismissal of Pipes, like the attempt to shoot Tom in a fit of rage (Chapter CIV), is indicative of how little Peregrine understands the nature of the relationship which should bind them. Even so, the hero has given some indication that he recognizes the need for relationships to have other than a financial basis; when Pipes saves Sophy from a fire at an inn, she rewards him with a gift of money, but Tom 'having consulted his master's eyes' refuses the present and Peregrine

> begged that Miss Sophy would not endeavour to debauch the morals of his servant . . . because he himself had such a particular value for the fellow, on account of his attachment and fidelity, that he should be sorry to see him treated on the footing of a common mercenary domestick. (p. 146)

Such scruples soon disappear, and throughout much of the novel Peregrine is not only careless of Pipes but actively encourages corruption by the bribery of other servants; only when endeavouring to bribe a nun does he, for the first time, find the 'art of corruption' ineffectual. Pipes, meanwhile, has very different notions; on rescuing Peregrine from Mr. Hornbeck, for instance, he declares:

> here am I, without hope of fee or reward, ready to stand by you as long as my timbers will stick together; and if I expect any recompence, may I be bound to eat oakum and drink bilge-water for life. (p. 317)

Even more important is Pipes's attitude to Peregrine in the Marshalsea. He first offers to share his savings with his master but although the hero is greatly affected by this fresh instance of Pipes's attachment, he declines the offer and

> paid his wages up to that very day, thanked him for his faithful services, and, observing that he himself was no longer in a condition to maintain a domestick, advised him to retire to the garison. (p. 683)

Pipes attempts to offer the money a second time but Peregrine commands him to desist and, says the narrator, Pipes was 'so mortified at his refusal, that, twisting the notes together, he threw them into the fire without hesitation, crying, "Damn the money" ' (pp. 683–84).

This total rejection of mercenary motivation in the master–servant relationship forces Peregrine in the sequel to reconsider his own values, though he remains obstinate for some time, declining even to accept reciprocal aid from those of his peers—Hatchway or Godfrey, for instance—whom he has previously assisted (Chapters CVII and CIX). Tom's attitude has made its mark, however, and it is entirely appropriate that when Peregrine does eventually agree to accept a loan from Hatchway, Pipes 'applying the whistle to his lips, performed a loud overture, in token of his joy' (p. 755). Pipes's role is essentially complete at this point and he scarcely reappears in the novel's closing pages. His part, however, has been an important one. Not only does he teach the hero by example, but in his rejection of financial reward and his willing assumption of a subordinate social position at all times, he acts out the social values the author suggests appropriate to his rank in an ordered, hierarchical society.

'[D]ecorum, order, and subordination'[30] were the qualities Smollett admired in his society, and throughout *Peregrine Pickle* he implies an ideal society which would greatly resemble that proposed by Pope in the *Essay on Man:*

> Heav'n forming each on other to depend,
> A master, or a servant, or a friend,
> Bids each on other for assistance call,
> 'Till one Man's weakness grows the strength of all.

> (ii, 249–52)

The need for reciprocity in social relationships is emphasized in Peregrine's changed attitudes at the end of the novel to Godfrey and Hatchway as well as to Emilia and Pipes.[31] Most important, though, is the need for the independence of the country gentleman implied both in Pope's poetry in particular and in the country party philosophy in general. When Peregrine emerges from the Marshalsea, he immediately takes up the suggestion that he should 'live absolutely independent' in the country, and

> could not help forming plans of pastoral felicity, in the arms of the lovely Emilia, remote from those pompous scenes, which he now detested and despised. He amused his fancy with the prospect of being able to support her in a state of independency. (p. 758)

Peregrine's experience, the narrator insists, has been purchased at extravagant cost, but now, as becomes 'a man of honour, sensibility and politeness', the hero declines to marry the only daughter, with a considerable fortune, of a neighbouring peer, pleading a previous attachment to Emilia. When they are married, Peregrine and Emilia appear together in London, and at court Emilia attracts the attention of the king himself, but when a nobleman who had deserted Peregrine in his misfortune now recognizes him again, the hero 'eyed him with a look of ineffable contempt, saying, "I suppose your lordship is mistaken in your man," and turned his head another way, in presence of the whole court' (p. 780). Justice is seen to be done, and the incidents assure the reader that Peregrine really has learned from his experience, resisting the very motives of venality and social ambition that had previously degraded him. It is no surprise that, in the concluding paragraph of the novel, Peregrine and Emilia depart for the country where they are to live, entering their estate 'amidst the acclamations of the whole parish' (p. 781). His moral and social education complete, Peregrine Pickle is indeed 're-established in that station of life which . . . he could fill with dignity and importance'—as an independent country gentleman.

NOTES

1. *The Adventures of Peregrine Pickle*, ed. James L. Clifford (London, 1964), p. 211. All further references appear in the text.
2. *The Letters of Tobias Smollett*, ed. L. M. Knapp (Oxford, 1970), p. 12.
3. Henry St. John, Lord Bolingbroke, 'A Dissertation upon Parties', *The Works of Lord Bolingbroke* (1841; rept. London, 1969), II, 168.
4. Ibid., i, p. 502.
5. *The Present State of all Nations* (London, 1768), II, 165.
6. Although Smollett wrote his satires in imitation of Juvenal, he refers in *Reproof* to 'Pope's immortal strain' and later, surveying recent literature, would assert that 'The satires . . . of Pope as yet are unequalled' (*The Present State*, II, 227).
7. There is good reason to think that Smollett consciously had his verse satires in mind when writing *Peregrine Pickle*, for when the hero turns poet he produces 'an imitation of Juvenal, and lashed some conspicuous characters, with equal truth, spirit, and severity' (p. 637); see also note 27 below.
8. *The Adventures of Roderick Random*, ed. Paul-Gabriel Boucé (Oxford: New York: Toronto: Melbourne, 1979), p. 228.
9. *The Present State*, II, 209.
10. James Boswell, *Life of Johnson*, ed. G. B. Hill, rev. L. F. Powell (Oxford, 1934), I, 491n.
11. Ibid., I, 492.
12. *The Present State*, II, 209.
13. Ibid. II, 123.
14. *Continuation of the Complete History of England* (London, 1766), I, 48.
15. *The Present State*, II, 213.
16. George M. Kahrl, *Tobias Smollett: Traveler-Novelist* (Chicago, 1945), p. 40.
17. *Travels through France and Italy*, ed. Frank Felsenstein (Oxford, 1979), pp. 251–52.
18. In *Peregrine Pickle*, Smollett wrote, 'every person of rank, whether male or female, was a professed gamester, who knew and practised all the finesse of the art' (p. 209); in *Travels through France and Italy*, he alleged that 'you seldom meet with a native of France, whether male or female, who is not a compleat gamester' (p. 55).

19. Henry Fielding, 'Jonathan Wild', ed. Leslie Stephens, *The Works of Henry Fielding* (London, 1882), V, 25.
20. *The Present State*, II, 217.
21. The 'Great Man' was perhaps the best known appellation of Sir Robert Walpole in opposition attacks on him, and though there is no suggestion that Peregrine's patron represents any particular individual, the epithet would have had an additional significance for Smollett's first audience.
22. *Continuation*, I, 317.
23. See above, p. 150.
24. *Works*, II, 398.
25. *The Expedition of Humphry Clinker*, ed. Lewis M. Knapp (London, 1966), p. 98.
26. When Smollett failed to get himself appointed physician to the army in Portugal in 1762, he wrote to John Moore representing his misfortune in terms very similar to those in which he had described Peregrine's experience and concluded by an assertion of his own desire for independence: 'The Secretary of war professed great Friendship and assured me I might command his best offices. I asked the Place. He expressed great Concern that I had not applied a week before. He said both the Physicians were appointed. This was true, but two other Physicians have been appointed since. You see how much I may depend upon the Friendship of this Gentleman. If my Health had held out, I would have buffeted the storms of Life without having Recourse to the Protection of any man. As it is, I hope no misfortune shall ever be able to tame the Freeborn spirit of, Dear Sir, Your affectionate humble Servt., T^s. Smollett' (*Letters*, p. 108).
27. It has not perhaps been sufficiently noticed how closely ten lines of *Advice* anticipate—in theme and narrative—this section of Peregrine's career:

> Shall I then follow with the venal tribe,
> And on the threshold the base mongrel bribe?
> Bribe him, to feast my mute-imploring eye,
> With some proud lord, who smiles a gracious lie!
> A lie to captivate my heedless youth,
> Degrade my talents, and debauch my truth;
> While, fool'd with hope, revolves my joyless day,
> And friends, and fame, and fortune fleet away;
> Till scandal, indigence, and scorn my lot,
> The dreary gaol entombs me, where I rot!

(ll. 39–40)

28. The narrator comments directly on this confusion elsewhere; for example, pp. 218 and 397.
29. The thematic relevance of the Memoirs of a Lady of Quality has already been mentioned (see above, p. 157), and Peregrine will shortly hear Lady V—— declare that 'I would rather give myself to a footman, than sell myself to a prince' (p. 474).
30. *Continuation*, II, 84.

31. This is emphasized also in the brief interpolated story, which Peregrine relates to his fellow-prisoners in the Marshalsea, of the surgeon who is revealed to be a Spanish grandee. In the tale, the surgeon's wife is afraid that her husband will now disown her but he immediately assures her that 'as she had shared in his adversity, she should also partake of his good fortune' (p. 735).

7

The Thematic Structure of *Ferdinand Count Fathom*

by PAUL-GABRIEL BOUCÉ

The technical structure of *Ferdinand Count Fathom*, the only one
the critics disdainfully examine, is clumsy, unbalanced by the
direct interventions of the author and above all by the incom-
patibility of the adventure story in the line of Defoe—'the novel
of roguery'—with the unfortunate incursion into the sentimental novel dominated by Richardson. But without wishing,
for all that, to make *Ferdinand Count Fathom* out a masterpiece, it
is still possible to discern, independently of the clumsy technical
framework, a certain thematic structure following a general
pattern determined by two closely linked factors, to wit
Fathom's social success and his amorality. In a first ascending
movement, which is far from being regular and unswerving, up
to Chapter xxxv inclusive,[1] Smollett shows the victories of Evil
and Fathom's rise in the social scale. Three stages can be
distinguished in this 'Rogue's progress'. Childhood, adolescence
and the arrival in Vienna, say the first ten chapters, constitute
Fathom's first ascent, important, but not reaching any extraordinary height. The sojourn in Vienna marks a temporary
culminating point, followed by a fairly rapid decline, leading to
Fathom's first nadir in Paris, which it is impossible to separate
from the stasis constituted by the interpolated story of Don
Diego. The stay in Great Britain, up to the social triumph of
Bristol Spring, represents the third phase, the one in which
Fathom reaches his apogee. The second movement, symmetri-

cal with the first, retraces the decline of the scoundrel and the final triumph of Good. But, there again, the development is not regular. Fathom's decline to his last nadir is swift and occupies only three chapters (xxxvi to xxxviii). Prison (xxxix to xli) forms a stasis similar to the first one in Paris, followed by a new moderate rise which culminates in Chapter xlix in the attempt at seduction perpetrated on Monimia. After this second stage in Fathom's decline, the final fall (artificially postponed by the sentimentality of the last ten chapters) is also very swift, since Fathom is in prison again at the end of Chapter lvi, this time without any hope of coming out of it. The absolute nadir having been reached, Fathom disappears from the novel, whose last ten chapters cannot appear on the same graph. It would be necessary to draw a supplementary graph of the adventures of Melvil, this time with virtue and happiness as co-ordinates. But such a task would be rendered difficult by the frequent and long disappearances of this character. The adventures of Melvil are circular, not linear. He returns, after the classic ordeals of the heroic cycle, to his point of departure, to wit happiness and fortune.

Smollett skims rapidly over Fathom's childhood and adolescence. Chapter ii, according to the heading, presents only a 'superficial view of our hero's infancy'. But already he outlines the themes which will subsequently be repeated and amplified. First of all, the major part languages will play in the formation and adventures of Fathom. His mother, a great chatterbox, talks English to him even when they are living in Prague (p. 11). This knowledge of English helps to strengthen the interest Count de Melvil already takes in him, as he is glad to hear the sound of his mother tongue (p. 17). The scraps of French Fathom then knows enable him to frustrate a plot (pp. 17–18). His ability to speak English makes it easier to gain access to Mademoiselle de Melvil (p. 23). Fathom has the linguistic gift of the great international crooks, since, after two years in Vienna, he speaks French and Italian extremely well. Rather oddly, no mention is made of Hungarian or German, but on his arrival in Paris in a cheap cosmopolitan ordinary 'he at once distinguished the high and low Dutch, barbarous French, Italian, and English languages' (p. 90). When, on his arrival in England, he is up against the magistrate and cannot make use of English because he has adopted the device of travelling incognito, he tries to plead his case 'successively in French, High-Dutch, Italian and Hungarian Latin' (p. 136) with no success, very much the reverse! This linguistic gift is closely associated with the flexibility of character and adaptability of Fathom.

The psychological and moral antithesis between Fathom and Melvil's son is strongly emphasized at least twice in these first ten chapters. While young Melvil is only interested in intellectual and athletic prowess, Fathom learns little at school, but already evinces remarkable social talents. Smollett contrasts the uncouthness and shyness of young Melvil, who for the moment despises the simperings dear to feminine society, with Fathom's innate aptitudes for gallantry, politeness and other external rituals of a static hierarchical society. The dialectic of reality and appearance is at the core of *Ferdinand Count Fathom*, as it is of the two previous novels. Fathom's fellow-student willingly allows him his little social successes 'while he himself [Melvil] was conscious of his own superiority in those qualifications which seemed of more real importance than the mere exteriors and forms of life' (p. 19). Behind the mirage of appearances, by which Melvil's father and later the young man himself allow themselves to be deceived, Smollett contrasts the fundamental egotism ('self-love', p. 20) of Fathom with the genuine qualities of heart which make life in society ('social virtue', ibid.) possible.[2] But, just as Smollett implicity criticizes women for their superficial judgement of young Fathom, it is none the less implicit, right from the beginning of the novel, that this society on which Fathom will wreak his ravages is guilty of having encouraged him. So, when Smollett underlines a second time the contrast between Fathom and Melvil, it is clear that society is ready to let itself be duped with a criminal credulity: 'he [Fathom] and the young count formed a remarkable contrast, which, in the eye of the world, redounded to his advantage' (p. 40).

The theme which dominates Fathom's adolescence is the precocious awakening of his sensuality. Probably Smollett wished to suggest that Fathom inherited his sensuality from his highly sexed mother, who married five times in the course of a single campaign (p. 7), not to mention the numerous other men she slept with. At about the age of twelve, Fathom has already spent the night in 'more effeminate amusements' (p. 20) than translating Caesar. In these conditions, it is not surprising that, at the age of sixteen, he tries to seduce Mademoiselle de Melvil, thanks to a carefully devised plan of amorous poliorcetics: 'the method of sap' (p. 24). Smollett often has recourse to the vocabulary of sieges, fortifications and military tactics to describe Fathom's amorous manoeuvres. This first attempt at seduction proves Fathom to be a born strategist in the wars of Venus but it ends at once in a defeat and an unforeseen success. Though Mademoiselle de Melvil remains icy, Teresa catches fire, or rather at last reveals her ardent passion (pp. 27–8). Here again it certainly seems that *Jonathan Wild* was not without influence on the conception of Teresa and Fathom, unless Fielding and Smollett borrow their ideas of sexual criminology from the common fund of Anglo-Saxon puritanism. Jonathan Wild's penchant for women is his only great weakness 'so naturally incident to men of heroic disposition; to say the truth, it might more properly be called a slavery to his own appetite' (Book iii, Chapter iv). Teresa, just like Laetitia in *Jonathan Wild*, 'was furnished by nature with a very amorous complexion' (p. 27), and Smollett calls these young lovers 'real voluptuaries' (p. 31). But whatever nightly revels Fathom and the maid-servant may have indulged in, Smollett describes with a puritanical fascination, not wholly devoid of complaisance, the psychological and physical methods leading up to this curious attempt at seduction. Fathom, the great amorous strategist (the military metaphor recurs again in this passage: ibid.), approaches Mademoiselle de Melvil through the intermediary of his mistress, Teresa. The latter has become his accomplice in the hope of sharing Mademoiselle de Melvil's fortune. In this systematic enterprise of seduction, the first but not the last in the novel, Fathom attacks on three fronts. First of all, he makes use of a limited, but quite effective knowledge of psychology, in this case the dynamic value of contradiction (pp. 32–4). He will use this psychological tool again to manipulate Melvil (p. 43). Next, he tries to play on Mademoiselle de Melvil's passions by exciting her sexual appetites (pp. 34–5) by licentious anecdotes and books. He had noticed beforehand that Mademoiselle de Melvil's temperament showed 'some marks of inflammability'

173

(p. 31). Smollett uses an earthy metaphor—'the warm luxuriant soil of youth' (ibid.)—which reveals all his puritanical mistrust of the impulses of youth. Lastly, he has recourse, like Peregrine, to aphrodisiac drugs (p. 34) to try, in vain, to seduce Mademoiselle de Melvil.

Right from the beginning of the novel, the problem of Evil, particularly in its sexual aspect, is definitely posed. But, in fact, Smollett does not question himself about the *origins* of Evil (apart from the few details about Fathom's heredity). He merely *states* the existence of amoral monsters, and then goes on to describe the ravages they are capable of causing in a society guilty of always being ready to let itself be hoaxed. Fathom, according to Smollett, who tries to adopt the irony of Fielding, is 'naturally a genius self-taught, in point of sagacity and invention' (p. 28). Behind the transparent ambiguity of the ironic inversion ('genius', 'sagacity', 'invention'), it is the insistence on the innateness of Evil ('naturally', 'self-taught') which is important. It is impossible to speak of a moral decline in Fathom, since, from the beginning of his life, this character is set, with no further explanations, on the level of complete amorality. Thus, in the enterprise of seduction conducted by Fathom and his mistress: 'All principles of morality had been already excluded from their former plan; consequently, he found it an easy task to interest Teresa in any other scheme tending to their mutual advantage, however wicked and perfidious it might be' (p. 35). In adopting an amoral character right from the first, Smollett condemns himself to describing a collection of heinous crimes, without being able to draw any gradation in perversity. Fathom, like the other scoundrels, in particular Ratchcali and Teresa, is a monolithic character, who does not develop, but is shattered at the end of the novel. Conversely, the faultless goodness of Melvil, and later of Monimia, makes them spectral beings, without real fictional consistence. The aseptic perfection of Monimia also kills almost any life in this character.

This antithetical duality involves the absolute necessity of duplicity in the villains of the novel. Without this duplicity all relationship between the 'good' and 'bad' characters would be impossible. *Ferdinand Count Fathom* is the novel of misunderstanding, sometimes spontaneous, more often provoked by Fathom and his acolytes. A stylistic examination of *Ferdinand*

Count Fathom would doubtless reveal the frequency of the prefix 'mis',[3] which is, in a way, the indication of the thematic continuity of the novel. The duplicity of Fathom helps or engenders misunderstandings. Thus the systematic inversion of reality is tinged with an irony which ends by becoming wearisome because it is of such a mechanical type. The incident of the copied translation (pp. 20–2) lacks neither psychological credibility nor logical coherence. The schoolmaster's misunderstanding, and above all Melvil's own father's, is only the beginning of a long series of injustices endured in all good faith by the innocent Melvil. When, later, the Count suspects his son of having stolen some jewels from his sister, the irony is triple. Fathom and Teresa are the guilty ones; but this time Fathom has nothing to do with it, the father immediately suspects his son; and, third level of irony, the father proposes Fathom to his son as 'a preceptor and pattern' (p. 39). The logic of this ironic concatenation is almost too rigorous to be acceptable.

The Hobbesian *credo* of the scoundrel with which Chapter x ends is a pedalpoint in these variations on the theme of Evil. The meeting with Ratchcali, the ideal confederate, will enable Fathom to put all these principles into practice in Vienna, a training ground and field of action more worthy of his talents than the closed world of Presburg.

This second stage (up to the beginning of Chapter xxvii, some eighty pages or so) marks a temporary decline in Fathom's social success. In spite of some little financial and amorous success, these sojourns in Vienna, in the Imperial and later the French army, and in Paris are dominated by failure. Fathom learns to his cost the many risks which beset the path of the professional crook. In spite of the mediocre quality of *Ferdinand Count Fathom*, it must be admitted that Smollett takes pains to vary the fortune of his hero, according to an alternation, artificial perhaps, but which at least has the merit of avoiding the equation: 'Evil = Social success', and its inverse.

Venus—and Mercury—rule Chapters xi–xvii inclusive, which provide confirmation of Fathom's greedy sensuality. But though he seduces Wilhelmina and her stepmother, these are paltry conquests and already mark a social setback for Fathom. His obscure birth denies him admittance to the same world as Melvil's, and Fathom has to be content with more middle-class game in a 'humbler sphere' (p. 44), which Smollett also calls 'an inferior path of life' (p. 45). These chapters, and all the manoeuvres of seduction with an eye to the main chance, are based on an antithesis: the hot-bloodedness of the two women and the cold-bloodedness of Fathom. Besides the well analysed animosity which sets the stepmother against the stepdaughter, Smollett takes care to stress[4] their ardent temperament. The stepmother has 'an increased appetite for pleasure' (p. 46), while Wilhelmina can pride herself on a 'complexion . . . very much akin to that of her stepmother: indeed they resembled each other too much to live upon any terms of friendship or even decorum' (p. 46). Fathom thinks above all of making profit out of this double love affair carried on at the same time at the price of a little invention and psychological agility. As he plans this operation with the cold-blooded tactics of a strategist, it is not surprising that the metaphor of besieging a city is continued throughout these pages.[5] Seducing Wilhelmina becomes an exercise in style, or rather in amorous rhetoric, cold, bombastic and artificial. On Fathom's side, there is no fire, no impulsive ardour. He fans the flames, but does not burn. Even in taking the precaution of informing his reader that Wilhelmina is 'an utter stranger to addresses of this kind' (p. 47) Smollett is unconvincing. Besides a feeling of improbability and monotony, this declaration of love gives an impression of disproportion between the verbal battery brought into action and the objective.

These pages (pp. 47–8) are such an accumulation of senti-mental clichés, even including those of pseudo-archaic pastoral eclogues, that it is permissible to wonder whether they do not constitute a satire, in the second degree, on the stupidity of Wilhelmina as well as of women in general. The technique of lying, the favourite weapon of his duplicity, remains in almost constant employment by Fathom. Ever since his first attempts with the Melvils, Fathom contrives to make use of the truth as much as possible even though he does not scruple to reverse its meaning and its consequences. Thus he ends by achieving his aim—getting possession of a very valuable gold chain—by making his victim believe he is doing her a favour (pp. 59–61).

Nevertheless, these dubious occupations are not without their risks. These range from the farcical but dangerous incident to terror, including the mortification of being duped. His double amorous intrigue involves Fathom in unpleasant situations, in which the frustration of interrupted love-making is mingled with the fear of being discovered by one or the other mistress.[6] Fathom is afraid, being naturally cowardly, and Smollett delights in describing his emotions in terms which are almost behaviouristic before their time, and indicate only physical or physiological reactions. Subsequently Fathom succeeds in overcoming his cowardice, when he is living in a military environment, and Smollett, on this occasion, adumbrates a psycho-sociological theory of the influence of environment (p. 75). Another untoward incident in Fathom's career: he gets cheated by Ratchcali at the very moment he was thinking of giving the latter the slip. Thus the theme of misunderstanding does not disappear from these pages. Misunderstanding acts sometimes in Fathom's favour, sometimes against him. He succeeds in deceiving not only the jeweller's wife and daughter but the worthy Viennese himself. When the latter at last begins to think that the necklace has been stolen by a member of his own family, his suspicions fasten (wrongly) on his own wife (p. 63). Fathom uses the flight of Melvil's valet to cover the theft he has committed himself. Melvil continues to take his companion for 'a mirrour of integrity and attachment; in such an exquisite manner did he plan all his designs, that almost every instance of his fraud furnished matter of triumph to his reputation' (p. 79). But this triumph is shortlived, for Ratchcali takes possession of Fathom's booty (p. 83). Smollett thus makes himself the interpreter of a certain picaresque socialism, in which money circulates by ways as hidden as they are unpredictable. Melvil, his valet, Fathom, Ratchcali and the swindlers on the other side of the Rhine who finally relieve the Tyrolean of his money (p. 144) form an original channel for the redistribution of property, itself considered as theft by Proudhon a century later. Need one add that Smollett observes this furtive circulation of liquid assets with regret rather than approval? Fathom, without being a model of stoical resignation, bears this setback fairly philosophically. Experience has taught him that even he can be the victim of a misunderstanding. This first adumbration of misfortune is repeated and developed in the account of his stay in Paris.

But, previous to this, Fathom endures the ordeal of terror,

described in the most celebrated pages of the book, to wit the journey through the forest by night and the meeting with the thieves who rob and murder travellers (pp. 83–9). There are few critics who have not praised the quality of this passage, even if they have not thought much of the rest of the novel. Hazlitt, in his *Lectures on the English Comic Writers*, is harsh about both the subject and the characters of *Ferdinand Count Fathom*, but admits that 'there is more power of writing occasionally shewn in it than in any of his works',[7] and he expresses his wholehearted admiration for the scene of the robbers in the forest. Scott has an equally unfavourable opinion of Fathom's moral depravity. Nevertheless, he is glad to draw attention to the excellence of the passage in question: 'The horrible adventure in the hut of the robbers, is a tale of natural terror which rises into the sublime; and, though often imitated, has never yet been surpassed, or perhaps equalled.[8] It is difficult to find direct precursors of Smollett in the literary use of terror. Shakespeare uses the unleashed elements in *King Lear* and *Macbeth* to emphasize the human storm, but the terror thus inspired is more a symbol than an end in itself. Perhaps it is possible to draw a parallel with the night in the entrenched camp, described by Defoe in *Captain Singleton* (1720). Besieged by a horde of ferocious animals, the shipwrecked men in the African bush combat the wild beasts and their terror, which is rapidly conjured up: 'The Moon was near the Full, but the Air full of flying Clouds, and a strange Hurricane of Wind to add to the Terror of the Night.'[9] Nearer to *Ferdinand Count Fathom* is the chapter Lord Kames entitles 'Of our Dread of Supernatural Powers in the Dark' in his *Essays on the Principles of Morality and Natural Religion* (1751). This essay (pp. 307–14) starts out from the fact that children and men fear the unknown. This fear works on the imagination which it thus predisposes to exaggeration. Lord Kames stresses that this terror is due 'entirely . . . to the operations of the imagination' (p. 314). He adds, as proof, that, in company, man is not afraid of the dark. Smollet's pages seem like a literary illustration of this theory, but no document proves that Smollett knew this work of Lord Kames's at that time.

A critical analysis relying very closely on the text makes it possible to detect the means employed by Smollett and thus to grasp more clearly the ends he set out to achieve. It matters little that readers nowadays, surfeited with literary, cinematic and, above all, atomic terror, may be inclined to smile at this scene—not to say scenario—which has since become classic. One must try to rediscover the original novelty of this passage. Smollett begins (p. 83) by giving a few rapid indications of the gloom, the silence, the solitude, without neglecting the psychological background, to wit, Fathom's dejection at the loss of the jewels. The fear mounts by degrees ('began', 'gradually'). Fathom's apprehensions take a more definite shape when the guide tells him of travellers murdered in these woods. Abandoned by the guide, Fathom is aware only of the dying away of the horse's hoofbeats and the rising gusts which announce the coming storm soon to burst in full fury (p. 84). Auditory sensations play nearly the most important part in Fathom's terror. In spite of being overcome with fear, Fathom is still able to think coherently and the intellectual vocabulary predominates in the last two paragraphs of this page. The two following ones (pp. 85–6) prove once again that Fathom too can be the victim of misapprehensions. The haven he thinks he has found is a den of thieves. Appearances deceive him, in spite of his almost professional mistrustfulness. The old woman answers him 'with such appearance of truth and simplicity, that he concluded his person was quite secure' (p. 85). The adventure of the strayed traveller might have been quite commonplace but for the discovery of a still warm corpse in an attic from which there is no escape, for the old woman has locked him in from outside. The manipulation of terror is extremely skilful. First, the prelude, in which fear, rather than terror, predominates; then the horror of the macabre discovery, but above all the nightmare feeling of being unable to escape, when Fathom knows that the same fate awaits him. As the great modern purveyor of horrific thrills, Hitchcock, stresses, it is not so much the unknown danger as the known and measured one which terrifies man. Panic gives way to anguish, and, for the first time, Fathom, at the approach of what he deems near and inevitable death, proves that his monstrous mechanism can, for a brief moment, be thrown out of gear when confronted with the monstrous. The comment is crisp, 'his conscience rose up in judgement against him' (p. 86), but it betrays Smollett's moral intention.

This scene of terror is undoubtedly less fortuitous than the critics have claimed. It is advisable, first of all, to relate it to the auto-dedication in which Smollett announces his intention of putting the psychological power of terror to profitable use. Consequently, the terror in this scene should, on a man other than Fathom, have had a cathartic effect. In Smollett's mind this journey through the forest and this night in the hut were a moral ordeal which should have halted Fathom on the path of crime. But the determination to survive soon reawakens all Fathom's ingenuity and he puts the corpse in the place he himself should have occupied in the bed. As he had foreseen, the old woman's assistants come and stab . . . a corpse. It is the turn of the robbers to be deceived by that sigh exhaled by the twice-murdered dead man. There is thus a certain balance of structure. Fathom has just let himself be deceived by Ratchcali. But he, in his turn, thwarts human wickedness in a far more dangerous situation. As he is not troubled with scruples, he robs the corpse, and this money will enable him to cut a better figure in Paris. The end of the scene (pp. 87–9) presents less interest. Fathom, in his turn, terrifies the old woman when he comes downstairs after the murderers have departed on another hunt. Irony resumes its rights. The old woman devoutly puts herself under the protection of all the saints. Fathom, after having got himself conducted, pistol in hand, to the nearest village, rewards his conductress with a little moral sermon. The interplay of ironies keeps events perpetually dovetailing into each other, at a very swift, but unobtrusive tempo. The old woman hastens to betray Fathom by having him accused of murder, but Fathom has prudently deemed it expedient not to linger in the village, and has thus thwarted the old vixen in advance. Smollett returns to the theme of terror (p. 88): noises and Fathom's frenzied imagination play the principal part. Finally, this passage has the merit of clearly expressing, not only the duplicity of the man, but also his duality. Fathom owes his life to his instinct of self-preservation—'an impulse that seemed super-natural' (p. 86)—but also to the swiftness of his mental reactions, intensified by the stimulus of a situation out of the ordinary. But is not terror the ironical falling back of intelligence on instinct? Smollett, the ironist, plays a double game, between the duality and the duplicity of his hero.

Having escaped from this adventure, Fathom is given a brief respite. Appearances and his own illusions combine to make him fall into the gravest error of his career up to now. He takes a master crook, Sir Stentor Stile, for a rustic fool whom he will be able to fleece. The game of dice (pp. 105–6) proceeds in a way that recalls the one in which Roderick (Chapter xiv) is the victim of the same kind of rogue. There again the thematic structure is very balanced. In a first section, Fathom, oversure of himself, is the victim of a sham country bumpkin whom he thought he could cheat. Stripped of everything, Fathom is determined to profit by this dearly bought lesson (p. 107). He survives by getting himself engaged as a violinist at the Opera and is thus transformed, against his will, into an attentive spectator of the fashionable world.

In these circumstances the interpolated story of the noble Castilian plays the part of a necessary stasis before the resumption of adventures in Great Britain. This story has often been condemned by critics,[10] but wrongly, for it makes an indispensable pause and serves as a thematic counterpoint of honourable deeds to the sordid adventures of Fathom. Don Diego de Zelos is doubly the victim of his misunderstandings. In Spain, first of all, where he is mistaken about the identity of Orlando-Renaldo, and where he believes he has sacrificed his wife and daughter to his Castilian sense of honour. Later, and in a more commonplace way, he is deceived by Fathom, to whom he entrusts his jewels to sell. Thus, far from being boring and irrelevant, the story is of a new type in Smollett's work because it sets the action going again (Fathom will be able to leave for Great Britain) and serves as a dramatic and thematic link between the adventures of Fathom and the love affair between Serafina-Monimia (Don Diego's daughter) and the young Orlando-Renaldo Melvil.

The sojourn in Paris reveals another literary quality of Fathom's. His duality and his duplicity meet in the ambiguity of his satirical function. He observes this cosmopolitan and French society (Chapters xxii and xxiii) where the corruption of morals does not prevent him from moving freely in it. Fathom, however reprehensible his deeds, judges with the cold lucidity of a man accustomed to take advantage of the weaknesses of others. The nocturnal brawl in a Paris brothel is more than a repetition of incidents in *Roderick Random* (Chapter xvii). It is an opportunity for Smollett to launch into a virulent satire on the French, their morals and their religion, without, for all that, sparing the national types of the Englishman and the German. The moral intention is so obvious that it threatens to turn the satirical verve into caricatural allegory. The bawd (p. 93) is less an ancient handmaid of Venus than a repulsive description of vice and disease. Smollett sketches, incidentally, a sexual typology. It is, of course, the Italian and the French priest who first decide to visit the brothel, whereas the more phlegmatic Dutchman withdraws from the party (ibid.). The Englishman and the German quarrel for the favours of the same beauty, and their remarks display the sarcastic arrogance of the one and the Teutonic fury of the other. But it is the violent anti-Catholic and Gallophobic satire that is most striking in these pages. The inmates go to Confession before the *concubitus*, and the priest, scolded by the brothel-keeper, kneels down before her to ask forgiveness. The ironic inversion verges occasionally on sacrilege, as the heavy-handed onomastic satire with which the priest is burdened indicates.[11]

Fathom's departure for Great Britain was prepared for on the thematic plane almost from the beginning of the novel. The importance of the English language in his adventures has already been evident. This linguistic attachment is reinforced, in Fathom, by a pragmatic patriotism. Great Britain appears to him as 'the Canaan of all able adventurers' (p. 77). The same biblical metaphor recurs when he contemplates the English coast from Boulogne, 'like another Moses reconnoitring the land of Canaan from the top of Mount Pisgah' (p. 128). The description of the wealthy English (pp. 129–30) and the analysis of the British national temperament (pp. 145–46) are doubly effective satires, since most of the observations are not lacking in perspicacity, and they are made by swindlers (Fathom and Ratchcali). Right from the first the two confederates are sure of making their fortune in a country where opulence, credulity and liberty offer them such lucky prospects (p. 146).

Fathom's great triumph is rapid, but of short duration (Chapters xxvii–xxxv inclusive, some forty pages). His rocket-like rise is almost too rapid, unless the swiftness of his success is not in itself an oblique satire on worldly infatuation, the wilful, social and sophisticated form of misunderstanding. The journey in the coach from Canterbury to London plays a triple role. First, as in *Roderick Random* and *Peregrine Pickle*, this little enclosed world is an opportunity for Smollett to present a satirical microcosm.[12] Secondly, the misunderstanding of which Fathom is the victim (Chapter xxix) will enable him to make the acquaintance of the young nobleman (pp. 136–37) who introduces him to London society (p. 148). Finally, the hasty seduction (Chapter xxx) of the innocent Elenor is relevant to both the thematic structure and the dramatic manipulation of the story.

With the help of Ratchcali (Chapter xxxi), Fathom's social ascent is dazzling, for the adventurer takes care to let the false treasures of his knowledge, his talent and his taste shine with all their deceptive glitter (pp. 148–49). The mirror of appearances ensnares good society like so many scatterbrained larks. Worldly success is heightened by a shameless financial exploitation for which it is rather hard to blame Fathom, since he is only taking advantage (he does not lack descendants today) of the craze for antiques. Now these rare pieces, jewels, Cremona violins, bronzes, medals, pictures, are all fakes. But the fascination and infatuation (p. 151) of his admirers is such that all critical judgement is suspended. Smollett was not the only man about that time to denounce the scandalous traffic in pseudo-antiques. Samuel Foote, a year before *Ferdinand Count Fathom*, had published a comedy in two acts (played without much success at Drury Lane in 1752), *Taste*, in which Carmine the painter and Puff the auctioneer divide the money of their dupes between them. In the prologue Garrick wrote this guilty boast of the auctioneer's:

> My best Antiquities are made at Home.
> I've *Romans, Greeks, Italians* near at hand
> True *Britons* all—and living in the Strand.

As such a success does not fail to arouse the jealousy of the swindlers, Fathom is exposed to their machinations. But, thanks to various stratagems, he succeeds in defending himself against appearances by the very play of appearances. This is the thematic significance of Chapter xxxiii, in which he puts his bullying adversary to flight by having recourse to a gory stratagem.

This social and financial success would not be complete without a conquest flattering to Fathom's demanding and perverse sexuality. The seduction of the unfortunate Celinda in Chapter xxxiv enables one to measure the experience Fathom has acquired since his (somewhat bungled) love affairs in Vienna. As a clearheaded Don Juan, he has quickly divined the hypersensitiveness of this young illegitimate daughter who is persecuted in her father's house. As in the forest, auditory sensations (pp. 160–61) play a major part in the awakening of Celinda's superstitious terror. The ruin of this young girl is complete, for not only does Fathom seduce her but to get rid of her more easily he makes her an alcoholic. Thus, just as Fathom's covetousness achieves its highest satisfaction, his sensuality wins its most complete victory. But it is precisely his taste for women that will be the ruin of Fathom. The sojourn in Bristol, where Fathom 'as usual formed the nucleus or kernel of the beau monde' (p. 165), marks the fatal apogee of his career as swindler and seducer.

The decline of the scoundrel cannot be symbolized, any more than his ascent, by an unbroken downward line. There again, Smollett arranges a level stage halfway which represents a second nadir before a partial reascent and the final fall.

The causes of this decline are simple. Betrayed by his carnal desires, Fathom, in his turn, is the victim of an adventuress, Mrs. Trapwell. The play of appearances and illusions is complicated by a triple irony. Mrs. Trapwell has married, thanks to a stratagem. Instead of complaining, her husband gives her to understand that they can both take advantage of an unpleasant situation and, fully agreeing with him she seeks a victim in Bristol. Finally, at a third level of irony, the husband wishes to make some money, but above all to get rid of this burdensome and wanton wife; of this the adventuress is unaware. Caught in the trap—*rem in re*—Fathom leaves some financial plumage in it but wins a fine feather in his Don Juan's cap (p. 171). This vain glory does not last long. The psychological and logical sequence of Chapters xxxvi and xxxvii has an inexorable precision. Pressed for money as a result of the trial, Fathom is imprudent enough to be a little too clever at cards. Ratchcali, too, makes a mistake, and, as a crowning piece of ill-luck, Fathom is recognized by Sir Stentor Stile, who has returned to London. His social decline is as swift as his ascent. He has lost the favour of the fashionable world (p. 173). Bled by the lawyer who defended him, sentenced to a fine of £1,500, abandoned by his friends, betrayed by his confederates, Fathom sinks to the depths in the space of a few hours (p. 181). The three following chapters (xxxix to xli) represent a stasis similar to Chapters xxv and xxvi. In the microcosm of the debtors' prison, Fathom is able to observe the realm of illusions, which file before his eyes like the shadows in Plato's mythical cave. Theodore,[13] the dethroned King of Corsica, or the pathetic illusion of power; Mungo Barebones,[14] or the theological mirage; Minikin, or the ludicrous demands of the point of honour, are fantastic puppets rather than genuine characters. Yet two of them (Theodore and Mungo Barebones) are people who had really existed. The technique of doubly indirect presentation of these characters (pp. 181–82) and the vigour and variety of the style make these pages one of the best passages in the novel.

The thematic significance of Fathom's providential liberation is twofold. Evil, aided by chance, can come to the help of Evil. Melvil, victim of an age-old confidence trick (p. 199) comes to help a hypothetical female relative confined in this prison. The unexpected result of this visit is the setting free of Fathom, who is recognized and promptly aided by Melvil. A second result of this apparently lucky chance (for Fathom) is that, confronted with Monimia, the adventurer promptly catches fire and forgets 'the prudential maxims he had adopted on his first entrance into life' (p. 201). Evil therefore carries within itself the power of thwarting and destroying itself. Fathom is the slave of a destiny inscribed in his flesh:

> In all probability, Heaven mingled the ingredient in his constitution, on purpose to counteract his consummate craft, defeat the villany of his intention, and, at last, expose him to the justice of the law, and the contempt of his fellow-creatures. (ibid.)

Chapters xliv to xlix have as their central theme the momentary triumph of misunderstanding. It is a series of variations, not lacking in psychological truth, on the problems of moral semiology, or rather the deciphering and interpretation of intentions. All the near-diabolic cleverness of Fathom consists in taking advantage of the financial difficulties against which Melvil is struggling (Chapter xliv) to sow mutual doubt in the minds of the lovers. It is fair to observe that Smollett avoids drawing up a Manichean table of responsibilities. If Fathom is guilty, Melvil and Monimia are partly so too, through the ill-advised pride which impels them to keep silent. The misunderstanding which, in their case, could have proved tragic, is a momentary paralysis of their social and psychological abilities to communicate. Moreover, Smollett implies that there is a purpose in Evil. Melvil, the young aristocrat who has led a coddled life, needs to suffer, to face up to the harassing problems of money. The author observes, not without irony, that Fathom 'was willing to let Melvil be better acquainted with adversity, which is the great school of life' (p. 205). The lesson is the same as in *Roderick Random*, though the adventures are very different.

Doubt soon arouses jealousy. From then on Melvil and Monimia behave like broken-down automata, immured in their silence and bitterness. Their actions succeed each other with the paralogical unreality of a nightmare, and their eyes no longer see except through 'the false medium of prejudice and resentment' (p. 214). As thematic counterpoint Smollett invokes professional and racial prejudice. Such is the meaning of the opposition between the heartless Christian usurers and the Jewish moneylender Joshua, who, contrary to all expectation, decides to help Melvil (pp. 224–29). The attempt to rape Monimia (pp. 236–37) had been preceded by a first error on the part of Fathom, who had declared his passion too soon, before Melvil had left England (p. 216). Monimia's haughty coldness only inflames Fathom's desire. Smollett ironically applies to Fathom the theory of contradictory passions which the latter uses to excite Melvil's resentment against the innocent Monimia (p. 217). Fathom's failure is due to Providence, but above all to the point of the sword with which Monimia, the noble daughter of a *hidalgo*, threatens him.

Taken in and rescued by Madame Clement, Monimia disappears from the novel, while Fathom sees his final downfall fast approaching. From Chapter l onwards, he changes his way of life. The 'zenith of his fortune' (p. 243) is past. He cannot resume the place he occupied in the fashionable world. After a few reflections, at once prudent and moral, on the passion for gambling which has seized English society (pp. 244–45), he decides to practise the medical profession, in other words to lower himself 'one step in the degrees of life' (p. 245). His sojourn in Tunbridge Wells is not lacking in irony. Whereas in Bristol Fathom had an unlooked-for medical success, in Tunbridge Wells he has to wage a fierce battle against colleagues already installed on the spot. Smollett launches a fresh attack against the infatuations of upper-class society (pp. 247–48), and the medical blindness of the patients as much as that of the doctors (Chapter li).

But, in spite of a few small successes, Fathom begins to pile up mistakes. In courting the daughter, once again, without realizing it at first, it is the mother who falls for him (p. 257). In London, there again, the new doctor has great difficulty in establishing a clientèle, in spite of the numerous and picturesque stratagems to which he resorts (pp. 259–60). For once the play of appearances deceives no one but Fathom himself, who has chosen, as his ally, an apothecary as rascally as himself. Fathom's bad luck takes a series of surprising turns which have manifold consequences. The amorous widow dies and the disappointed daughter vows implacable hatred against her ex-suitor (p. 262). A merchant, allured by the damsel's calumnies, and anxious to get rid of his wife, has recourse to Fathom's bad offices. Contrary to the merchant's expectations, as a result of a particularly violent treatment, the wife recovers. The husband promptly claims that Fathom intended to poison his wife, but this extraordinary cure earns Fathom a certain success (pp. 263–64). Another surprising turn: Fathom, impelled as usual by his demon of sensuality, seduces a clergyman's wife, whose liberal and mainly bookish education somewhat reminds one of Miss Williams's in *Roderick Random*. The young woman, overcome with remorse, confesses to her husband, who takes legal action against Fathom.

As a result of this scandal, Fathom's reputation and his clientèle vanish into thin air (p. 267). The three following chapters (liv to lvi) might, indeed, all bear the same title, 'his eclipse and gradual declination' (p. 267). In the previous chapters, it seems that Smollett wishes to suggest the tortuous ramifications of Evil, which alternately assume a positive and negative aspect for Fathom. In these last three chapters, it seems that he wishes, above all, to accentuate the rigorous, inescapable concatenation of mischances, the blind but also ambiguous form of Destiny, since Fathom's mischances prepare the way for the defeat of Evil and the final victory of Good. Smollett's recipe for making Fathom founder (definitely) is the same as the one employed for the momentary eclipses of Roderick and Peregrine: the acceleration and concentration of unfortunate incidents (ibid.).

But if this formula is therefore not new, there is nevertheless an appreciable difference in technique, due to the specific case of Fathom. On the one hand, even in this final decline, Smollett arranges a respite one might call a 'microstasis'. This is the story of the old female kleptomaniac hoaxed by Fathom, thus, on the thematic plane of the exploitation of evil by evil (pp. 271–73). Still impelled by his sensuality—the genetic form of transcendental Evil (p. 271)—and his cupidity, Fathom marries an ardent young widow. But he is mistaken about his wife's fortune. A plot between his father-in-law, a lawyer, and fellow charlatan who fears Fathom's rivalry results in having him thrown in prison, this time with no hope of getting out.

Now this ending lacks neither ingenuity nor irony. Fathom has been deceived on all fronts. He loses his wife, his reputation, his liberty and his hopes on a (false) charge of bigamy. The irony of systematic misunderstanding is thus reversed. For the first time, Fathom expresses remorse for his past crimes. But Smollett takes care to stress that from momentary remorse to lasting repentance there is all the long and arduous road of penitence to travel, a journey Fathom is far from inclined to take. It even seems that Smollett does all he can to minimize his hero's remorse in order to reduce it to no more than self-pity. Thus, Fathom's duality, duplicity and ambiguity are checkmated by a double-crossing lawyer (p. 281).

One may regret that Smollett, at the price of a simple imaginary chapter, did not then make Fathom disappear from the scene and wind up the sentimental sub-plot and its corollary, the story of the noble Castilian. But, at that time, the moral standards of the novel demanded the total ruin of the villain and, if he survived, his more or less convincing reformation. At the end of *Tom Jones*, Blifil is converted to Methodism, which, coming from the pen of Fielding, is perhaps as little flattering to Blifil as to Methodism. Technically, the last ten chapters over-weight and unbalance *Ferdinand Count Fathom*. But without wishing, at all costs, to salvage this novel whose end founders in a morass of boring sickly-sentimentality, it is possible to discern a certain thematic continuity between the adventures of Fathom and their sentimental appendix. In the first place, the theme of misunderstanding persists. Melvil comes to wish he had kept his illusions about Monimia (pp. 282–83) and when his sister tells him the truth about Fathom's activities, he begins by denying the evidence (p. 295). The hasty remarriage of the Countess de Melvil is yet another variation on the same theme (pp. 284–86). But there are other misunderstandings whose results are less painful. In his supposed coma, Melvil gives the appearance of being dead (p. 303). The illusion of a dream (pp. 305–6) prepares the way for the final reunion with Monimia, who has been hidden and cured by the worthy Madame Clement. There is even a wish, manifested in a way at once antithetical and parallel in both Melvil and Fathom, to cling to the unreal in order to make it easier to deny a reality which seems to them illusory. Such is Melvil's psychological reaction when he meets Monimia again (p. 329) and Fathom's when he is saved through the good offices of Melvil (pp. 358–59). Fathom believes himself the victim of a 'vision so perfect and distinct, as to emulate truth and reality' (p. 360). This morbid interplay of illusion and reality is emphasized on the stylistic and sentimental planes by the repeated use of oxy-morons which imply bitter-sweet delights and fantasies of love and death. Expressions such as 'pleasing anguish' and 'gloomy enjoyment' (p. 306) recur several times in these pages.[15] But the most striking and unexpected feature is the suggestion of necrophilia in Melvil's melancholy ravings. Sorrow is described by Smollett in the language of erotic excitement exacerbated by the frustration of sexual desire. As he approaches London 'his impatience became so ardent, that never lover panted more eagerly for the consummation of his wishes, than Melvil for an opportunity of stretching himself upon the grave of the lost Monimia' (p. 315). The references to an erotic pleasure derived from intercourse with the departed are even more explicit in the pages that follow. Melvil considers the first night he spends keeping vigil by the supposed grave of Monimia as a wedding-night (pp. 317–19, 323).

A second persistent theme is the interplay of illusions and prejudices. In this respect, the dénouement of the Castilian story is full of information about Smollett's intentions. Don Diego examines his conscience and deplores the murderous folly which impelled him to poison (at least, so he believes) his wife and daughter. But, above all, he condemns his haste, due to the vengeful demands of Spanish honour: 'I was guided by that savage principle which falsely we call honour: accursed phantome! that assumes the specious title, and misleads our wretched nation!' (p. 329). These declarations of Don Diego's do not however remove all anxiety for the honour of his name a few pages later (p. 341) although, a fresh contradiction, he has renounced the 'vindictive principles of a Spaniard' (p. 342). As to Don Diego's prejudices, the embryonic interpolated story (the frustrated loves of Charlotte and Valentine, pp. 345–50) provides a thematic counterpoint to them in a minor social key. Smollett is quite conscious of the possible parallel with Don Diego's story since Melvil tells his in order to persuade the intractable father. After Joshua, Melvil makes a positive plea, full of common sense, in favour of marrying for love rather than money ('mercenary and compulsive matches', p. 348).

The edifying end of the novel is in conformity with its thematic structure. The banality of this happiness awarded to the good and of the physical punishment (disease) and the moral one (repentance) of the wicked which concludes this story renders any continuation of the analysis pointless. A single feature, also unexpected, mars these last conventional pages to the point of repugnance. This is the lesson of latitudinarian tolerance given by Don Diego, hitherto the most rigid and monolithic of the good characters. In order to be able to marry Madame Clement, the benefactress of his long-lost daughter, he decides to be converted to Protestantism. Besides the haste of this marriage, which cannot fail to come as a dramatic surprise, thematically this decision makes Don Diego once again contradict himself, since the heretical religion of his daughter's suitor was at that time one of the main causes of his parental ire. But is it really a contradiction or a conversion? Don

Diego's sincerity compromises with a certain prudent casuistry. He hastens to declare that he will not make his conversion public until *after* his return from Spain, whither he is going to settle his family affairs and his affairs of honour. But, having made this reservation, it is only fair to point out that there is no trace of Protestant proselytism in Smollett. Don Diego condescends to embrace the Protestant faith rather than adopting it with fervent conviction. He is converted not so much for positive reasons as for lack of negative ones or, to quote his own words: 'though I am fully satisfied that real goodness is of no particular persuasion, and that salvation cannot depend upon belief, over which the will has no influence' (p. 363). What is striking about this moderate and tolerant profession of faith, is more the number of reservations and negations, implicit or explicit, than the positive ardour of the neophyte. Hence, though a concern for religion is not absent from *Ferdinand Count Fathom*, it remains subordinate to a level-headed rationalism. The only trace, a very faint one, of metaphysical anguish is Melvil's exasperated cry: 'sacred Heaven! Why did Providence wink at the triumph of such consummate perfidy?' (p. 316). The final happiness of the lovers reunited at last, such is Smollett's moral reply, since, like Richardson, he is a defender of ethical mercantilism. Happiness is *earned* through trials created by God and man. The supreme reward—one is strongly tempted to write 'the bonus'—is the carnal possession of Monimia, 'the well-earned palm of virtue and of constancy' (p. 351). A good sixty years before the conspirators of *Hernani*, Melvil might have murmured, '*Ad augusta per angusta.*'

NOTES

1. All references are to the 'Oxford English Novels' edition of *Ferdinand Count Fathom* (1753), with introduction and notes by Damian Grant (London, 1971), pp. xxvi + 384. For a study of the technical structure of *FCF*, see Paul-Gabriel Boucé, *The Novels of Tobias Smollett* (London, 1976), pp. 145–58.

2. On this subject, see M. A. Goldberg, *Smollett and the Scottish School* (Albuquerque, 1959), pp. 82–107, '*Ferdinand Count Fathom:* A Study in Art and Nature'. See also p. 23 for the description of the talents, superficial but prized in society, which Fathom acquires at as early an age as twelve. For global approaches to *FCF* see the following essays: T. O. Treadwell,

'The Two Worlds of *Ferdinand Count Fathom*' in G. S. Rousseau and P-G. Boucé, eds., *Tobias Smollett* (New York, 1971), pp. 131–53; Thomas Preston, 'Disenchanting the Man of Feeling: Smollett's *Ferdinand Count Fathom*', in Larry S. Champion, ed., *Quick Springs of Sense* (Athens, Georgia, 1974), pp. 223–39; and more recently John F. Sena's dramatic approach in his 'Fathoming Fathom: Smollett's Count as Malevolent Artist', in *Forum for Modern Language Studies*, xvi (1980), 1–11.

3. See in particular, in the first forty pages, pp. 22 (four times in one page), 35, 38.

4. See two other indications of this kind: p. 47 (Wilhelmina); p. 53, the stepmother, with an explanatory sentence addressed directly to the reader; also pp. 67–8.

5. See *FCF*, p. 45, chapter heading; p. 47, where this flag of surrender hoisted in a face constitutes a metaphor, to say the least of it, dubious; p. 59, 'Having thus kindled the train', a sapper's metaphor which Smollett uses again, in another sphere, p. 81 ('finds himself countermined').

6. See pp. 51–3, 55–6.

7. William Hazlitt, *Lectures on the English Comic Writers* (London, 1819), p. 232; see also p. 231.

8. Walter Scott, *The Lives of the Novelists* (London, 1910), p. 84.

9. Daniel Defoe, *Captain Singleton* (1720; rept. London, 1963), p. 123.

10. Saintsbury, for example, who does not at all like *FCF*, declares in his introduction, 'Few, I suppose, are much enamoured of the History of the Noble Castilian,' Navarre edn., 1925, VIII, xvi.

11. This priest signs himself 'Pepin Clothaire Charlé Henri Louis Barnabe de Fumier' (p. 99). The litany of Christian names is meant to ridicule the onomastic ostentation of the French (petty) nobility.

12. See Grant T. Webster, 'Smollett's Microcosms: A Satiric Device in the Novel', *Satire Newsletter*, v (Fall 1967), 34–7.

13. On Theodore de Neuhoff, see P. Wilding, *Adventures in the Eighteenth Century* (London, 1937; rept. New York), pp. 117–63.

14. See Earl R. Wasserman, 'Smollett's Satire on the Hutchinsonians', *MLN*, lxx (May 1955), 336–37, which identifies Sir Mungo Barebones as a caricature of the theologian John Hutchinson (1674–1737).

15. See in particular pp. 315–16, 'gloomy satisfaction'; p. 316, 'let me enjoy a full banquet of woe'; p. 319, 'woful enjoyment'.

8

Smollett and the Reader in *Sir Launcelot Greaves*

by JOHN VALDIMIR PRICE

The Adventures of Sir Launcelot Greaves deserves to be a better novel than it is. Smollett scholars and critics have, unsurprisingly, found much to praise in it, and Professor Boucé's percipient and sympathetic analysis is quite the most persuasive comment on the novel.[1] No one, however, is going to assert that its admirers are numerous, nor are they likely to be. Those of us who can find much to enjoy in Smollett have been frequently viewed with suspicion, but others have rated Smollett somewhere below George Gissing or Wilkie Collins (to choose authors from a safely different century). In any case, a scholar or critic setting out to write on Smollett can be presumed to be predisposed in the novelist's favour. Thoughts such as these conditioned me years ago to expect very little of *Sir Launcelot Greaves*, and I was consequently pleasantly surprised the first time I read it. When I came to read it again after an interval of several years, I was even more pleasantly surprised.

The critical fortunes of *Sir Launcelot Greaves* may be traced to James Beattie, who gave it his approval (a dubious benefit):

> Sir Launcelot Greaves is of Don Quixote's kindred, but a different character. Smollet's [sic] design was, not to expose him to ridicule; but rather to recommend him to our pity and admiration. He has therefore given him youth, strength, and beauty, as well as courage, and dignity of mind, has mounted him on a generous steed, and arrayed him in an elegant suit of

193

armour. Yet, that the history might have a comic air, he has been careful to contrast and connect Sir Launcelot with a squire and other associates of very dissimilar tempers and circumstances.[2]

Beattie's early notice has perhaps been the source of critical fixation on the quixotic pattern of the novel, to the detriment of its real merits. To be sure, Sir Launcelot regards himself as a latter-day knight errant, but he makes quite clear the differences between himself and the hero of Cervantes's novel when he is accused by Ferret of setting up as a modern Don Quixote:

> He that from affectation imitates the extravagances recorded of Don Quixote, is an impostor equally wicked and contemptible. He that counterfeits madness, unless he dissembles like the elder Brutus, for some virtuous purposes not only debases his own soul, but acts as a traytor to heaven, by denying the divinity that is within him.—I am neither an affected imitator of Don Quixote, nor, as I trust in heaven, visited by that spirit of lunacy so admirably displayed in the fictitious character exhibited by the inimitable Cervantes. I have not yet encountered a windmill for a giant; nor mistaken this public house for a magnificent castle: neither do I believe this gentleman to be the constable; nor that worthy practitioner to be master Elizabat, the surgeon recorded in Amadis de Gaul; nor you to be the enchanter Alquife, nor any other sage of history or romance.—I see and distinguish objects as they are discerned and described by other men. I reason without prejudice, can endure contradiction, and, as the company perceives, even bear impertinent censure, without passion or resentment.[3]

This early outburst must be kept in mind when we are assessing Smollett's aims and achievements. In the novel, behaviour like that of Don Quixote is associated with madness, and Sir Launcelot is not mad. His (temporary) eccentricity and idiosyncracy are the manifestations of a misguided heart, not the product of a diseased mind.[4] His emotions can be violent, and his love for Aurelia has been maliciously thwarted; but he is never incapable of distinguishing between illusion and the real world of his empirical sensations.

Smollett's own attitude towards the novel is by no means clear. Again, assessment of the novel has been hampered by the account given by Sir Walter Scott of its composition:

194

Smollett appears to have executed his task with very little premeditation. During a part of the time he was residing at Paxton, in Berwickshire, on a visit to the late George Home, Esq., and when post-time drew near, he used to retire for half an hour or an hour, to prepare the necessary quantity of *copy*, as it is technically called in the printing-house, which he never gave himself the trouble to correct, or even to read over.[5]

This account begs more questions than it answers. How often did Smollett 'retire'? Did he write full chapters, or only portions? How does Scott know that Smollett never corrected or read over his copy? Surely there would have been more inconsistencies in the novel than there are if the method of composition was so haphazard. Professor Knapp has, moreover, decisively proved, on factual grounds, that Scott's account cannot be trusted.[6]

Early comments like these of Beattie and Scott, and the absence of any later attempts to analyse their validity, have not encouraged careful assessment of the novel. Also, the temptation to find analogies with other quixotic novels of the eighteenth century, such as Charlotte Lennox's *The Female Quixote* (1752), has been great, and it has probably deterred readers from looking beyond these superficial elements for other more interesting features and effects in the novel. Different approaches and methods yield different results, but I think that some clue to Smollett's attitude towards his novel, its aims, and its relationship with its audience can be gleaned from his appeals to the reader, not only in the text, but in the chapter headings.

The authorial voice is at its most apparent in the chapter headings. Their tone varies from the straightforward ('VII. *In which the knight resumes his importance*') to the prescriptive ('VI. *In which the reader will perceive that in some cases madness is catching*'). These chapter headings are notably different in style from those in Smollett's other novels. For example, the sixty-nine chapter headings in *Roderick Random* (1748) are quite lengthy and written for the most part in the first person. Only the interpolated stories are not recounted as if by Roderick himself, and the headings tend to be shamelessly full of self-praise ('VI. *I make great progress in my studies—am caressed by everybody—my female cousins take notice of me . . .*'). The chapter headings thus contain a précis of the novel from the main character's point of view, and no direct appeal or allusion is made to the reader. Since the work is fictional autobiography, perhaps one would expect a direct approach, such as those found in spiritual autobiographies, but *Roderick Random* was Smollett's first novel, and in it he seems unaware of the potential inherent in the relationship between author and reader.

In *Peregrine Pickle* (1751), Smollett resorted to a neutral, third-person style in the chapter headings. Again, the 114 chapter headings merely summarize the story and give little hint of either Smollett's attitude or the main characters' attitudes towards the events.

Two years later, *Ferdinand Count Fathom* was published, and here the chapter headings are noticeably different from those in the earlier novels. The first one announces an attitude and a tone of self-confidence on Smollett's part that had not been present before; a certain ironic awareness of the role that Smollett as author is playing also emerges: 'I. *Some sage observations that naturally introduce our important history.*' To be sure, most of the short, if not abrupt, chapter headings merely summarize the plot in a perfunctory manner, but Smollett is much more aware of the reader than he had been when writing the chapter headings for his preceding novels. The reader is specifically addressed three times, in the headings to Chapters VIII, LVII, and LXV, but as there are sixty-seven chapter headings, this is not a high level of frequency.

In the twenty-five chapter headings of *Sir Launcelot Greaves*, the reader is addressed six times, more than in any other novel. This time, Smollett gives very little clue to the development of the story, or the actions of the characters, and he exhibits a penchant both for an ironic moral and ambivalent circumlocution. Since Smollett's last novel, *Humphry Clinker* (1771), is an epistolary novel and contains no chapter headings, it is worth looking at *Sir Launcelot Greaves*'s chapter headings in a little detail.

The reader is appealed to in the first heading, '*In which certain personages of this delightful history are introduced to the reader's acquaintance.*' Except for the word 'delightful', Smollett is neutral, but the attempt to predispose the reader in favour of the novel is so overt that it can hardly be called persuasive. In terming the work a history, Smollett is also employing a device familiar enough to readers of eighteenth-century novels, but his second chapter heading suggests that he was uncertain about the appropriateness of this analogy: '*In which the hero of these adventures makes his first appearance on the stage of action.*' It is a long step from a history to a play, and one might be tempted to see Smollett hopelessly confused about the kind of work he was writing.

The third chapter heading, however, perhaps gives us evidence that Smollett is deliberately playing with the reader's expectations and drawing the reader to an awareness of his relationship with the author as well as with the novel: '*Which the reader, on perusal, may wish were chapter the last.*' It can be asserted, though not argued, that Smollett, knowing that the novel was going to appear serially over a long period, establishes his control over his material and the reader by reminding us that the quixotic fantasy we are reading should not be taken too seriously. The third chapter is also the longest in the book, recounting the nativity and early youth of Sir Launcelot, and it would be unlikely that the reader would want the third chapter to be the last. Whatever the literary defects of *Sir Launcelot Greaves* may be, most readers and critics have found the first few chapters the best parts of the novel. Smollett's ironic confidence may derive from assumptions about human nature rather than from certitude about the narrative cogency of his story, but his object remains the same: furthering the reader's commitment.

Chapter three also engages the reader's interest in a theme which Smollett continues to develop throughout the novel, that of madness. Professor Boucé's sympathetic treatment of *Sir Launcelot Greaves*, and of the madness theme in particular, draws our attention to the relevance of the heading for chapter six, '*In which the reader will perceive that in some cases madness is catching.*' This chapter heading perhaps suggests that the thematic unity of Sir Launcelot's commencement and activities as a knight errant is more conscious than not,[7] and it certainly points the reader towards the 'correct' reaction to the chapter. In it, Captain Crowe, having heard the story of Launcelot's commencement and activities as a knight errant, decides that he wants to become one as well, which provides the opportunity for some mischief on the part of his companions. Thus, the chapter heading encourages the reader to understand that aberrant behaviour can easily set the wrong example for minds that are not very steadfast.

Because of the moral importance of the madness theme in the novel, Smollett is, I think, reminding his readers that his story is not merely entertaining, but can be instructive as well. The absence of overt moralizing tends to go hand in hand with artistic excellence: the reader redeploys the elements of his own experience in order to find a subjective correlative in that experience that gives meaning and value to what he is reading. Smollett uses his chapter headings for such purposes on several occasions, and they remind the reader of the serious contours in the novel.

Smollett addresses the reader in three more chapter headings, all of which share a similar phrase: 'XV. *Exhibiting an interview, which, it is to be hoped, will interest the curiosity of the reader*'; 'XVI. *Which, it is to be hoped, the reader will find an agreeable medley of mirth and madness, sense and absurdity*'; and '*Chapter the last. Which, it is to be hoped, will be, on more accounts than one, agreeable to the reader*'. Smollett used the phrase 'it is to be hoped' in a chapter heading on only one other occasion, in the heading to Chapter LXIV of *Ferdinand Count Fathom*: '*The mystery unfolded. Another recognition, which, it is to be hoped, the reader could not foresee.*' The ironic stance of these chapter headings in *Sir Launcelot Greaves* is a continuation and development of previous ironic conventions. Smollett's awareness of himself as an author keeping his secrets from his reader is both an eighteenth-century narrative convention as well as a mode of deferential self-assertion. Smollett wants the reader to respond to his writing on the reader's own terms, but he is willing to give him a few guidelines.

In *Sir Launcelot Greaves*, then, the role for the reader may be seen to be that suggested by Wolfgang Iser: 'While the eighteenth-century novel reader was cast by the author in a specific role, so that he could be guided—directly or indirectly, through affirmation or through negation—towards a conception of human nature and of reality, in the nineteenth century the reader was not told what part he was to play.'[8] This is more true of *Sir Launcelot Greaves* than any of Smollett's other novels, for he is nowhere so much a part of his own creation as in this work.

The fact that Smollett was having to attract and to hold his audience's attention for a period of about two years, from January 1760 to December 1761, may account for his persistence in reminding them of the part they have to play in reading the novel. No one had ever attempted such an ambitious serial novel before,[9] and an author about to embark on such a project might very well have wondered about his ability to retain his readers' commitment over an extended period. Equally, he might have wondered about the psychological and phenomenological abilities of a reader to sustain a process that one more often associated with shorter bursts of concentration or attention. Richardson's vastly longer *Clarissa* had been published in the space of just over one year (from 1 December 1747 to 6 December 1748), but it is about twelve times longer than *Sir Launcelot Greaves*. Its length alone (not to mention other features) makes demands on a reader that a shorter work over a longer period would find less easy to make. It is also worth recalling that Smollett had the aid of illustrations for his novel, and it was the first illustrated serial novel.[10]

Smollett's consciousness of the reader is thus at the forefront of his attention and his craft, and it emerges in the novel itself as well as in the chapter headings. More specifically, the reader is addressed directly at the ends of chapters, the first four, as well as chapters fourteen and seventeen. In addition, other allusions or statements are directed to the reader, who, if not so designated, is clearly the person Smollett has in mind. The appeals or addresses to the reader are of a frequency much higher in this novel than in any of Smollett's other novels; the reader is not so much 'implied' as presumed.

Smollett reveals himself to be aware not only of the reader's presence but actually inducts him into the novel at the end of the first chapter: 'But as a personage of great importance in this entertaining history was forced to remain some time at the door, before he could gain admittance, so must the reader wait with patience for the next chapter, in which he will see the cause of this disturbance explained much to his comfort and edification' (p. 7). In fact, the reader had to wait a good deal longer than Launcelot, the 'personage of great importance', who is admitted to the public house after a delay of a few minutes, while Smollett's readers had to wait a month to be edified and comforted. Smollett had told us in the chapter heading that the novel was 'delightful'; he now reminds us that it is 'entertaining' as well. The reader is thus given his instructions and can prepare himself psychologically for what is to follow.

There is also a rhetorical challenge set up in these words. The reader is after all free to decline the invitation to wait with patience (in fact, most authors would probably prefer a little impatience from their readers). The comic exaggeration of Launcelot's knocking at the door ('which threatened the whole house with immediate demolition') at least lets the reader know that the inhabitants of the Black Lion are in no danger. More importantly, the reader is also being conditioned to associate himself with Launcelot; he and the reader both must wait for others. Just as Launcelot bursts in on the assembled company at the beginning of the second chapter, so the reader is invited to immerse himself imaginatively in the novel and to join Launcelot as he makes his entry not only into the Black Lion but into the novel as well.

Though Smollett can thus be seen to invite the reader to identify with Sir Launcelot, he forestalls too much sympathetic identification and keeps the reader firmly an outsider. At the end of the second chapter, when Sir Launcelot has retired from the company, Tom Clarke succumbs to the entreaties of the surgeon to know Greaves's story, and Smollett concludes this chapter by saying that 'Tom, wiping his eyes, promised to give him that satisfaction; which the reader, if he be so minded, may partake in the next chapter' (p. 17). Now the reader is no longer strategically correlated with Sir Launcelot, but, like the surgeon, becomes a listener.

At the end of this chapter, then, the reader has been made the means by which an ingenious structural complexity is incorporated into the novel. The reader was at first introduced to various characters in the 'delightful history', and then encouraged to enter into the spirit of the story at the same time that Sir Launcelot makes his appearance. He is now taken a further step from the author and hears the author's account of his fictive character's account of Sir Launcelot's birth, early life, and commitment to knight-errantry. He is thus two steps removed from the creative process and must now piece together, imaginatively or intuitively, the information that he has at first-hand from the internal narrative of Mr. Clarke, and second-hand from the inferences that he makes from the raw data that Smollett gives him. This is all done economically, for Smollett has by now written only a small portion of his story, but he has already given notice to the reader that the narrative, though having many features that intersect with our subjective experience in the 'real' world, is nevertheless different in kind and degree from that experience. Only the pedestrianism of Smollett's style prevents him from imbuing these early episodes with the esthetic cogency that one would find in Dickens.

While Tom Clarke is, in his ponderous way, narrating the early history of Sir Launcelot, he is impertinently interrupted by Ferret, and as Smollett puts it, 'Discord seemed to clap her sooty wings in expectation of battle' (p. 30). Violence is not, of course, likely, and the comic contours are emphasized in the last sentence of this third chapter: 'But as the reader may have more than once already cursed the unconscionable length of this chapter, we must postpone to the next opportunity the incidents that succeeded this denunciation of war' (p. 30). Chapter III is the longest in the book, but a reader who had to wait for a month to learn of the consequences might not have cursed the unconscionable length but the unconscionable wait for the outcome.

The ironic point of this chapter conclusion is that Smollett has once again associated his readers with one of his characters, a different one this time. The altercation that seems about to ensue is in fact caused by a curse. Clarke is expatiating, quite irrelevantly, on the genealogy of Scipio, Sir Launcelot's horse, when Ferret exclaims, 'in a furious tone, "Damn your father, and his horse, and his colt into the bargain!" ' (p. 29). Having been initially associated with the hero of the story, the reader now finds himself, if he curses the unconscionable length of the chapter, associated with the disagreeable Ferret. It is easy to see that Smollett is ironically defending his narrative strategy by such a device. An alert reader would notice the association, and even a not-so-alert one, with a month to wait for the next instalment of the novel, might very well discover the implied association.

At the end of the fourth chapter, Smollett aligns the reader not so much with one of the characters as with the narrative technique itself. A 'hideous repetition of groans' has emanated from Timothy Crabshaw's room, so that Tom Clarke's recital of Greaves's background is again interrupted, and 'this accident naturally suspended the narration. In like manner we shall conclude the chapter, that the reader may have time to breathe and digest what he has already heard' (p. 41). Here, the reader's complicity is demanded at the same time that his pseudo-disapproval is invited. The reader may feel like indulging himself, Smollett implies, in a 'hideous repetition of groans' at the suspension of the narrative, but the ostensible narrator, using 'we' to align himself with someone other than those in the novel, disclaims any responsibility for what has passed. Who constitutes 'we' is deliberately ambiguous, but the usage is not, I think, merely editorial. Smollett wants the reader to act as if the narrative had a life of its own.

These early appeals and addresses to the reader, within the body of the novel, and in such frequency, are not to be found in any of Smollett's other novels.[11] An easy, but I think correct, explanation for them lies in Smollett's realization that he was attempting something unique in the history of English fiction, that is, extended and prolonged serial publication, accompanied by illustrations. The reader needed to be reminded of his importance as well as the effort that would be expected of him in keeping up with the story. Moreover, it was a device that Smollett had not used before, and it offered him an opportunity to extend his range and to give structural complexity and coherence to what otherwise would appear as a superficial piece of writing.

For the next ten chapters, Smollett all but forgets the reader, at least overtly, though he alludes to him or mentions him from time to time. At the end of chapter fourteen, however, he is once again ostensibly concerned with the reader's welfare and stamina. The escape and subsequent disguise of Aurelia Darnel from her uncle has been unfolded, and she is about to encounter Sir Launcelot, 'but as the ensuing scene requires fresh attention in the reader, we shall defer it till another opportunity, when his spirits shall be recruited from the fatigue of the chapter' (p. 119). The use of the imperative is Smollett's way of forcing the reader to associate himself with Aurelia and the intrigue necessary to let her escape from her uncle and a marriage that she does not want.

In a subsequent chapter, Smollett again exhibits this ironic concern for his reader's well-being, almost as if he is afraid that the story has dragged on too long. This is evident in the last sentence of chapter seventeen: 'But as we have already trespassed on the reader's patience, we shall give him a short respite until the next chapter makes its appearance' (p. 145). The reader naturally has very little choice in the matter, and original readers waiting for a month for the next instalment may have thought the respite long rather than short. However, two or three words in that sentence associate the reader with the characters and events in the chapter. In it, Captain Crowe, imitating Sir Launcelot's behaviour, assaults a group of farmers quite indiscriminately and without provocation. Litigation ensues, in which the most litigious of the farmers, Geoffrey Prickle, is effectively humbled by Sir Launcelot. It is a chapter in which Sir Launcelot's patience is tried, in which Captain Crowe has trespassed upon the king's highway, and in which the respite reached after justice has been done satisfies everyone concerned.

While I am not going to argue that *Sir Launcelot Greaves* is a great novel or an unjustly neglected masterpiece, I think it has a good deal more importance in the history of the novel than it has been given credit for. It is also an important landmark in Smollett's development as a writer. Smollett probably wrote more than any other author in the eighteenth century, and his writings cover a wider range than those of any other writer. His creative energies appear as a restless search for form. His first three novels were published within a space of just over five years. Between the publication of *Ferdinand Count Fathom* in February 1753, and the commencement of *Sir Launcelot Greaves* in January 1760, he published his translation of *Don Quixote* and a revised version of *Peregrine Pickle*, as well as a body of non-fiction. Several explanations have been put forward to account for the absence of a new piece of fiction from Smollett between 1753 and 1760, and most of them are plausible. I should like to add to these by suggesting that Smollett was too much of an experimenter, even an innovator, to try the same formula which he had used so successfully in *Roderick Random*, *Peregrine Pickle*, and *Ferdinand Count Fathom*.

In *Sir Launcelot Greaves*, Smollett reconsiders his narrative resources. The reader is encouraged or obliquely coerced into identifying with more than one character, and he is rhetorically associated with different characters at different times in the novel. This is a technique that Smollett was to exploit triumphantly in *Humphry Clinker*. There, the multiple point of view is achieved by epistolary correspondence, and the reader sees the same event through the eyes of different characters. The point of view in *Sir Launcelot Greaves* is shifted from character to character, and Smollett encourages the reader to respond to a given situation or development as if he were the character concerned. It is not particularly well done, partly because Smollett is relying on a rhetorical technique rather than a structural one (as in *Humphry Clinker*).

It is unfortunate that Smollett chose the quixotic pattern for his serial experiment, as the pattern has masked the narrative resources that he deploys in the novel, and it has become more of a stick to beat the novel with than anything else. I think it is unlikely that Smollett had planned the entire novel when he began writing, and the quixotic formula became more of a handicap than an asset as the work progressed. In 1760, it would have been apparent that only Charlotte Lennox had attempted a narrative use of the quixotic form with some success. Smollett, with a successful translation of *Don Quixote* and three well-received novels to his credit, might have thought that he could exploit the form in a better fashion. However, I think the major theme of the novel took over, and he found himself using the form as a means of saying something about madness and insanity, eccentricity and idiosyncrasy. The ironic inference that the reader is eventually cajoled into making is that Sir Launcelot's activities, while admittedly curious, are nevertheless a good deal less mad than those of many of the other characters. More importantly, Sir Launcelot is not guilty of immoral or uncharitable behaviour, while others, such as Justice Gobble, who is supposed to be a model of propriety and sanity, are. Sir Launcelot may be quixotic, but he is not wicked, and Smollett has made an important moral point: that the reader will do well to consider the possibility that good and evil can occur—all too often—in guises other than the conventional or expected ones. Sir Launcelot may appear to be mad, and is even so described, but his activities are prompted by value-charged motives, and his problem is that of finding a socially acceptable mode of behaviour that nevertheless accommodates his violent passions and his thwarted love.

Sir Launcelot Greaves thus reveals a new concern and commitment in Smollett to a story or plot animated and supported by moral principles. In reading *Peregrine Pickle*, it is sometimes difficult not to be a little distressed by the absence, or at least invisibility, of a hint from the author that Peregrine's behaviour is not always consistent with the highest ethical standards. (I am, of course, over-stating the matter, but the gestures towards morality in *Peregrine Pickle* often appear to be ritualistic obeisances and nothing more.) The same is true to a slightly lesser extent in *Roderick Random* and *Ferdinand Count Fathom*. In the latter novel, Smollett had delineated an impossibly vile character, and the overt moralizing in that novel contributes greatly to its failure as a work of the creative imagination. I think that Smollett was sensibly aware of this failure and tried to remedy the moral didacticism of *Ferdinand Count Fathom* by less obviously self-conscious devices in *Sir Launcelot Greaves*. In attempting to display a greater sense of moral awareness than he had before, he cultivated more assiduously the reader's co-operation and collaboration.

Some external evidence for this shift in Smollett's concern for moral values in his writings can be found in the *Continuation of the Complete History of England*, which he was writing and publishing at the same time as *Sir Launcelot Greaves*. In it, he writes of Samuel Richardson,

> The laudable aim of inlisting the passions on the side of virtue, was successfully pursued by Richardson, in his Pamela, Clarissa, and Grandison; a species of writing equally new and extraordinary, where, mingled with much superfluity and impertinence, we find a sublime system of ethics, an amazing knowledge, and command of human nature.

This comment may be helpfully contrasted with one on Fielding: 'The genius of Cervantes was transfused into the novels of Fielding, who painted the characters, and ridiculed the follies of life with equal strength, and propriety.'[12] Two rather obvious inferences may be made from these comments. While writing *Sir Launcelot Greaves*, Smollett had his mind on other matters (part of the time he was in prison), but he had been sufficiently impressed with Richardson's novels to single out their moral orientation as an important feature when he was writing about literature in his *Continuation*. For that reason Smollett perhaps wanted the marriage of Sir Launcelot and Aurelia to have far-reaching moral results: 'They were admired, esteemed, and applauded by every person of taste, sentiment, and benevolence; at the same time, beloved, revered, and almost adored by the common people, among whom they suffered not the merciless hand of indigence or misery to seize one single sacrifice' (p. 210). In none of Smollett's other novels do we find such an emphatic statement of the universally benevolent effects that marriage can have.[13]

If Smollett found the genius of Cervantes transfused into the novels of Fielding, was he attempting to make the same transfusion in *Sir Launcelot Greaves*? As I have suggested, I think he may have started out with that intention, but he quickly discovered that the adoption of a quixotic pattern or form did not necessarily ensure that the 'genius of Cervantes' would breathe life into his story. In Cervantes and Fielding it is not the superficial activities and peregrinations of the characters that count for so much, as the analyses and representations of human nature. In *Sir Launcelot Greaves*, Smollett exhibits a greater interest in the moral implications of his characters' activities and behaviour than he had in the earlier novels. It is, to be sure, only slightly greater, but he is unmistakably more concerned with the outward effects of behaviour than before. To a certain extent, comedy has given way to morality, sometimes too much so, and Smollett did not find for this novel a style of sufficient comprehensiveness to conflate moral guidance and narrative resourcefulness.

The novel thus falls into that well-filled category: interesting failures. At the risk of protesting too much, I should like to argue that it is more interesting than others in this category, including that other 'interesting failure' by Smollett, *Ferdinand Count Fathom*. It shows Smollett experimenting with form in order to find a means of displaying a new moral consciousness in his fiction. However limited its success may be, it led Smollett to the greatest of his creative achievements, *Humphry Clinker*. The work is also important in the history of the development of the novel, not just because of its serial, illustrated publication, but because in it Smollett proved that a reader's interest could be sustained over a long period and that there was a market for serial fiction. That the market was not fully catered for until much later does not invalidate Smollett's achievement.

The novel also indicates that authors were becoming increasingly aware of and sensitive to their audiences. New techniques and devices had to be found for coaxing the reader into the novel, both as observer and imaginative participant, and Smollett can be given some credit for at least showing the limitations of one approach. Finally, I think that the novel demonstrates, perhaps negatively, that without an underlying moral stratum of ideas about human nature and its moral constraints, fiction will lack cogency and coherence.

NOTES

1. Paul-Gabriel Boucé, *The Novels of Tobias Smollett* (London, 1976). My indebtedness to Professor Boucé's study, particularly to a paragraph on pp. 178–79, will be apparent.
2. James Beattie, 'On Laughter, and Ludicrous Composition', in *Essays* (Edinburgh, 1776), p. 605.
3. Tobias Smollett, *The Life and Adventures of Sir Launcelot Greaves*, ed. David Evans (London, 1973), pp. 12–13. Page references given in text hereafter.
4. On this point, I am in some disagreement with Professor Boucé; see particularly pp. 184–85.
5. Sir Walter Scott, *On Novelists and Fiction*, ed. Ioan Williams (London, 1968), p. 61.
6. Lewis Mansfield Knapp, *Tobias Smollett: Doctor of Men and Manners* (Princeton, 1949), pp. 228–30.
7. Boucé, p. 183.
8. Wolfgang Iser, *The Implied Reader* (Baltimore and London, 1974), p. xiii.
9. As Robert D. Mayo points out in *The English Novel in the Magazines 1740–1815* (Evanston, Illinois, 1962), pp. 276–78, it is important to remember that Smollett's novel was not the first piece of fiction to be published in parts, though *Sir Launcelot Greaves* was the first 'long piece of original fiction written expressly for publication in a British magazine' (p. 277).
10. The illustrations for *Sir Launcelot Greaves*, and for Smollett's other novels as well, have been expertly examined by Dr. Guilland Sutherland in her Ph.D. thesis, *Illustrations to Tobias Smollett's Novels, 1748–1832* (Edinburgh University, 1975).

11. In *Ferdinand Count Fathom*, one finds, in addition to the author's preface, a number of addresses to the reader, as well as the famous authorial outburst at the end of chapter 49. These are, however, different in style and structure from those in *Sir Launcelot Greaves*.

12. Tobias Smollett, *Continuation of the Complete History of England* (London, 1760–61), IV, 128, 127.

13. There are muted statements about the beneficial effects of marriage in *Roderick Random* and *Peregrine Pickle*, but none of these is so unqualified as the marriage of Sir Launcelot and Aurelia. Fielding's similar conclusion to *Tom Jones* is worth noting: 'And such is their Condescension, their Indulgence, and their Beneficence to those below them, that there is not a neighbour, a Tenant, or a Servant, who doth not most gratefully bless the Day when Mr. *Jones* was married to his *Sophia*.'

9

Appearance and Reality in *Humphry Clinker*

by R. D. S. JACK

It was Robert Giddings who suggested that the one moral point made in *Humphry Clinker* concerned the difference between appearance and reality. He did not himself develop upon this thesis and indeed indicated that Smollett 'seems for the most part unaware of it'.[1] But an overtly didactic approach to the theme would have been completely out of place in a work which makes its comments much more subtly.[2] I believe that various possible oppositions between appearance and reality are explored in *Humphry Clinker*, and that while they do not form the thematic core of a novel which self-evidently does not have a thematic core, an examination of this topic does lead to a more thorough understanding of the work.

To begin with, the two central narrative lines in the novel are examples of this opposition. Wilson who appears to be a poor actor and therefore wholly unsuitable socially as a marriage partner for Lydia is actually the son of a respected family and so an ideal husband! Humphry, the unwanted derelict, turns out to be Matthew's natural child. The novel contains two 'discovery' plots and in the simplest terms we move from appearance to reality; illusion to truth. But Smollett goes to some trouble to develop these basic situations and he does so in contrasting ways.

With Wilson, the audience is let in on the secret from the outset. In his own letter he indicates that he is concealing his true identity, while Lydia at an early stage writes, 'I am still persuaded that he is not what he appears to be' (p. 37).[3] The various disguises he chooses strengthen the idea of a man who is sustaining an illusion. He initially makes his living as an actor (a creator of illusions). He passes himself off as a seller of spectacles, thus keeping others in darkness by pretending to improve their sight. In short, he accepts that in order to gain his genuine ends he must adapt to a world which worships appearance. He does this so successfully that poor Lydia at the fancy dress party faints at the sight of a man dressed up as one of the characters Wilson had portrayed in the theatre and later when he actually rides past, she thinks he is a ghost, 'Good God! did he really appear? or was it only a phantom, a pale spectre to apprise me of his death?' (p. 349). On the one hand, therefore, he draws sincere characters into his world of illusion and deception. Lydia, after all, deceives her family in order to maintain the liaison. But more importantly he shows up a society which in many ways is anxious to accept the appearance and blind itself to the reality due to social prejudices. His subterfuge is occasioned by his refusal to go along with an 'arranged' marriage. Its success is largely sustained because people are guided in their judgements by preconceptions of class. Who would look for a man of respectable family among a company of players? The most extreme and most comic example of this sort of blindness is, of course, Jerry. So long as Wilson is an actor, he is beneath contempt—'I know not what to call him' (p. 36). As soon as he is a prospective landowner, he becomes 'one of the most accomplished young fellows in England' (p. 374). Wilson's answer, then, is actively to use the weapons of a prejudiced society against that society. His energetic embracing of his world of illusion serves to highlight a variety of more pernicious illusions harboured by others.

Humphry Clinker's situation is entirely different. As readers we are given no earlier hints of his true pedigree. We therefore accept him as the simple servant he believes himself to be. And Humphry's simplicity, even more than Wilson's acting, condemns the society around him as one which worships appearance and denies true worth. Admittedly it also makes him act foolishly as when he tries to rescue Matthew from a non-existent drowning but generally he stands out as a figure of simple virtue lost in a world which cannot understand honest values. Smollett uses a variety of techniques to underline this point. Most obviously there are direct character contrasts. His simple appearance and sincere love for Win are set against the dandified appearance and hypocritical wooing of Dutton. His honest (if naïve) Christianity is set beside Tabitha's egocentric brand of the same creed. ('God forbid that I should lack christian charity; but charity begins at huom', p. 190.) At other times his oppressed situation provides Matthew Bramble with the opportunity to expatiate on the way in which men pay lip service to ideals which in practice their every action contradicts. Such an instance occurs when first we meet Clinker and Matthew castigates the landlord as a 'Christian of bowels' (p. 113). This is a technique which works in reverse, for occasionally the straightforward vision of Clinker is used to reveal Bramble's own besetting prejudice—his rigidly hierarchical vision of society. Thus when the master orders his servant to cease preaching on the grounds that such an occupation ill befits one of the lower orders, Clinker, with apparent naïvety, counters:

> May not the new light of God's grace shine upon the poor and ignorant in their humility, as well as upon the wealthy and the philosopher in all his pride of human learning? (p. 170)

From the moment he appears, rejected as a man because of his poverty and as a postilion because his trousers split, Clinker is relentlessly used to indicate the hypocrisy and the superficiality of those values which permeate society—that is, both the appearance which conceals a directly contradictory reality and the appearance, overconcern with which, causes false, prejudiced attitudes. The two combine in the scene where Humphry is arrested, an incident which reminds one of the Morality dramas at the stage where Vice rules and Dame Chastity is confined to the stocks as a whore. What society is this in which the most honest of men can be convicted as a thief? What degree of prejudice must have existed in the minds of those spectators who see sure signs of villainy in a face which is 'the very picture of simplicity'? (p. 178) What double standards exist in a court of law whose presiding judge sends to jail a man whom he knows innocent? What hope is there for integrity when the hesitation

211

of simplicity is construed as prevarication and religious reservations on man's generally sinful nature seized upon as proof of
particular guilt? This is a court of justice in appearance only. It
is also a microcosm of that larger society which is characterized
by prejudice, the worship of externals, deceit and hypocrisy. In
their different ways the passive Humphry and the ingenious
Wilson underline this fact.

In terms of the initial distinction between reality and appearance, we have three rather different levels. There is first of all
the simple dramatic opposition we have just been discussing.
But this 'discovery' element on the narrative level has introduced two further approaches to the theme. There is the level of
hypocrisy and deceit in which the truth is known and a 'mask'
consciously created in order to make others accept that 'mask'
for the 'face'. The perpetrators of such situations inevitably feed
on the folly of another group who see only the surface and
accept it with no desire to probe deeper. Their dedication to
worldly values obscures their vision, leaving them a prey both
to the trickery of the manipulators and to the surface attractions
of the new, luxurious, town society which Smollett appears to
have distrusted so much. One group deserves the other. One
presents a false appearance in order to obscure the reality; the
other accepts false appearances sometimes wilfully, sometimes
due to folly. Clearly Smollett is arguing that such behaviour
characterizes much of British society in the later eighteenth
century. The next portion of this study will be concerned with
this, ultimately moral, argument and I shall be arguing that he
sees falsity of this sort in individual characters, in a wide variety
of institutions and in the deepest human relationships of friendship and love.

The third level is the most complex of all and in a sense it may
appear to go beyond the opposition between reality and appearance. There are five letter writers in *Humphry Clinker*.[4] Each
writer views life and frequently identical situations in life very
differently. If Matthew, Jerry, Lydia, Win and Tabitha each
observes Bath and paints for us a picture which bears no
resemblance to that presented by the others, where then is the
reality, where the appearance? In the final part of this article I
shall endeavour to show first of all how Smollett does introduce
this idea of 'appearance' as vision—people, events, countries

viewed through the prejudices and preconceptions of a variety of observers. But I shall also, through an analysis of his literary techniques, prove that he usually guides us towards a more balanced overview, using our knowledge of the characters, their social positions, their agreements and disagreements to achieve this end.

The novel is, of course, full of hypocrites. Many of the most memorable prove to be Tabitha's suitors. Sir Ulic Mackilligut feigns an extreme passion for her, but his true motives are perceived by Bramble early on. 'He is said to be much out at elbows; and, I believe, has received false intelligence with respect to her fortune' (p. 77). This is indeed the case[5] and on discovering the true state of her purse the ingenious knight extricates himself from the situation by kicking her beloved dog Chowder, a sin for which there is no possible forgiveness. The Scottish advocate Micklewhimmen is an even more extreme example of the hypocritical suitor. He begins by learning her governing obsession of the moment and professes to share it:

> As for Mrs. Tabitha, his respects were particularly addressed to her, and he did not fail to mingle them with religious reflections, touching free grace, knowing her bias to methodism, which he also professed upon a calvinistical model. (p. 207)

If Mackilligut was a hypocrite in love, Micklewhimmen's whole life is based on hypocrisy. His addresses to Tabitha have no serious intentions beyond making his life in Scarborough more comfortable. He feigns lameness so that people will cater for his every need. He drinks medicine which proves to be claret and generally fools the majority of the company into a spirit of sympathy and servitude. The complete falsity of his position is ludicrously revealed during the fire. The supposed invalid is one of the first to escape, 'running as nimble as a buck along the passage' (p. 208). And when Tabitha seeks his aid, he just pushes her down, ironically in so doing uttering one of her own favourite phrases, 'Na, na, gude faith, charity begins at hame' (p. 209). Despite his later desperate, sophistic attempts to justify his behaviour, he is finally seen by all in his true colours.

It is, however, undeniably the case that Tabitha attracts such

213

hypocrites because her all-consuming desire for marriage blinds her to their true natures. She sees them as she wants them to be and so is the perfect gull. She also indulges in her own brand of hypocrisy. Once the possibility of matrimony emerges, she will forsake all her apparent principles. As Bramble puts it:

> Though she is a violent church-woman, of the most intolerant zeal, I believe in my conscience she would have no objection, at present, to treat on the score of matrimony with an Anabaptist, Quaker, or Jew; and even ratify the treaty at the expense of her own conversion. (p. 94)

Even the freethinking Lismahago's direct questioning of Christian tenets meets with little opposition from the pious spinster, who has decided *a priori* that he is 'a prodigy of learning and sagacity' (p. 232). Primarily, however, Smollett presents her as the sort of person who accepts 'appearances' if they are pleasing to her and has no desire to probe deeper. Indeed, she goes further and interprets the most obvious situations in an entirely fallacious manner, albeit consistent with her ruling passion. It does not need a hypocrite to mislead Tabitha. She is quite capable of misleading herself when faced with honesty. The most obvious instance of this occurs when Barton begins his rather timid wooing of Lydia. Both Matthew and Jerry see clearly the true nature of the young man's desires. Both also see the malicious role being played by Lady Griskin. But poor Tabitha errs at the outset:

> she mistakes, or affects to mistake, the meaning of his courtesy, which is rather formal and fulsome; she returns his compliments with hyperbolical interest. (p. 127)

and remains entirely deluded until the ludicrous/pathetic finale.

It is no coincidence that Win, who has largely modelled herself on Tabitha, can also be misled by appearance in matters of the heart. The flamboyantly dressed, glib-tongued Dutton, by appealing to her desire to rise above her station, briefly wins her away from Clinker. In situations of this sort Smollett is not only attacking those who, for selfish purposes, present a false mask to the world; he is also satirizing those whose prejudices, ruling passions or even simple naïvety make them over-anxious to accept illusion for fact.

That said, the hypocrites in *Humphry Clinker* outnumber the gulls. Often too their hypocrisy is not set against folly but integrity. Serle may have been over-generous to Paunceford initially but his quiet stoicism in the face of his erstwhile protégé's complete ingratitude can only arouse admiration. Smollett skilfully contrasts the two characters. The one, once wealthy now poor; the other rising from poverty to riches. The one solitary; the other surrounded by gay company. The one even now refusing to denounce his friend; the other proclaiming his gratitude in words to others but staunchly avoiding any private confrontation or any practical return for all the benevolence he has been shown. The world of *Humphry Clinker* is one in which deviousness triumphs with great regularity, leaving honesty to suffer.

On a broader level, the worlds of law, politics and literature are shown to be false; further clear symptoms of a society in which appearance belies reality. Clinker's court case has already been mentioned but it deserves more detailed treatment because in it Smollett mounts a brief but powerful satire on the state of the law in England.[6] Everything is the opposite of what it appears to be. The innocent Clinker is accused of robbery by a man who himself turns out to be a thief. He is defended by Martin, the highwayman who is guilty of the very crime for which Clinker is being tried. The judge, with all his appearance of power, is in fact powerless. Legally he cannot deny the sworn evidence of the postilion. He cannot even grant Clinker bail but must send him to jail. This is in spite of the fact that he and everyone else with any influence in the court KNOW his innocence, the postilion's knavery and the true identity of the guilty party. What we are seeing is a grotesque charade, but one which could conceivably result in wrongful execution.

We are also told that the Judge and Martin who oppose each other in the court room and should be sworn enemies, given the conflicting nature of their chosen professions, are in fact on quite intimate terms:

> Sometimes they smoke a pipe together very lovingly, when the conversation generally turns upon the nature of evidence. (p. 182)

There is a sense in which the image of the 'club' which this evokes, applies to the court situation generally. There are those (like Martin) who are members and know the rules. There are others (like Clinker) who are not and do not. The former argue and manipulate; the latter are bewildered and oppressed. For the first group the 'rules' sometimes seem to become an end in themselves, the whole activity is a sort of game in which rhetorical skills are valued above the facts of the case. For the second group everything is much more grave for in the end it is their lives which may be at stake.

Thus the opposition between appearance and reality in the court of Justice Buzzard could scarcely be more clearcut nor the implied satire more damning. An uninitiated observer would suppose the honest Clinker dishonest, the roguish postilion an earnest upholder of the law, the actual highwayman a clever lawyer expertly handling a difficult case, and the ineffectual judge all-powerful. As he observed the knowing looks passing from judge to defender, from thief-taker to thief-taker or heard the matter of fact, sometimes even lighthearted, tones of the major participants, he might be forgiven for thinking he was involved in some complex but essentially enjoyable game rather than watching a serious trial. But above all he would take a cynical act of complete injustice for the fair verdict which, on the most superficial level, it appears to be.

When Smollett turns his attention to politics, the opposition between reality and appearance is no less stark. Bramble and Jerry are taken to a levee arranged by the Duke of N——.[7] The whole event is itself a facade; a repetition of the sort of occasion held by the Duke when he possessed real power. Now, however, he is rejected and despised by the government of the day. His few remaining friends go through the motions as before 'to support the shadow of that power, which he no longer retains in substance' (p. 142). What appears to be a momentous political occasion is in fact a meaningless assembly.

Jerry and Bramble go there at the invitation of Barton, whose political and personal naïvety serves to highlight the deviousness of his fellow politicians. Their main companion is Captain C——, whose character and career reintroduce the theme of appearance and reality in highly complex fashion. To Barton, he is 'a man of shrewd parts' (p. 142), highly valued by the government. More reliable sources suggest that he was a fraudulent merchant who then became a spy in the English cause. Disguised as a Capuchin he hazarded his life in both France and Spain, gaining important information for the government. Jerry's letter, however, strongly suggests that he is a double agent; that he really is a priest and that his true allegiance lies with France. Their guide, therefore, is a man whose whole livelihood depends on deception and it would appear that he is in fact deceiving the very people who believe he is deceiving on their behalf.

But the major point stressed by Smollett in this vignette of British politics is that where one would expect wisdom, folly rules. He emphasizes this in a variety of ways, all bearing on the theme of reality and appearance. The Duke of N—— proves himself a complete buffoon, mistaking the identity of nearly everyone at his own gathering:

> So saying, he wheeled about; and going round the levee, spoke to every individual, with the most courteous familiarity; but he scarce ever opened his mouth without making some blunder, in relation to the person or business of the party with whom he conversed; so that he really looked like a comedian, hired to burlesque the character of a minister. (p. 145)

So idiotic is he that a Turkish guest actually mistakes him for a professional fool, holding it a great marvel that Britain is ruled by a 'counsel of ideots' (p. 144).

The comments of Captain C—— strengthen this impression. He explains at great length how the government in their planning for war proved themselves unaware that Cape Breton was an island. In his opinion:

> They are so ignorant, they scarce know a crab from a cauliflower; and then they are such dunces, that there's no making them comprehend the plainest proposition. (p. 143)

For only one contemporary politician does he have any respect and that is C—— T——.[8] But while the others appear wise yet are in fact foolish, Townshend belies truth in another way:

> There's no faith to be given to his assertions and no trust to be put in his promises. (p. 146)

In the legal world Bramble and his friends were faced with a facade of justice behind which lurked bribery, corruption and inadequate laws. In the political world they visit a man who clings to the appearance of power. They do this in the company of someone who appears to be a loyal Englishman but who is in all probability a double agent. They learn that behind the appearance of wisdom lies folly; behind promises and protestations of friendship lie falsity and political opportunism. Once more, briefly and poignantly, Smollett has indicated the great gap that exists between the appearance and the reality; the mask and the face.

The situation proves to be very much the same in the world of letters. Matthew and Jerry discover at least five different ways in which writers and scholars present a vision of themselves which is at odds with reality. There is first of all the conflict between the vision of the writer presented in his works and his private personality. Matthew in particular is upset to discover that one writer whose works he had read with particular pleasure, proves to be a dogmatic idiot, who can find reasons to condemn every other author except himself. And the more widely he mixes with men of letters, the more disillusioned he becomes. Fine ideas on paper may originate from petty, spiteful individuals intent only on self-advancement. As he writes to Dr. Lewis, 'For my part, I am shocked to find a man have sublime ideas in his head, and nothing but illiberal sentiments in his heart' (p. 138).

Related to this is the opposition between reputation and ability. In London Jerry is invited to meet the leading wits and professors of the day. The wits he finds insipid, confessing that he had 'never passed a duller evening in (his) life' (p. 149). The professors parade their love for argument and tedious long-winded explanations, but in so doing also reveal their ignorance. Wherever he and Matthew go it is the same story. Men of reputed genius prove boring companions and generally where they have been led to expect intelligence, open discussion and generosity of sentiment, they find ignorance, superficial conversation and intense personal jealousies.

Another and more glaring example of reality and appearance in conflict is uncovered at the lunch given by S——.[9] There, a number of minor writers are assembled. Almost without excep-

tion they have devised glaring eccentricities, hoping in this
manner to draw attention to themselves. Each of these eccentricities is completely at odds with the true character of the
individual concerned. Thus one wears spectacles despite
having particularly fine eyesight; another affects crutches
'though no man could leap over a stick with more agility'
(p. 157); a third pretends to hate the country, although he was
brought up there. They do these things because they are aware
that without idiosyncrasies they would be revealed for the
ordinary, boring people they are. As such they are perfect
representatives of a literary society, which the novel presents as
second-rate and hypocritical.

This falsity extends to their work. We learn that a book which
deals with the niceties of the English language has been written
by a Piedmontese; that a treatise on practical agriculture has
been completed by a man who 'had never seen corn growing in
his life' and that another mastermind has just finished a study of
his travels through Europe and Asia without himself venturing
out of London. All of these studies bear the appearance of long
research and serious thought. They turn out to be mere fantasies dreamt up by men whose own lives are as deceitful as the
literature they produce.

On a personal level too they prove as expert as either lawyers
or politicians at pretending friendship, while nursing envy or
hatred in their hearts. This is most fully explored in Jerry's
description of S——'s party. We learn that every one of his
literary visitors is indebted to him in some way. As he talks with
them, the relationships appear to be uncomplicated and generous. Yet Jerry is soon to learn that a high proportion of the
critical abuse S—— has suffered in fact originated from the
pens of these very men.[10] His companion attributes such
behaviour to one source above all others. 'Envy (answered
Dick) is the general incitement' (p. 164). This is to echo a
judgement made earlier by Matthew, whose first encounter
with the London literati had led him to ponder on the same
subject:

> I am inclined to think, no mind was ever wholly exempt from
> envy; which, perhaps, may have been implanted as an instinct
> essential to our nature. (p. 138)

The literary world in *Humphry Clinker* is indeed a world of jealous factions, where minor criticisms lead to lifelong enmities; writers cannot bear to hear others praised and boost themselves by denigrating their rivals. Also, from a whole variety of angles, it is a world of appearance, peopled by men who create false images of themselves, show no integrity in their writing and gain reputations wholly at odds with their true ability. In letters, in politics and in law it is the image which is all important. True values are of secondary importance.

It is, I believe, because Smollett was so concerned with the theme of reality and appearance in *Humphry Clinker* that he devoted so much of the later part of the novel to a series of visits at which his central characters received starkly contrasting examples of hospitality. Hospitality is the outward, the social sign of friendship and love. In Scotland the group had uniformly received warm receptions. Indeed the only criticism proffered was that perhaps the Scots prided themselves too much on their hospitality.[11] Now in England between 30 September and 8 October, Bramble visits four different households. At the first, Lord Oxmington's, all is appearance. The meal is 'served up with much ostentation' (p. 321), but his Lordship only uses the event to demonstrate his own affluence and influence. He dismisses his guests as unfeelingly as he had treated them throughout the meal. There is no trace of real friendship here, as Bramble's furious reaction underlines.

The second visit, to Baynard, is in many ways similar. Once more the meal is ostentatious. It is composed almost entirely of foreign dishes; lacqueys stand behind the chairs and there is a veritable 'parade' of plate and china. Yet the rudeness shown by Mrs. Baynard, her aunt and son is even more extreme than Oxmington's. The difference lies in the disposition of poor Baynard. Crying, 'Friendship is undoubtedly the most precious balm of life!' (p. 333), he endeavours, despite his henpecked position, to make his old comrade welcome. But his infatuation for his wife has led him into a world in which 'appearance' is all. His house, once pleasant, has been extravagantly re-modelled according to her fashionable (if execrable) architectural tastes. His estate, once profitable, has been turned into walks, shrubberies and an economic disaster. The number of servants has been dramatically increased solely to impress others. And the poorer Baynard in fact becomes, the richer he must appear to be. His own genuine feelings remain but the world into which he invites Bramble and his company is false in every other particular as the ostentatious, friendless hospitality underlines.

The third visit, to Sir Thomas Bullford, in many ways represents an advance on the earlier ones. The pervading spirit is one of mirth; the meal appears to be more than adequate and his wife proves as friendly and genuine as Mrs. Baynard had been offhand and false. Yet we are still not in a world of genuine love and friendship. Bullford's guests are there primarily to promote his own enjoyment. He is more concerned with making them sources of laughter through his talent for practical joking than caring for their needs. It is, in this context, important that the meal, though good, is used as a practical joke, which convinces one guest that he is about to die. It is true that when Lismahago turns the tables on Bullford, the latter takes it in good spirit, but basically we have an egocentric host and, once more, the appearance of friendship rather than the genuine thing. After all, as Jerry points out, 'the greatest sufferer' (p. 346) of the baronet's wit is likely to be Bramble, whose health is not robust enough to stand the shocks and 'night-alarms' in which Bullford glories. A true friend would have understood this and desisted from self-indulgence.

Thus, before introducing the novel's three marriages, Smollett has used three contrasting visits to highlight the various false forms friendship and love may take. He has done this by continuing to examine, although in a different context, the opposition between appearance and reality. In the fourth and last visit, to Dennison, he presents the positive vision. Dennison's life-style contrasts in particular with that of Baynard. He is married to a loving wife completely lacking in pretentiousness. Instead of ruining a flourishing estate, he has turned one on the verge of ruin into a profitable enterprise. Instead of living beyond his means in order to keep up with the neighbours, he lives within his means and scorns their opinion of his household.[12] Now at last Bramble and his companions find hospitality, friendship and love free from pretence of any sort.

So far the oppositions between appearance and reality have

seemed quite clear and I think there is no doubt that Smollett intended to satirize eighteenth-century Britain, and in particular eighteenth-century England, as a land dominated at every level by false or superficial values. But he does choose to do this by presenting the opinions of five clearly contrasted characters. Of these at least three present misleading visions of themselves to society. Bramble's affected misanthropy conceals the heart of a sentimental philanthropist. Tabitha's prudery and extreme religious enthusiasm hide the passions born of long frustration. And Win in her letters depicts herself as a tight-lipped confidante before revealing to Molly every detail of gossip known to her. Each of the five sees his own 'reality' and often the definitions of that reality differ sharply. This is most obvious when they are visiting towns and passing comment on them. For Lydia, Bath is a place of wonder and romance:

> an earthly paradise. The Square, the Circus, and the Parades, put you in mind of the sumptuous palaces represented in prints and pictures; and the new buildings, such as Prince's row, Harlequin's row, Bladud's row, and twenty other rows, look like so many enchanted castles, raised on hanging terraces. (p. 68)

For Jerry, it is primarily an exciting social centre:

> I am, on the contrary, amazed to find so small a place so crowded with entertainment and variety. (p. 78)

For Bramble, viewing it with the eye of aged cynicism, it is 'the very centre of racket and dissipation' (p. 63), a gaudy show, signifying primarily the breakdown of a society in which everything and everybody had its appointed place. For Win it is where she dropped her petticoat and achieved a new worldly vision which places her in a position of superiority to Molly Jones: 'But this is all Greek and Latten to you, Molly' (p. 73). Tabitha's comments suggest that Bath as such makes no impression on her at all. She is more concerned with the practicalities of running the home in Wales and curbing the generosity of her brother to his servants. Yet she is writing formally to her housekeeper and the letters of the others strongly suggest that Bath, like any other place on earth, is merely a source of hypothetical husbands.

Each of these visions is the truth for its creator and on one level reality is what any individual chooses to believe. Smollett is, therefore, exploring a rather different aspect of the reality/appearance problem. In a sense there are as many Baths as people to view them. What is the truth about the town for Lydia is almost exactly the antithesis of the truth for Matthew. Smollett even introduces in Lismahago a character whose nature drives him to believe that the most evident truths are falsities, arguing his paradoxical convictions with great energy and ingenuity:

> I believe in my conscience he has rummaged, and read, and studied with indefatigable attention, in order to qualify himself to refute established maxims, and thus raise trophies for the gratification of polemical pride. (p. 237)

Yet Lismahago's sincerity is never seriously called into question. He is the most extreme example of the relativity of vision; one for whom each apparent truth must be, *a priori*, a falsity. The more obvious a situation appears to be, the more emphatically will Lismahago argue the contrary case.

But does Smollett leave us there? Does he simply say there is no absolute truth, just a number of perspectives? I do not think his position is as extreme as that, although he does patently argue that Bramble's Bath is as real for him as Lydia's for her. Perhaps a second comment on Lismahago will help to explain his position. Jerry also sums up the man's nature:

> The lieutenant was, by this time, become so polemical, that every time he opened his mouth out flew a paradox, which he maintained with all the enthusiasm of altercation; but all his paradoxes favoured strong of a partiality for his own country. (p. 237)

In each case (as here) we are given careful outlines of the prejudices, education and nature of the characters whose opinions dominate the book. Lismahago, as a man who questions 'appearances' in a society which fosters falsity in so many forms must and does strike the note of truth with some frequency. When he argues against Bramble that the Union has done nothing but ill for the Scots, we sense that he is in many instances right. But we know his love of paradoxicality and his intense patriotism and so realize that he is probably over-stating.[13] In a similar way we know Lydia's confined upbringing and the romantic novels on which she has been nurtured. We consider her vision of Bath in that light. Bramble's ill-health and defensive misanthropy; Win's superficiality and Tabitha's governing obsession—all these are made clear to the reader and his judgements are tempered by that knowledge.

But such breadth of vision combined with the knowledge of individual idiosyncrasies can also work in the opposite way, arguing for incontrovertible truths as well as conditioned responses. When Bramble nearly dies everyone is overcome with relief at his recovery. Here the disparity of character argues for the fact that undeniably he is a good and lovable man. If Tabitha and Lydia, Jerry and Win (not to mention Humphry) all lament then the ultimate benevolence of this self-styled misanthropist can be in no doubt. The case is the same with Clinker. Everyone, although for different reasons, vouches for his worth and integrity. For Jerry, he is 'honest Humphry' (p. 185), a man for whose courage and loyalty he has the highest esteem. For Matthew, his 'character is downright simplicity, warmed with a kind of enthusiasm, which renders him very susceptible of gratitude and attachment to his benefactors' (p. 186). He wins over Tabitha after making such a bad impression initially. In her opinion, he is 'a sober civilized fellow; very respectful, and very industrious; and . . . a good Christian into the bargain' (p. 132). Even Lydia terms him 'a deserving young man' (p. 297), while Win expresses her admiration in the most extreme fashion possible by marrying him. The very different personalities of the letter writers guarantee that when they do agree on any topic, the reader is unlikely to arrive at a different conclusion.

If Smollett sometimes uses unanimity of vision to guide his readers' reactions, he also uses what I shall, for convenience, term 'inversion of vision', for the same purpose. If someone's most confirmed prejudices are overturned, this is strong evidence that the influence upon him or her is real. It is in this sense that I believe *Humphry Clinker* to be, on balance, a book written with a bias in Scotland's favour. Not because Lismahago argues so ingeniously, for Lismahago's character is built on ingenuity and paradoxicality. Nor because Smollett drops any pretence at narrative continuity to focus on the country's characteristics.[14] But because in Scotland, Bramble the cynic at times begins to sound like Lydia in his romanticism and enthusiasm:

> I should be very ungrateful, dear Lewis, if I did not find myself disposed to think and speak favourably of this people, among whom I have met with more kindness, hospitality, and rational entertainment, in a few weeks, than ever I received in any other country during the whole course of my life. (p. 267)

He sees Loch Lomond and finds it 'romantic beyond imagination' (p. 286). These reactions contrast so markedly with his jaundiced opinions of Bath, London and Scarborough that we feel Scotland must really possess the qualities he attributes to it.

Sometimes too, we are faced with comments which, although apparently opposed, are in fact complementary. Both Win and Tabitha, for example, discuss the position of servants in Scotland. Here we have an initial inclination to believe the former. For the most part she is presented as foolish and impressionable but she is herself a servant. Just as we might be prepared to accept Jerry's assessment of University life or Bramble's comments on estate management in preference to the views of the others, so in this case we know that she alone has first-hand experience of the situation. And for Win, although the Scots are 'civil enuff' (p. 257), she is horrified by their treatment of menials: 'the sarvants of the country . . . are pore drudges, many of them without shoes or stockings' (p. 257). Her horror is only matched by Tabitha's enthusiasm. She finds the whole situation admirable and wonders why their enlightened approach is not more widely practised:

> . I don't see why the servants of Wales shouldn't drink fair water, and eat hot cakes and barley cale, as they do in Scotland, without troubling the botcher above once a quarter. (p. 313)

We know, however, that one of Tabitha's principal aims in life is to keep the lower orders existing on the most minimal expense account possible. Paradoxically, therefore, her approbation serves to strengthen rather than oppose Win's evidence. Given the social situation of the one and the known prejudices of the other, it becomes clear that Scots treat visiting gentry with overpowering kindness but that their servants are resolutely kept in penury.

To 'unanimity of vision', 'inversion of vision' and 'opposed but complementary visions', we might add finally the 'development of vision'. It is true that most of the characters in *Humphry Clinker* do not change much throughout the novel despite the many experiences which befall them.[15] The major exception to this rule is Lydia. Naïve, idealistic and easily led at the outset, she becomes gradually more forceful and realistic as the journey progresses:

> There is such malice, treachery and dissimulation even among professed friends and intimate companions, as cannot fail to strike a virtuous mind with horror; and when Vice quits the stage for a moment, her place is immediately occupied by Folly, which is often too serious to excite anything but compassion. (p. 348)

These words were not penned by Bramble, as one might have supposed, but by Lydia towards the end of her travels. Her opinion confirms the viewpoints of her uncle and brother but it is more striking because it comes from one who, at the outset, saw romance and sincerity everywhere. It is her experience of society which has transformed her outlook and we sense that she cannot be wrong.

If we apply all this evidence to the topic of reality and appearance, we may say that on one level Smollett does argue that everyone's perception of reality differs. As Donald Bruce notes, 'Much of *Humphry Clinker* is a bland statement of the subjectivity of human outlook.'[16] At the same time, using the techniques I have analysed, Smollett gives the reader an 'overview'. This 'overview' is not imposed. The reader is invited to enter and sympathize with the opinions of each letter writer. They are all, in their own ways, lovable. But he is given insights into their strengths and limitations; their visions and prejudices. In any situation, therefore, he can weigh up the comparative authority of each writer's evidence. In this way Smollett uses the breadth of his chosen epistolary form to guide us towards the truth as he sees it. By drawing together a variety of limited outlooks he provides us with a varied and convincing picture of British life in the late eighteenth century. Behind all the 'appearances' we perceive a reality.

NOTES

1. Robert Giddings, *The Tradition of Smollett* (London, 1967), p. 149.
2. I cannot agree with the allegorical interpretation of the work advanced by M. A. Goldberg in *Smollett and the Scottish School* (Albuquerque, 1959): 'But symbolically, the expedition is a moral journey which culminates in the *expediting* or *freeing* of Humphry Clinker from the fetters of poverty, hunger, nakedness, and anonymity', p. 153.
3. All quotations and page references are taken from *Humphry Clinker*, ed. Angus Ross (Harmondsworth, 1978).
4. This excludes the single letter written by 'Wilson' to Lydia from Gloucester.
5. Win is the conveyor of this false information as she reveals in her letter to Molly (Bath, 26 April).
6. Later he deals much more favourably with the legal system in Scotland.
7. Thomas Pelham-Holles (1693–1768), Duke of Newcastle.
8. Charles Townshend (1725–67), Chancellor of the Exchequer in Pitt's second ministry.
9. Smollett himself.
10. Much of Smollett's unpopularity derived from the fact that for some time he was director of the influential literary journal *The Critical Review*.
11. 'I am afraid that even their hospitality is not quite free of ostentation' (Matthew to Lewis; Edinburgh, 8 August).
12. Laurence Brander, *Tobias Smollett* (London, 1951), notes, 'Matthew Bramble, in his letters about Dennison and Baynard, expresses the eighteenth-century nostalgia for the ideal country life, the craving for a well-ordered society based on the perennial round of toil on the good earth.' It is a nostalgia which Smollett appears to have shared to some degree.
13. Louis L. Martz, *The Later Career of Tobias Smollett* (Yale, 1942), argues persuasively that 'The satire of England and encomium of Scotland may well represent Smollett's attempt to reconcile himself with those of his countrymen who were offended with *The Present State of All Nations*' (p. 130). But Smollett does find much to criticize in Scotland in *Humphry Clinker* and he is careful to make its most voluble protagonist (Lismahago) a man whose views are suspect for the reasons noted above.
14. See M. A. Goldberg, *op. cit.*, p. 163.
15. See Robert Giddings, *op. cit.*, p. 144. 'There is one important aspect of character lacking, however, and this is development. Matthew Bramble's character does not develop as, for example, Peregrine's does.'
16. Donald Bruce, *Radical Doctor Smollett* (London, 1964), p. 55. But he also comments that 'since it allows for the variations of prejudice and opinion, the book is all the more valid as a survey of England [*sic*] in the late eighteenth century.'

Notes on Contributors

ALAN BOLD was born in 1943 in Edinburgh where he attended university and trained as a journalist. Since 1966 he has been a full-time writer and visual artist. He has published many books of poetry including *To Find the New*, *The State of the Nation* and *This Fine Day* as well as a selection in *Penguin Modern Poets 15*. He has edited *The Penguin Book of Socialist Verse*, *The Martial Muse: Seven Centuries of War Poetry*, the *Cambridge Book of English Verse 1939–75*, *Making Love: The Picador Book of Erotic Verse*, *The Bawdy Beautiful: The Sphere Book of Improper Verse* and *Mounts of Venus: The Picador Book of Erotic Prose*. He has also written critical books on *Thom Gunn and Ted Hughes*, *George Mackay Brown* and *The Ballad*.

PAUL-GABRIEL BOUCÉ was born in 1936 in Versailles and belongs to a Cotentin family. He was educated in France, Britain and the U.S.A. (Dijon; Maidstone; Phillips Academy, Andover, Mass.; Lyons). After two years as a Naval Reserve officer he was, in 1963, appointed lecturer in English literature at the Sorbonne where he took his D.Litt. in 1970 on Smollett's novels. Since then he has always taught at the Sorbonne, and, in 1971, was appointed Professor of eighteenth-century English literature. Professor Boucé has published extensively on Smollett and the eighteenth-century novel: he is co-editor (with G. S. Rousseau) of *Tobias Smollett* (1971), editor of the 'Oxford English Novels' critical edition of *Roderick Random* (1979), and author of *The Novels of Tobias Smollett* (1976). He is currently editor-in-chief of *Etudes Anglaises* and editor of *Sexuality in Eighteenth-century Britain*. He is Former Visiting Fellow, Wolfson College, Cambridge.

DAVID DAICHES was born in Edinburgh in 1912 and educated at George Watson's College (Edinburgh), the University of Edinburgh, and Balliol College, Oxford. He has held academic posts at Oxford, Chicago, Cornell, Cambridge and the University of Sussex (of which he was one of the founders in 1961). He is the author of over forty works of criticism, biography, autobiography, literary and cultural history, including *A Critical History of English Literature*, *The Novel and the Modern World*, *Robert Burns*, *The Paradox of Scottish Culture*, *Scotland and the Union*, *Edinburgh*, *Two Worlds* (autobiography). He holds honorary degrees from the Sorbonne, Brown University (U.S.A.), Edinburgh, Sussex and Stirling. Professor Daiches (F.R.S.L., F.R.S.E.) is now Director of the Institute for Advanced Studies in the Humanities of Edinburgh University, an Honorary Professor of Stirling University, and Professor Emeritus of the University of Sussex. He is Gifford Lecturer for 1982–83.

ROBERT GIDDINGS was born in Worcester in 1935 and educated at the universities of Bristol and Keele. He has been Lecturer in English and Communication Studies at the City of Bath Technical College since 1964; and was Fulbright Exchange Professor, St. Louis, Missouri, from 1975–76 and Tutor, the Open University, 1971–81. His publications are *The Tradition of Smollett* (1967), *You Should See Me in Pyjamas* (1981) and (with Elizabeth Holland) *J. R. R. Tolkien—The Shores of Middle-Earth* (1981). He contributes to the *New Statesman, Dickens Studies Newsletter, Tribune, New Society, Music and Letters, New Tolkien Newsletter*; and broadcasts and writes scripts for the B.B.C. and I.T.V.

DAMIAN GRANT was born in London in 1940, and attended London University where he completed an M.A, on Smollett in 1966. Since then he has been a lecturer in English literature at Manchester University, teaching for a year abroad (Tunis) in 1975–76. He contributed a study of *Realism* to the 'Critical Idiom' series in 1970 and edited *Ferdinand Count Fathom* for the 'Oxford English Novels' series in 1971. His *Tobias Smollett: A Study in Style* appeared in 1977. Damian Grant has also published poems and articles on modern poetry in various journals.

R. D. S. JACK was born in Ayr in 1941 and educated at Ayr Academy. He graduated from Glasgow University and is now Reader in English literature at the University of Edinburgh. His publications include *Scottish Prose 1550– 1700, The Italian Influence on Scottish Literature* and *A Choice of Scottish Verse 1560–1660.*

JOHN VALDIMIR PRICE was born in 1937 in Lamesa, Texas, and attended the University of Texas. After teaching for three years in California he took up a post in 1965 at the University of Edinburgh where he is currently Senior Lecturer in English literature. He is author of *The Ironic Hume* (1965), *David Hume* (1968) and *Tobias Smollett: The Expedition of Humphry Clinker* (1973); he is co-editor of Hume's *A Letter to a Gentleman* (1967) and editor of Hume's *Dialogues Concerning Natural Religion* (1976). He is currently preparing a book on sexual manners and morality in the eighteenth-century novel.

IAN CAMPBELL ROSS was born in Bristol in 1950 and is a graduate of the universities of Sussex, Dublin and Edinburgh. He was Lecturer in English literature at the University of Birmingham from 1975 to 1977 since when he has been Lecturer in Modern English at Trinity College, Dublin. He has written frequently on eighteenth-century fiction, most recently on the Irish novel before 1830. He is preparing an 'Oxford English Novels' edition of *Tristram Shandy.*

TOM SCOTT was born in 1918 in Glasgow and attended Thornwood Primary School, Partick, and Hyndland Secondary. In 1931, as a result of the slump, the family moved to St. Andrews where he attended Madras College, leaving school when fifteen. He worked first in a butcher's, learning much about farm and peasant life as a result, then became a builder's apprentice.

He owes much of his real education in this period to school and university friends, beginning to write seriously in his late teens. Conscripted in 1939 into the R.A.P.C. at Perth, he saw service in Nigeria for two years. His first poems were published in 1941 in London where he settled for ten years till 1954. Tom Scott found his Scots voice in 1950 and with it his sense of direction as a writer, having become dissatisfied with his work in English. He has published six volumes of verse (with as many yet to publish), a critical study of *Dunbar*, and some children's books; he has edited several anthologies (including *The Penguin Book of Scottish Verse*) and contributed to many journals. He feels he has suffered much from the irresponsibility of publishers in Scotland and the English bias against Scots. In 1957 he went belatedly to Edinburgh University taking first an Honours M.A. then a Ph.D. in literature. He says he exists 'as a freelance writer, largely on air'.

K. G. SIMPSON was born in Ayrshire and is a graduate of Glasgow University. Since 1969 he has been a lecturer in the Department of English Studies at the University of Strathclyde, specializing in the teaching of the development of the novel and the literature of the period 1900–50. He has published articles on Smollett, Galt, Burns and eighteenth-century Scottish literature; on Stevenson and Home's *Douglas*. He is interested in the Scottish experience of the movement of ideas in the eighteenth century and is currently researching the literature of the Scottish Enlightenment.

Index

233